Campus Crisis Management

Eugene L. Zdziarski II,
Norbert W. Dunkel,
J. Michael Rollo, and Associates

JB JOSSEY-BASS

Campus Crisis Management

A Comprehensive Guide to Planning, Prevention, Response, and Recovery

BICENTENNIAL
1807
WILEY
2007
BICENTENNIAL

John Wiley & Sons, Inc.

Published by Jossey-Bass
A Wiley Imprint
989 Market Street, San Francisco, CA 94103-1741   www.josseybass.com

Jossey-Bass books and products are available through most bookstores. To contact Jossey-
Bass directly call our Customer Care Department within the U.S. at 800-956-7739,
outside the U.S. at 317-572-3986, or fax 317-572-4002.

Jossey-Bass also publishes its books in a variety of electronic formats. Some content that
appears in print may not be available in electronic books.

Library of Congress Cataloging-in-Publication Data

Zdziarski, Eugene L.
    Campus crisis management : a comprehensive guide to planning, prevention,
response, and recovery / Eugene L. Zdziarski II, Norbert W. Dunkel, J. Michael Rollo,
and associates.
        p. cm.
    Includes bibliographical references and index.
    ISBN-13: 978-0-7879-7874-7 (cloth)
    ISBN-10: 0-7879-7874-4 (cloth)
    1. Universities and colleges—United States. 2. Emergency management—
United States. I. Dunkel, Norbert W., 1956- II. Rollo, J. Michael. III. Title.
LA226.Z39 2007
378.73—dc22   2006100387

Printed in the United States of America
FIRST EDITION
HB Printing   10 9 8 7 6

The Jossey-Bass
Higher and Adult Education Series

Contents

Preface   ix
Eugene L. Zdziarski II, Norbert W. Dunkel,
and J. Michael Rollo

About the Authors   xv

Part I: Understanding Crisis Management

1. The Impact of Crisis   3
   J. Michael Rollo and Eugene L. Zdziarski II

2. The Crisis Matrix   35
   Eugene L. Zdziarski II, J. Michael Rollo,
   and Norbert W. Dunkel

Part II: Crisis Management in Practice

3. Crisis Management Teams   55
   Grant P. Sherwood and David McKelfresh

4. Developing a Crisis Management Plan   73
   J. Michael Rollo and Eugene L. Zdziarski II

5. Crisis Communication   97
   Cynthia J. Lawson

6. Working with Emergency Personnel and   121
   Outside Agencies
   Norbert W. Dunkel and Linda J. Stump

7. Psychological First Aid in the Aftermath   145
    of Crisis
    Wayne Griffin

8. Crisis Training   183
    Maureen E. Wilson

Part III: Lessons from Crisis Management

9. Environmental Crises   207
    Pat Whitely, Jacinta Felice, and Kevin Bailey

10. Facility Crises   231
    Tom Brown, Craig Allen, Jim Conneely,
    and Claire Good

11. Human Crises   255
    Brent G. Paterson, Lee E. Bird, Suzanne M. Burks,
    Cindy K. Washington, Tom Ellett, and Anthony Daykin

Part IV: Maintaining a Crisis
Management Focus

12. Contemporary Issues in Campus Crisis   285
    Management
    Beth Hellwig-Olson, Merna Jacobsen,
    and Azfar Mian

13. Where Do We Go from Here?   329
    J. Michael Rollo, Eugene L. Zdziarski II,
    and Norbert W. Dunkel

Appendix: Crisis Debriefing   337
    Daryl Johnston

Index   343

Preface

Colleges and universities have always confronted difficult issues: individuals in need of assistance, catastrophic weather events, and accidents and other unplanned crises. But in the past several years numerous highly visible events that have taken place on or around college and university campuses have required more than the usual attention. In particular, in fall 2005, the Gulf Coast was hit hard by two catastrophic hurricanes. These storms changed how colleges and universities plan for crisis management. It is no longer a matter of a single institutional plan; rather, plans for interinstitutional agreements are now being developed. Colleges and universities have revisited old response protocols in an effort to update them with more contemporary practices and procedures.

Today, campus officials must consider their relationship with their home city and county when responding to large-scale events. Campuses cannot ignore the fact that they may become terrorist targets because they house governmental research facilities, animal research facilities, nuclear materials, and the like.

Campus Crisis Management provides a framework in which to hold discussions about the subject on college and university campuses and offers a comprehensive guide to campus crisis management. The book describes the individuals who should be considered when developing a campus plan. When these individuals come to the table it is important first to understand the types of events they must consider.

This book discusses how to consider comprehensive crisis management planning as a year-round effort, offering examples, samples, and forms. Still, of course, it remains the responsibility of campus staff to develop approaches specific to their campus environments.

The inspiration for this book came from the experiences of the three editors. We have—fortunately, or unfortunately, as it may be—collectively experienced many crisis events throughout our careers. Although we read, write, and speak on this topic professionally, we found no publication that provides a comprehensive presentation of what campus staff should consider in crisis management. Through our experiences we also recognized that there are a number of experts in areas specific to crisis management. We were able to engage these individuals from the public and private sectors to share their knowledge and experiences in the volume's chapters.

Overview of the Contents

Campus Crisis Management is organized into four parts. Part One helps readers understand the concept of crisis management. In Chapter One, Mike Rollo and Gene Zdziarski introduce the impact of crisis management and provide a definition of crisis in the scope and context of the academic community. They share information on crisis management as a process and offer a brief history of crises in American higher education. In Chapter Two, Gene Zdziarski, Mike Rollo, and Norb Dunkel explain the need and value of developing a comprehensive crisis management system and introduce the *crisis matrix*, a typology that can be used to identify types of crises and how each interrelates and influences the crisis management process.

Part Two explores crisis management in practice. In Chapter Three, Grant Sherwood and Dave McElfresh explore crisis team structure, membership, operations, and training. Special attention is

given to the changes in team member roles depending on the type
and nature of the crisis based on the crisis matrix. In Chapter Four,
Mike Rollo and Gene Zdziarski present a comprehensive approach
for developing a campus crisis management plan, including conducting a campus crisis audit, writing a basic crisis management
plan, and developing crisis protocols for common events based on
the crisis matrix. Cynthia Lawson, in Chapter Five, discusses the
importance of identifying appropriate institutional spokespersons
and strategies for working with the media. She also offers the strategies for effective communication with internal and external constituencies in times of crisis. In Chapter Six, Norb Dunkel and
Linda Stump examine how campus staff work with emergency personnel services and other outside agencies. In Chapter Seven,
Wayne Griffin discusses stress management; attending to the mental health needs of campus community members and caregivers is
an essential component of any crisis management system. In Chapter Eight, Maureen Wilson offers an extensive set of resources,
including sample plans, checklists, case studies, and the like, that
readers can use in training their campus crisis management teams.

Part Three, which includes Chapter Nine, Ten, and Eleven,
offers lessons learned from real situations. The editors called upon
individuals from several U.S. campuses to share their experiences
and knowledge of specific, highly visible events. Edited by Norb
Dunkel, these vignettes provide insight into the issues and challenges and offer an opportunity to learn from the experiences of
others. In Chapter Nine, Pat Whitely, Jacinta Felice, and Kevin
Bailey share their experiences with environmental crises. In Chapter Ten, Tom Brown, Craig Allen, Jim Conneely, and Claire Good
share their experiences with facility crises. In Chapter Eleven, Brent
Paterson, Lee Bird, Suzanne Murks, Cindy Washington, Tom Ellett,
and Anthony Daykin share their experiences with human crises.
Campus staff have much to learn from these individuals, who have
firsthand knowledge of major events. Following each of the crises is
a list of questions for reflection and discussion.

Part Four, containing the last two chapters of the book, offers additional thoughts, provides unique crisis situations, and advances ideas on the future of crisis management. In Chapter Twelve, Beth Hellwig-Olson, Merna Jacobsen, and Azfar Mian discuss four new and unique crisis situations for college and university campuses, including celebratory violence and security of information technology, and offer practical guidance and direction. In Chapter Thirteen, Mike Rollo, Gene Zdziarski, and Norb Dunkel offer concluding remarks and summarize the key elements of crisis management systems and the future of crisis management.

The Appendix, provided by Daryl Johnston, reminds us that when the crisis is over and the recovery is well under way, it is time for the campus to take a step back and debrief the process. The debriefing checklist it contains focuses on continuous improvement rather than finding fault.

Acknowledgments

A number of people contributed to the completion of this book. First, we want to thank the chapter authors for agreeing to provide their expertise and knowledge—in several cases having to relive very difficult events of the past. Their endurance and sensitivity will always be remembered.

David Brightman of Jossey-Bass deserves our special thanks. He worked with us to craft a book that is important and vital to campus communities.

Gene Zdziarski wishes to thank his wife, Cheri, and daughter, Laura Ann, for their understanding and support whenever the phone rings in the middle of the night or when he is called away in the middle of some other activity because of a campus crisis. It is only because of the strength and love of those at home that we can be effective in providing assistance to others in their critical times of need. He also extends his thanks to his friends and colleagues at Texas A&M University and the University of Florida. The selfless manner in which these individuals have given of themselves to serve the campus community in times of need is truly inspiring.

Norb Dunkel wishes to thank his wife, Kim, and son, Nicholas, for their continuing support of his writing, travels, and professional involvement. He also wishes to thank the following colleagues for reading the crises summaries and developing lists of questions for reader learning and development: Sharon Blansett, Diane Porter, Rob Holland, Kathy Hobgood, Julie McMahon, Lisa Diekow, Mark Hill, Azfar Mian, and Vince Roberts. Finally, he wishes to thank his staff at the University of Florida for their dedication and attention to detail in the management of the housing operation.

Mike Rollo wishes to thank his wife, Amy, for her support and encouragement of his taking on this important project in addition to his other professional responsibilities. He also wishes to thank the staff of the University of Florida's Division of Student Affairs for their commitment to caring for students and their families under the most difficult circumstances.

January 2007   Gene Zdziarski
Gainesville, Florida   Norbert W. Dunkel
                                      Mike Rollo

About the Authors

Eugene L. Zdziarski II is dean of students at the University of Florida. Prior to coming to the University of Florida, Zdziarski served as associate director of student life at Texas A&M, where he was responsible for the coordination and training of the Division of Student Affairs Critical Incident Response Team and was heavily involved in the response to the 1999 Bonfire collapse. At the University of Florida, he chairs the Division of Student Affairs Trauma Response Team and serves as a member of the University Counseling Resource Network and a member of the University of Florida's Emergency Operations Team.

Zdziarski received his bachelor's of science degree from Oklahoma State University, his master's of science degree from the University of Tennessee at Knoxville, and his Ph.D. from Texas A&M. His dissertation was titled, "Institutional Preparedness to Respond to Campus Crisis as Perceived by Student Affairs Administrators at Selected NASPA Member Institutions."

Zdziarski is the regional vice president for Region III of the National Association of Student Personnel Administrators (NASPA) and has previously served as the chair of the NASPA Task Force on Crisis Management and Violence Prevention. He regularly speaks at national, regional, and state meetings on campus crisis management. He appeared on a nationally broadcast satellite video-conference on campus crisis response and coauthored the training workbook for the videotape series Preparing for Crises on Campus. He has written several feature articles for NASPA *NetResults* and was a coeditor of *Crisis Management: Responding from the Heart.*

Norbert W. Dunkel is director of housing and residence education at the University of Florida. Prior to coming to UF in 1988 he held administrative positions at South Dakota State University and the University of Northern Iowa. His primary responsibilities include serving as chief housing officer for 7,552 students in residence halls and 1,700 students and family members in 980 graduate and family housing apartments. He oversees an operation of 750 employees with an operating budget of over $38 million.

Dunkel codeveloped the University of Florida Trauma Response Team, which was first deployed during the series of student murders that rocked Gainesville in 1990. He also codeveloped the University Counseling Resource Network as an integral part of the University of Florida disaster plan. He is a member of the University of Florida Trauma Response Team, University Counseling Resource Network, and the University of Florida's Emergency Operations Team.

Dunkel is currently vice president of the Association of College and University Housing Officers-International (ACUHO-I). He has authored or edited nine books or monographs and over forty chapters or articles on topics related to campus housing. He has served as a consultant at over twenty universities and colleges and testified before congressional committees on two occasions. In 2004, he received the ACUHO-I James C. Grimm Leadership and Service Award and the NACURH Ken Stoner Award, both national recognitions. In 2005, he received the ACUHO-I Presidential Service Award.

J. Michael Rollo has spent the majority of his career in higher education at the University of Florida. Beginning in 1980 he served as assistant dean and director of student judicial affairs for eight years, and subsequently was associate dean of students until 2000, when he became associate vice president for student affairs. During a twenty-month period spanning 2003–04, he served as interim vice president for student affairs. While still associate dean he was involved in the University of Florida's response to the Gainesville murders—when a serial killer stalked the university community. This led to his involvement with the university's trauma response team, which he chaired for eight years. Currently he is vice president for student affairs at Florida Gulf Coast University in Fort Myers.

ADDITIONAL AUTHORS

Wayne Griffin is clinical associate professor and associate director at the University of Florida Counseling Center. He received his doctor of philosophy degree from the Counselor Education Department at the University of Florida in 1993 and his doctor of ministry from Columbia Theological Seminary in 1980. He has taught undergraduate and graduate level courses and developed the graduate-level course Trauma and Crisis Theory: A Survey of Theory, Response Models, and Techniques. He is a licensed mental health counselor, clinical supervisor, and nationally certified crisis responder and trainer for the National Organization of Victim Assistance. He is on the board of directors of the Florida Crisis Team and has served on state and national teams responding to disaster. He has presented on topics related to the impact and assessment of trauma and best practices for crisis intervention at state and national conferences.

Merna Jacobsen is the coordinator of organizational and staff development for the Division of Student Affairs at Texas A&M. Previous positions in higher education include director of the Tointon Institute for Educational Change, director of the Center for Professional and Organizational Development, and director of the Teacher Induction Partnership Program, all at the University of Northern Colorado. In addition to her work in higher education, she has worked as a trainer, consultant, facilitator, and mediator for twenty years. Her work takes her throughout North America and across the globe.

Jacobsen has conducted extensive research on the leadership dilemmas faced by and strategies used by university administrators during campus crisis and tragedy. She is a contributing author to a text on mentoring programs for beginning teachers and recently coauthored an article on Texas A&M's Academy for Student Affairs Professionals for Leadership Exchange, a NASPA publication. She holds a B.S. in education from Montana State University and an M.A. in speech communication from the University of Northern Colorado.

Daryl Johnston is the director of the Institute of Public Safety at Santa Fe Community College in Gainesville, Florida, and the chief of police for the college's police department. With over three decades of law enforcement experience, he has also served with the Gainesville Police Department, including as interim chief of police in 1999, and at the University of Florida Police Department.

Johnston has extensive experience in crisis management. In 1990 he was the on-scene commander at the first homicide scene of the 1990 Gainesville student murders. He is also a member of Florida's State Working Group on Domestic Preparedness for planning for response to terrorism. At SFCC, Johnston developed the crisis management team concept, which adapts the Incident Command System to a college structure.

Johnston has a B.A. in public safety from the University of West Florida and a master's degree in adult education from the University of Florida, and has done doctoral work in higher education at UF. He has made national presentations on crisis management to the League for Innovation in Community College and the International Association of Campus Law Enforcement Administrators, and has contributed to chapters and articles on crisis management.

Cynthia J. Lawson, who has over twenty-five years of experience in public relations in both higher education and at a Fortune 500 company, has headed the marketing and communications departments at several universities, including Eastern Michigan University, the University of Arkansas at Little Rock, and Texas A&M. More recently, she was vice president of communications and strategy development at the University of North Carolina, and currently is assistant to the chancellor for marketing and communications at the University of North Carolina, Wilmington.

The public relations teams she has managed have received numerous awards for many of their publications, videos, and public relations strategies. Rated as one of the top three CASE speakers in the nation for several years in a row, Lawson has presented "Crisis Communications: The Bonfire Tragedy" at more than one hundred national and international workshops and conferences, from Canada to South Africa. She provides consultation services to cities and municipalities on their communication preparedness in response to a terrorist incident. She authored *Effective Crisis Communications*, a set of instructional materials for the National Emergency Response and Recovery Training Center.

David McKelfresh is the director of employee development and assessment for housing and dining services, and is also an assistant professor in the Student Affairs in Higher Education graduate program at Colorado State University. McKelfresh received his master's degree at Colorado State University and his Ph.D. at the University of Northern Colorado.

Azfar Mian is the associate director of administrative services in the Department of Housing and Residence Education at the University of Florida. In this role he maintains the offices of assignments, graduate and family housing, network services, and information technology support for the department. In his tenure at the University of Florida and Kent State University he has automated a variety of manual processes and developed strategies to increase customer satisfaction, productivity, and efficiency. He has been invited as a consultant in IT venues and been involved in academic initiatives work. He has coauthored articles for the *ACUHO-I Talking Stick*, contributed to ACUHO-I's Twenty-First Century Project, and authored a chapter on technology in the ACUHO-I publication *Foundations: Strategies for the Future of Collegiate Housing*.

Beth Hellwig-Olson is dean of student services at Gonzaga University. Before coming to Gonzaga University in 2000, she held positions at the University of Northern Colorado, Colorado State University, Montana State University, and New Mexico State University. She earned her Bachelor of Arts in Pre-Law/Political Science at New Mexico State University, her master's of education in student affairs and higher education from Colorado State University, and her doctor of philosophy in college student personnel administration from the University of Northern Colorado.

At Gonzaga University she coordinates the residence life on-call emergency response process, cochairs the Trauma Response: University Support Team (TRUST), cochairs the Sexual Assault Response Team (SART), chairs the Hate/Bias Incident Response Team, and sits on the Gonzaga Crisis Response Team.

Grant P. Sherwood retired, in January 2005, from his administrative and faculty roles at Colorado State University after serving in a variety of capacities for thirty-seven years. Most recently, he was an assistant vice president for student affairs and associate professor in the School of Education. He has worked extensively with campus auxiliary services and on a national basis was president of the National Association of College Auxiliary Services (NACAS) in 1995. As a faculty member, he served as director of the Student Affairs in Higher Education master's degree program at Colorado State for over fifteen years.

Linda J. Stump is director of the University of Florida Police Department. She is the first female police chief at a public university in the state of Florida. A native of Lafayette, Indiana, she holds a bachelor's degree in criminal justice and corrections from Ball State University and a master's degree in higher education administration from Purdue University, and is also a graduate of Florida and Indiana law enforcement academies and the FBI National Academy.

Stump started her law enforcement career in 1984 as a trooper with the Indiana State Police and joined the University of Purdue Police Department a year later. She was a member of Purdue's Task Force on Women's Issues; Purdue's sexual-assault prevention program, Partners in Prevention; and the Tippecanoe County, Indiana, Domestic Violence Task Force.

Currently, she is the chair of the Alachua County Law Enforcement Executive Board and vice chair of the Regional III Domestic Security Task Force. She has extensive law enforcement experience in large-event security with both the Purdue University and the University of Florida police departments.

Maureen E. Wilson is associate professor in higher education and student affairs at Bowling Green State University. She earned a B.S.B.A. in business administration and communication arts at Aquinas College in Michigan, an M.A. in college and university administration at Michigan State University, and a Ph.D. in higher education and student affairs at Ohio State University. She has worked in student affairs at the College of William and Mary in Virginia and the University of South Carolina-Columbia and on the faculty at Mississippi State University. Wilson coedited the *ASHE Reader on College Student Development Theory* and has authored several chapters and articles. She received the Annuit Coeptis and Emerging Scholar awards from ACPA and the Outstanding Contribution to Student Affairs Through Teaching Award from NASPA IV-East. She is chair of the ACPA Professional Preparation Commission. Working many years in residence life provided plentiful opportunities to learn about crisis management, and she has taught and published on the topic as well.

Incident Review Authors

Craig Allen is the director of housing at Tulane University. He was the director of housing and residence life at Seton Hall University during the 1990 fire. He received his B.S. in marketing at the State University of New York at Oswego and his M.A. in higher education/student personnel at the University of Arizona. He has written articles on crisis management and fire safety for NASPA *NetResults*, the MACUHO newsletter, and ResLife.Net. He has made presentations at annual conferences such as MACUHO, ACPA, and ACUHO-I, and has been a guest speaker at several institutions on the topic of crisis management and fire safety.

Kevin Bailey is the assistant vice president for student affairs at Tulane University with responsibility for judicial affairs, crisis management, student-neighborhood relations, fraternity and sorority programs, new student programs, leadership development, and parent and family programs. Earlier, Bailey worked at Millersville University of Pennsylvania, Bowling Green State University, and the University of North Carolina at Charlotte. He has held leadership positions in both NASPA and ACPA and currently serves on the executive council of ACPA. Bailey holds a doctorate in higher education administration from Bowling Green State University. His undergraduate and master's degrees are from Indiana University of Pennsylvania.

Lee E. Bird is currently vice president for student affairs at Oklahoma State University. She received her doctorate from the University of Arizona in 1991. She has worked in some aspect of student affairs for twenty-seven years. She was the president of the national board of directors for the Association of Student Judicial Affairs and continues to present nationally on topics related to student development, First Amendment rights of students, judicial affairs, sexual harassment, and staff training. She is a lifelong volunteer with groups such as FEMA, American Red Cross–Disaster Relief Services, Habitat for Humanity, the St. Cloud Hospital Emergency-Trauma Center, and the Leukemia-Lymphoma Society of Oklahoma.

Tom Brown, director of the Student Life Office at Virginia Tech, has worked in student affairs for twelve years. He provides institutional leadership to the "on-call" protocol and training, oversees the university response to off-campus crisis, and chairs the Student Affairs Care Team.

Suzanne M. Burks is director of university counseling services at Oklahoma State University. She received her B.S., M.S., and Ph.D. from OSU, completing her doctorate in 1990. Burks has worked in student affairs for twenty-seven years. She is a licensed professional counselor and an adjunct instructor in the counseling psychology department at OSU. She was a volunteer after the Murrah Building bombing in 1995 in Oklahoma City, debriefing rescue workers. She was president of the board of directors of Stillwater Domestic Violence and currently is on the board of directors of Starting Point II, a nonmedical detox center in Stillwater, Oklahoma. She is also a volunteer team counselor for the OSU women's soccer team.

Jim Conneely is vice president for student affairs at Eastern Kentucky University. He received his doctorate from Georgia State University in 1992. He has worked in many aspects of student affairs for twenty-three years. He was president of the Southern Association for College Student Affairs and continues to present nationally and write on topics related to student affairs, university housing, organizational issues in student affairs, and leadership development.

Anthony Daykin began his career in law enforcement with the Tucson Police Department in 1972. During his twenty-eight-year career there he had various assignments, including K-9 handler and trainer, and commanded many of the functions of the department, including community services, investigations, field services, information services, and administration services. He earned a bachelor of arts in management from the University of Phoenix and a master's of education from Northern Arizona University. He is also a graduate of the FBI National Academy and the Senior Management Institute for Police. He retired from the Tucson Police Department as an assistant chief to take on the role of chief of police for the University of Arizona in August 2000.

Tom Ellett is the assistant vice president of residential education at New York University. He received his doctorate from Fordham University's Educational Leadership, Administration, and Policy program. His dissertation focused on the role of residentially based learning communities in urban settings.

Jacinta Felice is associate director for the south campus of the Department of Resident Life at the University of Maryland-College Park. Previously, she served as the associate director of residence life at Syracuse University. She has been codirector of the Association of College and University Housing Officers–International National Housing Training Institute, which is housed at the University of Maryland-College Park, for the past five years.

Claire Good is the associate vice president for student affairs and dean of students at Eastern Kentucky University. She received her doctorate in counselor education from the University of Arkansas in 2002. Good spent the first fifteen years of her career in student affairs working in various positions, from resident hall director to interim director of university housing at Northwestern State University in Louisiana, the University of Arkansas at Monticello, and the flagship campus of the University of Arkansas in Fayetteville. She has been employed at Eastern Kentucky University since September 2003.

Brent G. Paterson has been associate vice president for student affairs at Illinois State University since April 2001. In this capacity, he supervises the career center, disability concerns, student counseling services, and student health services. He is also responsible for divisionwide strategic planning, assessment, and finances. As associate vice president, he coordinates crisis response in the Division of Student Affairs. Previously, he was a member of the student affairs staff at Texas A&M University for seventeen years, where he served in various roles. He was the dean of student life and adjunct associate professor of educational administration at Texas A&M University immediately prior to moving to Illinois State University.

Cindy K. Washington is a licensed professional counselor in the state of Oklahoma. She currently works as a clinical counselor at University Counseling Service at Oklahoma State University. Before taking this position, she worked as a bereavement counselor at Judith Karman Hospice in Stillwater, Oklahoma.

Pat Whitely serves as vice president for student affairs at the University of Miami. She has held this position for eight years. During Hurricane Andrew, she lived on campus for four weeks; at the time, she was associate director of residence halls. Whitely has been at the University of Miami since 1982. She is active in the National Association for Student Personnel Administrators and has received numerous awards from students for her work at the University of Miami.

Campus Crisis Management

Part I

Understanding Crisis Management

The Impact of Crisis

J. Michael Rollo and Eugene L. Zdziarski II

Thanks to the variety in institutions of higher education today, opportunities abound for enriching student lives and enhancing our society by educating and preparing the next generation of leaders and citizens. Regardless of their background, precollege preparation, interests, or social status, students have opportunities to interact, learn, and experience life in all its wonder and intricacies. *Urban, rural, public, private, large, small, faith-based, secular, commuter, residential,* and other terms are used to categorize our institutions. Yet despite our tendency to separate institutions into groups that seek to establish commonalities across what appears to be a diverse array of entities, one absolute that binds them all together is their core of students, faculty, and staff who live and learn at their campuses. With this interplay of people and institutions, the inevitable reality is that incidents and events that are characterized as crises are certain to occur. The impact of crises on the facilities and the institutions' ability to accomplish their educational mission must be addressed, but it is the human side of the equation that begs our attention as educators committed to serving our communities.

Today's Ethic of Care

Historically, educational institutions' control of student behavior and ability to function in loco parentis were the standards by which we measured our relationship to students and our commitment to the families who placed their children in our charge. That outdated legal relationship no longer guides our actions or philosophical positions. However, it did lead us to a modern institutional commitment to caring, respect, and concern for our students' growth and development (Rhatigan, 2000).

This transition from legal guardian to caring educator has been gradual, and we remain connected despite our arm's-length legal relationship with students. Bickel and Lake (1999) describe the death of in loco parentis as resulting from the civil rights movement, when students increasingly distanced themselves from universities and colleges and challenged institutions' ability either to control their behavior or to intercede in their personal lives. This distancing between students and institutions led to a period in which the institutions acted as "bystanders." As a result of increasing legal challenges and court decisions, institutions had no legal duties to students and were not responsible for harm (Bickel & Lake, 1999). Institutions seemed helpless to influence student life, and they struggled in the court of public opinion as student populations began to appear more disruptive and in need of greater direction and guidance. The need for some protection from harm, some entity to which to look for assistance, has led us to a new model, prevalent on campuses today, whereby it is believed that we have a duty to care for the students in our charge. Although some see this as a return to in loco parentis, it is more likely a period of transition, as a new relationship between students, their families, and the institutions that serve them evolves to address today's expectations. The legal decisions that continue to refine this relationship must be monitored constantly and used to update the policies and procedures we follow in serving our students. However, the underpinning of this relationship, regardless of how we characterize or label it, is the ethic of care. Caring for the individual, providing support to those who can benefit from attention to their needs, and enhancing the human experience as educators and mentors underlie much of what we do in higher education. It may be the most important value we hold to direct our actions and responses during times of crisis, when tragedies overwhelm us as individuals and communities.

By basing our actions on an ethic of care for our students, staff, and faculty when we respond to crises, we put a human face on our institution. Although we all want our problems, concerns, and personal issues to matter to the institution, the institution as a bureaucracy tends to operate on its own set of values and priorities to accomplish its mission regardless of individuals' personal needs. If the institution is to be successful in responding to crises over the long run, it must reach out to its constituencies with compassion, concern, and sensitivity to the situation at hand. The staff charged with first response must be free to engage the community affected by the tragedy without restrictions. The spokesperson for the institution, whether it is the president, a member of the media relations staff, or any number of possible administrators, must be able to speak directly to the affected communities about the desire to help ease any suffering or loss.

At some institutions it is expected that this will occur as a matter of course. Families choose to send their children to smaller institutions with the belief that they will receive more personalized attention there. Although many assume this is a clear expectation among parents of children at private colleges or universities, public institutions are not free from this expectation either. At large institutions, although there may be a desire for personal attention, there is also likely a realization that students will be more anonymous on campus. The irony is that, in times of crisis, especially large-scale events, larger institutions are more likely to have the resources to respond to the situation whereas the small, "caring" institutions can easily be overwhelmed by the scope and complexity of the tragedy. Indeed, when the large, "impersonal" institution does respond with care and compassion, the benefits of this unexpected response are dramatic. Inability to respond compassionately may be expected from a large bureaucracy, but it is totally unacceptable at a small institution, especially if it has presented itself in its recruitment of students as a supportive environment.

Regardless of the size of the institution or expectation of the constituencies, the impact of the institutional response over time is profound. Did the college or university reach out to the student and his or her family and friends? Did the institution assist the academic department, and was the staff able to work through a difficult loss? Was there a sense of support and compassion among the staff? The emotions that arise out of these interactions go home with families and are shared with neighbors and friends. Stories of care and concern are told in residence halls and other living units, passed between students, and handed down to next generations. They are conveyed in the departments and help form a network of support among the staff and faculty as they return to their normal routines.

The converse is, of course, also true. The families who are helped but not cared for, interacted with but not embraced, responded to but not engaged, will return to their homes with a much different sense of what happened. The faculty or staff member who returns to the classroom or office with no sense of concern from the institution has no opportunity to enlarge the institution's role as a community that cares for its members, one that reaches out to others in time of need and responds with compassion and dignity.

Lessons Learned from Experience

Over the past fifty years, as advances in technology have expanded the reach of televised media and communications, campus tragedies have become more prominent in our lives, regardless of where they occur. Our understanding of what can occur on college campuses affects our planning and preparation. Several specific incidents stand out—not so much for their uniqueness as for the impact they have had on our thinking and response to subsequent events, even when they are relatively minor in comparison. Neither the size nor the location of the institution, nor the scope of the crisis, has been as important as the impact of these crises on our collective communities of higher education.

University of Texas at Austin, 1966

The Texas Tower at the University of Texas at Austin stands as one of the most dominant landmarks on a college campus in the United States. At 307 feet, its height, in comparison to other buildings in the area, draws your eye to it immediately. Although not as tall as the nearby state capitol building, it is built on higher ground and thus gives the appearance of being taller (MacLeod, 2005). Constructed in 1936 as a centerpiece of the campus and community, it has, unfortunately, since 1966 been indelibly linked to the actions of Charles Whitman on August 1 of that year. After murdering his mother and wife earlier in the day, at approximately 11:30 A.M. he entered the tower with a footlocker full of weapons and ammunition and proceeded to the observation deck on the twenty-eighth floor. Over the span of the next ninety-six minutes, he killed fourteen people and injured dozens, using skills that had earned him a sharpshooter's badge while serving in the U.S. Marine Corps (MacLeod, 2005).

Although neither the first nor the last shooting on a college campus, this incident stands out for its undeniable impact on the community and the nation. On-site television coverage of news events was still developing. In 1966, a television camera was a bulky and cumbersome apparatus to use and most television crews were still using film to capture images for delayed broadcasts, but with an incident of this magnitude in a state capital with established local media, details were provided immediately to the local population by way of on-site radio coverage ("KLBJ: The Story of Austin Radio," n.d.). Students and area residents recall tuning in to the radio and hearing about the tragedy as it unfolded (Preece, 1996). Despite being warned to stay away by local radio reporter Neal Spelce, who was crouched behind his mobile broadcast unit in the shadow of the tower, area residents, including students, instead loaded their high-powered deer rifles and headed to campus to return fire alongside local police officers (Preece, 1996; MacLeod, 2005). Later, film shot by Gordon Wilkinson, a reporter from KTBC, captured the definitive images of the tragedy, including images of the wounded and interviews with students who risked their lives to rescue fellow students (Brown, 2006).

Just one week earlier, it had been discovered that Richard Speck had killed nine student nurses in their dormitory in Chicago. With this event still in mind, the media's on-site coverage of the Austin killings turned the nation's attention to that campus. The August 12, 1966, cover of *Life* magazine—one of the standards by which we as a nation gauged the importance of an event in that era—showed a photo of the Texas Tower taken by Shel Hershorn through the bullet-shattered glass of a store window in Austin; it connected us all to the incident ("Texas Store Window Shattered by Sniper," 1966).

In addition to an increasing sensitivity to this type of tragedy on campuses, police agencies across the nation began developing a new type of response. The first Special Weapons and Tactical Teams (SWAT), created at that time, were believed to be a direct response to this incident (Snow, 1996). These teams forever changed our university security operations.

Kent State University, 1970

Reaction to the military draft of college-age men was beginning to manifest in larger and more violent disruptions on college campuses in some communities. The internal conflict between their ambivalence toward the war in Vietnam and a desire to serve their country as their parents had during World War II was growing. On the campus of Kent State University in Ohio over a four-day period in May 1970, the demonstrations escalated in violence and destruction. Windows in local businesses were smashed, the ROTC building on campus was burned to the ground, and the National Guard was brought in to control the situation. On May 4, the university banned a planned noon rally, believing that the National Guard's presence made the demonstration illegal. Shortly after noon, the demonstrators (described as a core group of about five hundred and as many as two thousand "cheerleaders" who came to show support) began to throw rocks at the National Guard troops, who had ordered them to disperse. Through clouds of tear gas, the troops moved forward to disperse the crowd with loaded weapons, and after retreating to the top of Blanket Hill, turned and fired into the crowd. Four students were killed and nine wounded in a period of thirteen seconds (Lewis & Hensley, 1998), and the now-famous Pulitzer Prize–winning photo of Mary Vecchio, a fourteen-year-old runaway, screaming over the body of Jeffrey Miller was splashed across the front pages of newspapers and magazines around the country (Tuchman, 2000).

Campuses would never be the same again. Antiwar efforts expanded, students who had previously been ambivalent about the issue were galvanized to action, and new allies of the core antiwar demonstrators added their support. Campuses closed or canceled classes for varying periods of time to minimize additional disruption, but the trust between the students and the institutions they attended was damaged significantly and would require years to repair. In some cases, it never has been repaired.

Lehigh University, 1986

In April 1986, Jeanne Clery, a nineteen-year-old freshman, was brutally raped and murdered in her residence hall room on the campus of Lehigh University. The person accused of the crime and ultimately convicted and sentenced to death in the state of Pennsylvania was a student at Lehigh who had entered through a series of propped-open doors in the girls' residence hall (Clery & Clery, 2001). This personal tragedy of the Clery family became the centerpiece of a national initiative by her parents to require colleges and universities to report the occurrence of crimes in their campus communities to prospective students and families. Their efforts were fueled by the belief that colleges and universities were routinely hiding and covering up violent crimes to protect their institutions' reputations. Sympathetic legislators agreed with them, and through the lobbying efforts of Campus Security Inc., a nonprofit organization founded by the Clerys, created the Crime Awareness and Campus Security Act of 1990. This legislation and its evolution since 1990 into what is now known as the Jeanne Clery Disclosure of Campus Security Policy and Campus Crime Statistics Act, has changed the nature of the discussion on college campuses at orientation programs, putting front and center the expectations of today's parents regarding the responsibility of institutions to protect and warn their children about potential harms.

That doors are sometimes propped open in a residence hall should come as no surprise to anyone who has ever lived or worked in a living unit on a college campus. Helping young people understand the security risks of living away from their families for the first time is an ongoing challenge for student affairs and campus safety officers. It was the Clerys' position that many of our colleges and universities did not take this responsibility seriously before their daughter's death. Whether colleges and universities were doing a good job or not in this area is no longer an issue. The personal tragedy of the Clery family, which initially affected only a small circle of family and friends, now affects us all as all campuses, and especially student affairs professionals and public safety officers, are required to be accountable to families and students as risk managers. This incident lives on with us every day on college campuses since 1986. Connie and Howard Clery have achieved their goal: their daughter lives on in our collective memory and has helped avert subsequent tragedies like theirs.

Pan Am Flight 103, 1988

In the early evening of December 21, 1988, international terrorism first touched U.S. college campuses when Pan Am Flight 103 exploded at thirty-one thousand feet and crashed to the ground in pieces in and around Lockerbie, Scotland. Among the dead were eleven citizens of Lockerbie and 259 passengers, including students from numerous institutions returning home for the Christmas holidays from study abroad ("Bombing of Pan Am Flight 103 Over Lockerbie," 2000). Syracuse University had the largest contingent, with thirty-five students, but others studying through the Syracuse program brought the tragedy home to their campuses and homes outside the spotlight shining on Syracuse (*Victims of Pan Am Flight 103*, n.d.). As at Kent State and UT-Austin, the power of the media and the visual images of the horror of an airplane crash connected us all. Video of smoking wreckage, the seared earth in Lockerbie where the fuselage had hit, and the largest piece of the 747 fuselage lying in a field near the town, demanded our attention and sympathy. The latter image continued to be shown repeatedly on the cover of news magazines and as backdrops in subsequent news stories and is so closely identified with the tragedy that it has become an icon of this sort of event. The story took on a life of its own, with theories of conspiracy and collusion by governments, mismanagement, and poor security on the part of Pan Am, and numerous human interest stories featuring mistaken notifications of death, changed travel plans that resulted in survivors who had taken other flights, and the unending pain and suffering of the families who lost their loved ones so unexpectedly due to a terrorist act.

Once again, the scale of this tragedy and its impact on our campuses changed the way we view our off-campus experiences but also affected our sense of safety from forces in the world that until this incident seemed far away. Although new and dreadful terrorist acts have occurred more frequently in the years since, we can still look back at this incident as the beginning of a new era in the American realization of international terrorism and its effects on our country. Where since the end of World War II we had felt impervious to attacks, we were now entering a period of highly visible, high-impact, media-conscious terrorism that targeted our citizens, and by relation, our students and learning communities.

The University of Florida, 1990

The age of the twenty-four-hour news channel and satellite television trucks that allowed any story of local significance to immediately become a national story dawned in August 1990, when the bodies of four students at the University of Florida and one from nearby Santa Fe Community College were discovered over a five-day period in Gainesville. The ensuing onslaught of media attention in the midst of a police investigation to identify and capture what appeared to be a serial killer led to widespread panic among students and families connected to Gainesville. The attention brought to bear on the institution forced it to spend significant financial and staff resources to respond to a public only loosely connected to the university. What had been the cover of a magazine and a series of newspaper articles immediately following the 1966 incident in Austin in 1990 turned into two weeks of daily news conferences, false arrests, repeated broadcast of videotape of bodies on gurneys being removed from apartments, human interest stories about fear and panic in the community and university, sensationalized television talk shows, and law enforcement efforts to stop rumors of secret morgues and unreported additional deaths ("Students at University of Florida," 1990).

The university's use of the media to communicate with the public was also new. It took advantage of the massive interest by the national and state media. Coordination of official responses by the central administration allowed the university to tell its story of concern and support to all who wanted to listen and ultimately allowed the students to return to campus and resume normal operations despite an unresolved police investigation. The national media was forever tied to subsequent events on college campuses, regardless of their scope. No photo opportunity or sound bite was out of reach, and in fact, all were available for immediate broadcast and publication as events unfolded. This was in marked contrast to the response to a similar incident at Florida State University that had occurred back in 1974, when one Saturday night Ted Bundy murdered two women in a sorority house on that campus. The university staff had all day Sunday to prepare before the national and state media descended on Tallahassee on Monday. But in 1990, it became clear that this kind of time to plan a coherent and consistent response was no longer available. The planning now had to become part of any campus's general preparation for responding to tragedy and crisis.

The University of Illinois at Urbana-Champaign, 1991–92

Not all crises come in forms visible to the naked eye. Over a fifteen-month period spanning 1991–92, the University of Illinois at Urbana-Champaign (UIUC) and surrounding communities were stalked by a sinister yet invisible killer: *meningococcemia*. A bacterial infection that begins with flu-like symptoms causes an inflammation of the lining of the brain and the spinal cord or blood infections. Treatment with antibiotics during the earliest stages of the infection are usually successful, but because the symptoms resemble those of the flu, effective treatment may be delayed, causing devastating results in some cases ("University of Illinois," 1991). The group living conditions of many student populations, such as in residence halls or Greek letter chapter houses, exacerbate the potential for transmittal of the infection. Coupled with substantial misinformation about meningitis, the fear of contagion and harm resulted in a health crisis for the institution that required a large-scale response. Meanwhile, eight students at UIUC and one at neighboring Parkland College were infected with meningococcemia, and tragically, three died. Yet fifty-seven hundred students at UIUC were given oral antibiotics after the first two students died in 1991, and over the next year, eighteen thousand more were given free vaccinations in an attempt to stop the spread of the infection and ease the tension in the community ("Meningitis Scare Prompts Vaccinations," 1992).

Subsequent to this incident, some states, under focused lobbying by drug companies and interest groups, have required colleges and universities to inform incoming students of the increased risk of infection associated with living in high-density communities like residence halls in an attempt to have more of them vaccinated prior to enrollment. As new vaccines are developed, this particular type of large-scale health crisis may disappear. However, the ability of institutions to mobilize their resources to respond to health crises remains an important piece of any crisis preparation. With bioterrorism now a strong concern at the Department of Homeland Security, large-scale events and high-visibility populations of young people at colleges and universities make attractive targets for release of toxins and viral agents that could quickly cause widespread health crises.

California State University-Northridge, 1994

Each region of the world has its own unique natural disasters to which local residents must respond. The U.S. Gulf Coast and East Coast must prepare for hurricanes, whereas parts of the Midwest must be ready to respond to tornados or heavy snow. The West Coast is forever linked in the public's mind to earthquakes and their devastation.

On January 17, 1994, Southern California experienced a 6.7 magnitude earthquake with its epicenter only a mile from the California State University-Northridge (CSUN) campus. At the time considered the most costly natural disaster in U.S. history, with damage estimated at up to $40 billion (Rodrigue, Rovsi, & Flace, 1997), this tragedy is viewed as a case study in how to recover effectively. Over the next eight years, in the words of former CSUN President Blenda Wilson, the university was "not just back—better" (Sodders, 2004).

Throughout Los Angeles the devastation was overwhelming, with over 114,000 buildings damaged, nine thousand injuries, and seventy-two deaths, including two CSUN students. Particularly hard hit (though not suffering the greatest damage in the area) was the CSUN campus: all 107 buildings were either damaged or destroyed, at a resultant cost of $400 million. Despite the damage, CSUN opened the spring semester only four weeks late with classes being taught in tents, trailers, inflatable buildings, even on fields. Extraordinary actions and a total commitment to recovery were necessary for this to occur in so short a time span. For example, at one point, Susan Curzon, dean of the library, rode a cherry picker to the fourth floor of the condemned computer center and rescued the only set of complete computer tapes containing the registration records of all CSUN students ("Northridge Quake Anniversary," 2004). Over sixty-thousand books had to be reshelved in the main library building, which had been heavily damaged.

The emotional impact on the community and the campus was substantial, forcing many residents to leave the area and placing heavy debt burdens on those without insurance who chose to rebuild. The Federal Emergency Management Agency (FEMA) played a big role in helping fund the recovery, with all the usual bureaucratic complications of documenting need and recovery costs. FEMA provided $63 million as the federal share of the $320 million needed to restore the campus. The financial impact of a crisis can put at risk an institution's future ability to function at any level, or at best, can affect it negatively by draining resources for growth that must be used just to rebuild to status quo.

University of Wyoming, 1998

Sometimes personal tragedies transcend an incident and become the basis for a new awareness about unresolved problems in our society on a national scale. Much like the events surrounding Jeanne Clery's death, this is how the events in Laramie, Wyoming, played out over the weeks surrounding what at first glance seemed a single act of bigotry and violence against a young man named Matthew Shepard. Shepard died after being brutally beaten, tied to a fence, and then abandoned in a remote area outside of Laramie. During the course of the investigation, the public would discover that two men who had masqueraded as gay men to gain the confidence of the openly gay Shepard had given him a ride from a local bar (Hurst, 1999). The subsequent explosion of grief and anger, coupled with the onslaught of homophobic reactions from across the nation, brought this horrible act to the forefront of our collective consciousness. Inside of a few days, this deeply personal family tragedy became a cause for the LGBT community to rally around and point to as an example of the ongoing prejudice against gay and lesbian Americans.

The institution became subject to a media problem of different proportions. Now, in addition to the television and print media seeking photos or video and sound bites to fill the twenty-four-hour news channels, the public weighed in across the Internet, overwhelming the computer and human resources of the University of Wyoming. Thousands of e-mails, both in sympathy for Matthew Shepard and expressing hatred and bigotry toward homosexuals, inundated the institution's mail servers. The overload served as a de facto denial of service attack on users of the university network. In the first twenty-four hours alone, Shepard's parents received over two thousand e-mails ("Murder Charges Planned," 1998). As a result, the institution was unable to respond effectively using the resources that many of us had come to rely on as our default communication methods to share information and respond to our constituents. Electronic mail and Web sites lost their usefulness during this crisis and this affected the institution's ability to respond effectively.

Texas A&M University, 1999

When our students share cherished traditions, we assist in maintaining them as opportunities to develop teamwork and leadership and provide a connection across time for our campuses to establish a sense of belonging. Many traditions are intimate and personal for those involved, others based on legends or folktales from the institution's past. Others still may be highly ceremonial, requiring direct engagement by the community as participants or on-site observers.

Until 1999, one of the most profoundly unique traditions on a college campus was the annual Bonfire, held at Texas A&M University during the week leading up to the football game with the University of Texas. Hundreds of students would organize into highly structured units to share in the honor of participating in a ninety-year-old tradition that was without equal.

As is often the case with campus tragedies, they happen despite the best efforts of dedicated and well-meaning professionals to avoid them. Preparation for different contingencies and thoughtful and carefully managed risk management reviews provide us with a sense of security. But in the early morning of November 18, 1999, all the planning and careful preparation by generations of students, faculty, and staff came crashing down when twelve individuals lost their lives in the tangle of logs that had been the Bonfire construction site.

The ubiquitous availability of cell phones spread word of the tragedy quickly through the campus and the state. Recovery and identification of the injured and killed took place under the glare of emergency lighting and curious and concerned bystanders. Electronic intercepts of communications between students and among university staff by local media caused information to be released prior to notification of kin, further damaging the university's image. As at the University of Wyoming, communication systems including e-mail and telephone lines were overwhelmed, putting yet more stress on the campus community's support system ("Bonfire Collapse," 1999). With this increasingly frenetic intrusion by outside media, the institution's ability to respond effectively and in a timely manner was eroded. Resources had to be reallocated from direct service to the community to focus instead on communicating with the many constituencies that demanded attention. The loss of the twelve individuals at Texas A&M led to the loss of a very special student experience, the Bonfire, for future generations of students, and it took something away from the institution that it will probably never regain.

New York City–Washington, D.C.–Shanksville, Pennsylvania, 2001

Planning, training, and preparing for campus crises require an ongoing and inward focus on available resources that can be brought to bear on foreseeable incidents. No one imagined that what we all saw on our television sets on September 11, 2001, would ever happen. How could we have prepared our country or our students for the trauma inflicted on New York, Washington, and the Pennsylvania countryside? What was a clear and immediate danger and horror to the citizens directly affected by these terrorist acts became a crisis of faith in our personal and national security when the towers of the World Trade Center collapsed as rubble right before our eyes on live television.

Not in two generations—and then with a one-month delay before film of the attack on Pearl Harbor became available to the public—had the U.S. citizenry been shocked in this manner (Schoenherr, 2001). It appeared on that day that "everyone was a New Yorker" and the nation grieved together. College campuses across the United States became places of mourning, with traumatized individuals and hurriedly organized ceremonies of remembrance arranged by staff as worried and concerned as all other citizens. Fearful families struggled to reunite while airline service was totally disrupted with the uncertainty of our safety. There appeared to be no end in sight from an enemy characterized as far away and at the same time living among us. A war with an enemy we did not understand had begun, and we began to realize it would affect us for the rest of our lives, and most likely the lives of our children too. Our society entered a permanent state of crisis, with color-coded warnings and dire predictions of subsequent terrorist acts. University campuses were no longer islands of scholarship and learning for our best and brightest. They were now "soft targets" in a war without traditional battle lines, and our crisis plans became immediately obsolete.

Hurricane Katrina, 2005

The hurricane season that runs from July to November of each year has taken on increased national interest with the advent of twenty-four-hour weather stations and news coverage. Watching a disaster approach for weeks via satellite imagery, with hourly updates of the destruction it causes along the way, becomes mesmerizing to the residents in its path. After Andrew (a Category Five hurricane) hit South Florida in 1991, campuses had become more conscious of the impact a major storm could have on their lives. The devastation to Miami and three of its higher education institutions (the University of Miami, Florida International University, and Miami-Dade Community College) have been studied since that time to help us prepare for the possibility of another event of this magnitude. Little did we know that the benchmark we used as the worst possible situation would be surpassed.

Katrina began as a Category One hurricane, striking the Florida coast just north of Miami and killing twelve people on August 25, 2005. After crossing the Florida Peninsula, it gained strength, and after briefly becoming a Category Five storm, struck the central Gulf Coast near Buras-Triumph, Louisiana, on August 29, 2005, as a Category Three, with sustained winds of 125 miles per hour. Possibly the largest hurricane of its strength ever recorded, it caused destruction all along the Gulf Coast from Mississippi to Louisiana, in some cases obliterating entire communities (Hurricane Katrina Timeline, 2005). But Katrina will forever be remembered for the impact it had on New Orleans as a storm surge breached the levee system that protected the city from Lake Pontchartrain and the Mississippi River and flooded a significant part of the city in up to ten feet of water. Over 1 million people were displaced, destruction was estimated at as much as $75 billion, over eighteen hundred deaths occurred, and much of the city of New Orleans was abandoned as unlivable. As of December 2005, over four thousand residents were still unaccounted for, with many presumed dead. If the residents still unaccounted for are reclassified as deaths, Katrina may ultimately be considered the second most deadly hurricane in U.S. history (Brunner, 2005; Pickrell, 2005).

The infrastructure of New Orleans was in ruins. In addition to losing such basic services as water, security, transportation, and sanitation, the educational system across the city disappeared, the result of either rising water or the evacuation of students. With the destruction so complete, the institutions of the city were unable to reopen even after the levees were repaired and the water was finally pumped back into Lake Pontchartrain. Students at the city's universities (Tulane, Loyola, Xavier, Dillard, Southern, and the University of New Orleans, to name the most prominent) sought enrollment in institutions across the country, and many institutions opened their doors to them as "walk-ins" or "temporary transfer students." The institutions themselves were left to rebuild without a significant portion of the staff and faculty, who were also unable to return to their homes. Over $200 million in damage to Tulane and the loss of tuition income for the fall semester forced the university to lay off 230 faculty and terminate five undergraduate programs and more than half of its doctoral programs. Eight nonrevenue NCAA athletic programs were also terminated (Johnson, 2005). The three historic African-American universities were hit harder than Tulane and the University of New Orleans and had fewer resources with which to recover. Dillard University, Xavier University, and Southern University shared $1 billion in flood and fire damage affecting over eight thousand students. Dillard at one point floated in upwards of ten feet of water and lost three residence halls to fire. At Southern University, Chancellor Edward Jackson conjectured that all eleven buildings on their campus would have to be replaced at a cost of $500 million (Romano, 2005).

Although all the institutions reopened for spring semester, only about 73 percent of the students formerly enrolled at the city's four-year institutions returned. Dillard University's campus remained closed, but the university was able to secure one-third of the rooms at the Hilton to house the thousand students who reenrolled. Tulane, Xavier, and the University of New Orleans, even with repairs, used trailers provided by FEMA placed in parking lots and playing fields to house staff and students, as housing in the city remained in short supply. Predictions aside that more students will continue to return the institutions to pre-Katrina enrollment levels, all of the institutions continue to this day to face a daunting task to full recovery. The impact of this loss of fiscal and human resources will forever change them all and may indeed force the closure of the weaker ones if substantial financial assistance is not obtained. Scott Cowen, president of Tulane University, stated: "This is the most significant reinvention of a university in the United States in over a century" (Johnson, 2005). Delgado Community College had only half of its 17,400 students return in the spring, and two technical schools in the city were unable to open in spring 2006. With a student population made up primarily of local residents, it is understandable that the recovery may be longer for these institutions as the citizens of New Orleans must first return and restore some normalcy to their lives before they can begin the task of balancing work, family, and a college education (Konigsmark, 2006).

One of the few bright spots to be found in this tragedy was the remarkable level of interinstitutional cooperation and collaboration. Almost immediately, public and private institutions across the nation opened their doors to displaced students so that they could continue their education during the recovery process. The Tulane University Medical School moved to Baylor University to continue its programs, and due to the lack of patients in New Orleans in a drastically reduced city population, remained there after the reopening. Help even came from inside New Orleans, as Tulane and Loyola Universities offered space to Dillard and Xavier to assist them in their successful efforts to reopen in spring 2006. The American Council on Education (ACE) and the National Association of College and University Business Officers (NACUBO) jointly developed

CampusRelief.org. Described on this Web site as "Campus to Campus Disaster Assistance," it serves as a clearinghouse of information for students, faculty, staff, and institutions to assist in the recovery and relocation process. As college campuses face new challenges, this service may continue and possibly grow in usefulness and importance to institutions.

Despite the devastation and personal tragedy that resulted from Katrina in Louisiana and the other Gulf Coast states, this new collaboration between institutions has offered an opportunity for universities and colleges with differing missions to focus on the role they all view at their center: providing postsecondary instruction to students on a residential campus. Lessons can be shared, and now it appears that even resources can be shared, among institutions that before Katrina seemed divided by an uncrossable chasm formed through history, traditions, and culture. Tragedy and crisis have a way of changing how we view the world around us. Even universities—so set in their ways and committed to following their own agendas—can be moved to new models of service and teaching when given the opportunity.

What Is a Crisis?

History has shown that campus crises have had a significant impact on higher education—our students, their families, and society as a whole. Having just listed a series of crisis events, the temptation is to plunge forward with the assumption that everyone knows what a crisis is. But the reality is that how we define crisis varies significantly from one individual to another and from one institution to another. For example, everyone has probably heard a colleague describe a particularly difficult workday as one spent "running from one crisis to the next." In our culture we also use terms like *midlife crisis*, *identity crisis*, or *marital crisis*. In addition, the media often offers such news story headlines as "Middle-East Crisis" or "Crisis in [Insert Any Country]." But how can the same word be used to describe one individual's workday, a challenging life transition, a war that has affected the global community for decades, and the complex and wide-ranging disaster caused by Hurricane Katrina? Although each of these examples conveys a general understanding of the concept of crisis, the specific meaning clearly varies greatly.

The same is true in the professional literature on crisis and crisis management. Although there is general agreement and understanding of the concept, there is no common or widely accepted definition of the word (Auerbach & Kilmann, 1977; Coombs, 1999; Hermann, 1972). Each author seems to develop his or her own unique definition. Some of the more frequently cited definitions of crisis are these:

- "An organizational crisis (1) threatens high-priority values of the organization, (2) presents a restricted amount of time in which a response can be made, and (3) is unexpected or unanticipated by the organization" (Hermann, 1963, p. 63).

- A crisis is "an unstable time or state of affairs in which a decisive change is impending—either one with the distinct possibility of a highly undesirable outcome or one with the distinct possibility of a highly desirable and extremely positive outcome" (Fink, 1986, p. 15).

- A crisis is "a disruption that physically affects a system as a whole and threatens its basic assumptions, its subjective sense of self, its existential core" (Pauchant & Mitroff, 1992, p. 12).

- A crisis is "a major unpredictable event that has potentially negative results. The event and its aftermath may significantly damage an organization and its employees, products, services, financial condition, and reputation" (Barton, 1993, p. 2).

Characteristics of Crisis

Although similar in concept, each of these definitions emphasizes different characteristics that the authors felt were important to explaining and understanding the concept. These characteristics often influence how organizations and individuals interpret or perceive a crisis. If we examine these definitions, we can find some common characteristics: a negative event or outcome, the element of surprise, limited response time, disruption of operations, and a threat to the safety and well-being of people. Further discussion of these characteristics can be helpful as we seek to understand the nature of crisis and develop a definition of crisis management that is appropriate for the college and university setting.

Perception of the Event or Outcome

Most people would describe a crisis as being a negative event or having a negative outcome. A crisis event often poses a threat to an organization or institution. It can threaten an organization's mission and goals, its people, its financial status, its reputation, or its continued existence.

It can also be argued, however, that a crisis can be both a positive and a negative event. Steven Fink (1986), sometimes referred to as the father of modern crisis management theory, suggests that a crisis can have either a desirable or an undesirable outcome. He claims that a crisis is not necessarily bad, but involves the elements of "risk and uncertainty" that people generally attribute to negative outcomes (Fink, 1986, p. 15). He notes that the Chinese symbol for crisis is a combination of two words—*danger* and *opportunity*. How an organization responds to and resolves a crisis can clearly have an impact on its future. Herein lies the importance of effective crisis management.

Element of Surprise

Another characteristic often associated with a crisis is the element of surprise. This characteristic, however, is frequently debated in the literature. Some authors (for example, Barton, 1993; Hermann, 1963, 1972; Holsti, 1978; Phelps, 1986; Seymour & Moore, 2000) suggest that crises occur suddenly and without warning, making them unpredictable. Critics of these definitions (such as Billings, Milburn, & Schaalman, 1980; Irvine & Millar, 1996; Koovor-Misra, 1995) note that a situation need not come as a surprise to constitute a crisis. For example, the existence of a hurricane is known several days before it strikes and provides organizational leaders with an opportunity to prepare a response. The prior knowledge and opportunity to prepare do not make it any less of a crisis.

The element of surprise is an important part of Hermann's (1963) definition of crisis. According to his definition, surprise means not only that a specific contingency plan does not exist to respond to the event but also that there is a lack of recognition that such an event could even occur. However, it is this reference to lack of recognition or anticipation of a crisis that causes others to disagree (Coombs, 1999). Crisis is inevitable, and sooner or later all organizations will be struck by one. Although some crises do provide warning signs, crises are often unpredictable. Yet despite their unpredictability, crises should not be unexpected or unanticipated. Instead, institutions must conduct a thorough audit of their environment and identify the various types of crises that they might face as well as the impact that these crises would likely have on them.

Limited Response Time

Closely associated to the element of surprise is the idea that crisis situations provide organizational leaders with a limited time period in which to respond. In the midst of a crisis, administrators must formulate a response, make decisions, and take action quickly to avert or at least contain it. Again, Hermann (1963) articulates this aspect of crisis when he states that crisis "presents a restricted amount of time in which a response can be made" (p. 64).

It is because of this limited response time that the existence of a crisis management plan is so important. Administrators need to be able to respond quickly and take decisive actions when a crisis occurs. These actions can have a far-reaching effect on the institution, its people, its resources, and even its existence. There is little time to carefully weigh each decision and consider the long-term impact of that action. A well-developed crisis management plan addresses the anticipated decisions that will need to be made and actions that will need to be taken during a particular type of crisis and thus allows administrators to focus on the issues or decisions that are unique to the given incident.

Interruption of Operations

Another frequently mentioned characteristic of crisis is that it interrupts the normal operations of an organization. Seymour and Moore (2000) describe crisis as "the disruption of normal patterns of corporate activity by a sudden or overpowering and initially uncontrollable event" (p. 10). Pauchant and Mitroff (1992) also describe crisis in terms of a disruption. They note that crises not only disrupt organizational systems but can disrupt an organization deep into its core.

One of the primary goals of any crisis management plan is to return the organization to normal as quickly as possible. A good crisis management plan guides the institution through the process of resuming normal operations and supports the students, faculty, and staff in their transition back to their academic routines.

Threat to Safety and Well-Being

Although crises can have a significant impact on organizations, one of the main reasons why crisis management in higher education is so important is because crises pose a threat to the safety and well-being of the members of the campus community. No matter the specific type that occurs, almost all crises pose a threat to one or more members of the campus community. Although threats exist everywhere in society, the thought that something bad can happen at an educational institution seems to create the greatest sense of concern for us, perhaps because our campuses contain such a wealth of human capital. Students come to college to complete their education and prepare themselves to enter the real world as productive members of our society. These young, talented people have so much potential. They are just beginning their lives, and the thought that something might threaten those lives—cut them short and prevent them from ever fully reaching their potential—is something that all of society finds deeply disturbing.

In addition, college campus faculty and staff are some of the best and brightest minds our society has to offer. The faculty and researchers in our communities hold the keys to society's future. Through them, new discoveries are made that shape our lives and our way of living. Through them, our students are taught and prepared for their careers and their place in society. Again, the thought that something could happen to these brilliant teachers and scientists deeply concerns us all.

So, above all, protecting the safety and well-being of the people in our institutions is a principal objective of crisis management.

Crafting a Common Definition of Crisis

These common characteristics of crisis provide us with a better understanding of the term. Once we have a common definition and language that can encompass the array of possibilities, we have a foundation on which we can begin to plan for the uncertainties that will inevitably occur over time. As a guide for us to move forward with this discussion and for our purposes in this book we will use the following definition of crisis:

> A crisis is an event, which is often sudden or unexpected, that disrupts the normal operations of the institution or its educational mission and threatens the well-being of

personnel, property, financial resources, and/or reputation of the institution (Zdziarski, 2006, p. 5).

The unique aspects of each crisis will require us to respond differently. The severity, location, magnitude, and visibility of an event must be addressed in the context of the institution's ability to respond. Yet also influencing an institution's ability to respond is the impact of our perception of the event. A crisis for one person or organization may be a routine situation for another. Differences between institutions and organizational units thus also shape our perceptions of what a crisis is. A large public university in a metropolitan area will likely perceive a crisis event differently than will a small private liberal arts college in a rural community. The staff's perception of a crisis adds layers of detail to how crisis is defined at each institution. In addition, the organizational structure and culture of an institution will also affect how it defines crisis.

The following list provides examples of definitions of crisis gleaned from crisis management plans from institutions around the country.

Rivier College

A "crisis" is any condition or situation that directly disrupts the College's ability to continue normal operation in whole or in substantial part and that requires immediate, dynamic action to enable the College to resume normal operation within the shortest time possible.

Indiana University

A crisis threatens:

- The integrity of the institution or its activities

- Life and/or property

- Welfare of campus community

Concordia University

A crisis event includes the following:

1. Death on campus or at a university-sponsored event

2. Any student, faculty, or staff death, any near fatal accident or incident, any serious attempted suicide; any major harassment (racial/sexual) incident or the like

3. Serious damage to college property (including arson)

4. Other incidents unique to the campus demanding special attention but not involving the above, such as serious injury to a visitor or extraordinary damage to community property by students

5. Other incidents which in the judgment of the President, Vice President of Student Life, or Executive Vice President require or would benefit from the crisis team

Indiana University–Purdue University, Division of Student Affairs

The death or severe injury to a student, or other significant crisis situations involving students while on campus. When assistance is requested [the definition also includes] incidents off campus.

Virginia Tech, Division of Student Affairs

Crisis includes the following situations:

1. Death of a student

2. Serious (life-threatening) injury or illness of a student

3. Any situation in which a parent or news reporter is already involved or will be before the next day

4. Any situation which requires immediate action by the Dean of Students' on-call staff member

5. Any emergency which is clearly out of normal limits

Conclusion

How an institution or organizational unit defines crisis has a significant impact on the crisis management system it develops. It affects who will determine when and how a crisis management plan is activated, who will be part of the crisis management team, and what the specific protocols and procedures for responding to a crisis will be. In developing a crisis management system it is important for the staff tasked with this effort to define crisis in a way that emphasizes characteristics and attributes that are meaningful and appropriate to their organizational unit and campus community.

References

Auerbach, S. M., & Kilmann, P. R. (1977). Crisis intervention: A review of outcome research. *Psychological Bulletin, 84*(6), 1189–1217.

Barton, L. (1993). *Crisis in organizations: Managing and communicating in the heat of chaos*. Cincinnati: South-Western Publishing.

Bickel, R., & Lake, P. (1999). *The rights and responsibilities of the modern university*. Durham, NC: Carolina Academic Press.

Billings, R. S., Milburn, T. W., & Schaalman, M. L. (1980). A model of crisis perception: A theoretical and empirical analysis. *Administrative Science Quarterly, 25*, 300–316.

Bombing of Pan Am flight 103 over Lockerbie. (2000, May 18). Retrieved October 19, 2006, from http://www.history1900s.about.com/library/weekly/aa051800a.htm.

Bonfire collapse Texas A&M University: College Station, Texas-November 1999. (1999). Technical Report Series-USFA-TR-133. FEMA/U.S. Fire Administration. Retrieved November 2, 2006, from http://www.usfa.dhs.gov/downloads/pdf/publications/tr-133-508.pdf.

Brown, P. (2006). *Newsman captured Tower shooting in era before live TV*. Retrieved October 19, 2006, from http://www.news8austin.com/content/news_8_explores/ut_tower_shooting/?ArID=167765&SecID=552

Brunner, B. (2005). *Hurricane Katrina*. Retrieved October 19, 2006, from http://www.infoplease.com/spot/hurricanekatrina.html.

Clery, H., & Clery, C. (2001). *What Jeanne didn't know*. Retrieved June 5, 2005, from http://www.securityoncampus.org/aboutsoc/didn'tknow.html.

Coombs, W. T. (1999). *Ongoing crisis communication: Planning, managing, and responding* (Vol. 2). Thousand Oaks, CA: Sage.

Fink, S. (1986). *Crisis management: Planning for the inevitable*. New York: American Management Association.

Hermann, C. F. (1963). Some consequences of crisis which limit the viability of organizations. *Administrative Science Quarterly, 8*, 61–82.

Hermann, C. F. (1972). Threat, time, and surprise: A simulation of international crises. In C. F. Hermann (Ed.), *International crises: Insights from behavioral research* (pp. 187–211). New York: Free Press.

Holsti, O. R. (1978). Limitations of cognitive abilities in the face of crisis. In C. F. Smart & W. T. Stansbury (Eds.), *Studies in crisis management* (pp. 39–55). Toronto: Butterworth.

Hurricane Katrina timeline. (2005). Retrieved October 19, 2006, from http://www.cbc.ca/news/background/katrina/katrina_timeline.html.

Hurst, J. C. (1999). The Matthew Shepard tragedy: Management of a crisis. *About Campus, 4*(3), 5–11.

Irvine, R. B., & Millar, D. P. (1996). *Debunking the stereotypes of crisis management: The nature of business crisis in the 1990s*. Institute for Crisis Management. Retrieved October 13, 2006, from http://www.crisisexperts.com/debunking_main.htm.

Johnson, C. (2005). *Tulane scales back post-Katrina*. Retrieved October 19, 2006, from http://www.cbsnews.com/stories/2005/12/09/katrina/main1113504.shtml.

KLBJ: The story of Austin radio. (n.d.). Retrieved June 5, 2005, from http://www.klbjfm.com/about/index_history.aspx.

Konigsmark, A. R. (2006, January 1). New Orleans universities seeing real homecoming. *USA Today*. Retrieved October 19, 2006, from http://www.usatoday.com/news/education/2006-01-09-new-orleans-universities_x.htm?POE=NEWISVA.

Koovor-Misra, S. (1995). A multidimensional approach to crisis preparation for technical organizations: Some critical factors. *Technological Forecasting and Social Change, 48*, 143–160.

Lewis, J. M., & Hensley, T. R. (1998). The May 4 shootings at Kent State University: The search for historical accuracy. *Ohio Council for the Social Studies Review, 34*(1), 9–21.

MacLeod, M. (2005). *Charles Whitman: The Texas Tower sniper*. Retrieved June 5, 2005, from http://www.crimelibrary.com/notorious_murders/mass/whitman/tower_6.html.

Meningitis scare prompts vaccinations. (1992). *Chronicle of Higher Education*. Retrieved July 10, 2005, from http://chronicle.com/che-data/articles.dir/articles-38.dir/issue-26.dir/26a00703.htm.

Murder charges planned in beating death of gay student. (1998). Retrieved July 11, 2005, from http://www.cnn.com/US/9810/12/wyoming.attack.03/ index.html.

Northridge quake anniversary: Looking back, future plans. (2004). Retrieved July 10, 2005, from http://www.nbc4.tv/news/2766157/detail.html.

Pauchant, T. C., & Mitroff, I. I. (1992). *Transforming the crisis-prone organization: Preventing individual, organizational, and environmental tragedies.* San Francisco: Jossey-Bass.

Phelps, N. L. (1986). Setting up a crisis recovery plan. *Journal of Business Strategy,* 6(4), 5–11.

Pickrell, J. (2005, September 21). *Hurricane Katrina: The aftermath.* Retrieved November 2, 2006, from http://www.newscientist.com/channel/earth/ hurricane/dn9960.

Preece, F. (1996). *August 1st and other things.* Retrieved June 5, 2005, from http://www.austinprop.com/Whitman.htm.

Rhatigan, J. J. (2000). The history and philosophy of student affairs. In M. J. Barr, M. K. Desler, & Associates (Eds.), *The handbook of student affairs administration* (pp. 3–24). San Francisco: Jossey-Bass.

Rodrigue, C. M., Rovsi, E., & Flace, S. E. (1997, September). *Construction of the "Northridge" earthquake in Los Angeles' English and Spanish print media: Damage, attention, and skewed recovery.* Paper presented at the Southern California Environment and History Conference, Northridge, CA.

Romano, L. (2005, October 1). New Orleans's black colleges hit hard. *Washington Post,* p. A1. Retrieved October 19, 2006, from http://pqasb.pqarchiver.com/ washingtonpost/access/905124741.html?dids=905124741:905124741&F MT=ABS&FMTS=ABS:FT&fmac=&date=Oct+1%2C+2005&author= Lois+Romano&desc=New+Orleans%27s+Black+Colleges+Hit+Hard.

Schoenherr, S. (2001). *Pearl Harbor attack—1941. World War II timeline.* Retrieved June 5, 2005, from http://history.sandiego.edu/gen/ ww2timeline/prelude23.html.

Seymour, M., & Moore, S. (2000). *Effective crisis management: Worldwide principles and practice.* London: Cassell.

Snow, R. L. (1996). *SWAT teams: Explosive face-offs with America's deadliest criminals.* New York: Plenum Press.

Sodders, L. M. (2004, January 17). A better CSUN: Looking at campus's progressive decade. *LA Daily News,* p. N3. Retrieved July 10, 2005, from http://www.dailynews.com/Stories/0,1413,200~30561~1896551,00.html.

Students at University of Florida struggle to cope with grisly murders. (1990). *Chronicle of Higher Education.* Retrieved July 10, 2005, from http://

chronicle.com/che-data/articles.dir/articles-37.dir/issue-02.dir/
02a00102.htm.

Texas store window shattered by sniper. (1966, August 12). *Life Magazine*.
Retrieved June 5, 2005, from http://www.life.com/Life/search/covers.

Tuchman, G. (2000). *Kent State shootings remembered*. Retrieved October 19,
2006, from http://archives.cnn.com/2000/US/05/04/kent.state.revisit/
index.html.

University of Illinois immunizes 5,700 after 2 meningitis deaths. (1991, February).
Chronicle of Higher Education. Retrieved July 10, 2005, from http://
chronicle.com/che-data/articles.dir/articles-37.dir/issue-23.dir/
23a00204.htm.

Victims of Pan Am Flight 103 (n.d.). Retrieved October 19, 2006, from http://
web.syr.edu/~vpaf103/index.html.

Zdziarski, E. L. (2006). Crisis in the context of higher education. In K. S. Harper,
B. G. Paterson, & E. L. Zdziarski (Eds.), *Crisis management: Responding
from the heart* (pp. 3–24). Washington, DC: NASPA.

2

The Crisis Matrix

Eugene L. Zdziarski II, J. Michael Rollo, and Norbert W. Dunkel

In the previous chapter we reviewed the impact that crisis has had on college and university campuses. We saw how it has affected our students, their families, and society as a whole. We also explored what a crisis is and offered a definition of crisis that addresses many of its common characteristics. Yet as we seek an understanding of crisis and crisis management, if we set about listing all of the events that can result in a crisis we very quickly come to the realization that the possibilities are endless. Just reviewing our own history shows that whatever was possible—and in some cases unimaginable—has already occurred. What could be next? How can we prepare or plan for events that we cannot conceive of?

In this instance it becomes instructive to develop a taxonomy of types of events that allows administrators to conceptualize appropriate responses to a variety of incidents. In the previous chapter, some of the most sensational and overwhelming crises in higher education were identified. These examples provide us with a sense of the scale a crisis can reach despite our best-laid plans. Fortunately, these types of incidents tend to be relatively rare, and many of us will not be touched by an event of this magnitude in our entire careers. However, we administrators of colleges and universities need to function like firefighters. Firefighters prepare and train constantly for something they hope will never happen. We spend our professional lives preparing to work on an important task—responding to a major crisis—while hoping that it never comes. Yet the natural course of events on a college campus provides us many smaller and more manageable opportunities to practice our basic skills, develop and test protocols, and learn from our mistakes. If we pay attention to these smaller events that seem to occur endlessly, we can begin to see all of the pieces that will be needed when a large-scale event comes upon us. Thus, perceiving crisis response as a scalable resource is an important element in any institutional crisis management plan.

Furthermore, linear thinking when responding to a crisis can be limiting and result in lost opportunities to help those affected. For this reason, it is more useful to think of personal and institutional crises as a matrix of interrelated and dynamic events.

The Crisis Matrix

The crisis matrix (see Figure 2.1) is a conceptual model developed to provide a basic framework for assessing a crisis, determining its impact on the campus community, and identifying considerations

Figure 2.1. The Crisis Matrix

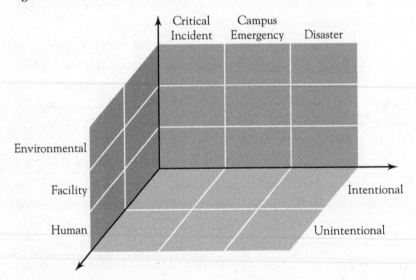

in responding to the crisis. The matrix comprises three dimensions: level of crisis, type of crisis, and intentionality of crisis. It can be visually represented as a cube, with the edges serving as axes of the three dimensions. Where a crisis falls within each of these dimensions will determine the types of issues or contingencies a campus must consider in its crisis management process and provide benchmarks to measure its need for resource allocation and deployment.

Level of Crisis

The first dimension of the crisis matrix is the level of crisis. By *level*, we mean the scope or magnitude of the crisis. In this model we identify three levels: critical incident, campus emergency, and disaster.

Critical Incidents

Not all crisis events affect the campus as a whole. Some affect a segment or portion of the campus in very significant ways but do not disrupt normal operations of the institution overall. These types of crisis events are identified in the matrix as *critical incidents*. A critical incident is an event whose initial impact is limited to a specific segment or subgroup of the institution.

Campuses tend to be well-versed in responding to critical incidents. Narrowly focused on one or more individuals, a living unit, a student organization, or an academic department, these incidents tend to be manageable by existing resources on many campuses. The regular occurrence of these sorts of events provides the campus with many opportunities for learning. Critical incidents include such things as a student suicide attempt, the death or serious injury of a faculty member due to a car accident, or a facility fire.

The basic response during any crisis comes back to focus on the actual person affected. Regardless of the scale of the crisis, it is the human element that we address consistently throughout the process. To varying degrees, physical, emotional, and spiritual well-being are keys to recovery in even the most minor incident. Therefore, all of the same services and processes that will be brought to bear in a larger crisis can be developed and honed during these smaller events. Relationships between on- and off-campus services can be developed and refined. Weaknesses in communication, cooperation, and coordination will become apparent and can be addressed.

For all these reasons, it is important that campuses plan and pre-pare for critical incidents and develop appropriate systems and teams. Critical incidents provide real-world opportunities to test and train for large-scale events. It is also important to realize that incidents that are mismanaged can easily grow and become full-blown crises. In sum, despite their small scope, critical incidents should not be overlooked.

Campus Emergencies

A *campus emergency* is defined as an event that disrupts the orderly operations of the institution or its educational mission. Such an event affects all facets of the institution and often raises questions about shutting down for a period of time. In terms of scope or mag-nitude, a campus emergency requires an institution-wide response to address multiple issues.

In a campus emergency, outside resources, particularly services that assist with public safety, are often needed to support on-campus services that may be stretched to the breaking point. The lack of a fully staffed counseling center, an Employee Assistance Program (EAP), a public safety unit, or a functioning emergency on-call sys-tem, will limit the ability of an institution to provide care if a sub-stantial number of individuals are affected. This is especially problematic at smaller or nonresidential institutions, because the infrastructure may not be in place to adequately provide the full array of necessary services or the size of the response capability may be insufficient for the need.

Large-scale demonstrations, riots at sporting events, a possible serial killer, tornadoes or approaching hurricanes, urban unrest, and the like, may all be contributing factors in an institution's ability to continue functioning and thus warrant designation as a campus emergency. Well-prepared and well-trained campuses that have had experience with previous such crises can be helpful to a sister institution that is experiencing one for the first time. Because of the campuswide scope of the event, sometimes caregivers and management are affected significantly along with the institution, which can compromise its ability to respond.

Disasters

Finally, some crisis events have a major impact well beyond the borders of the campus. This level of crisis is referred to as a *disaster*. A disaster disrupts not only institutional operations and functions but those of the surrounding community. During such crisis events, resources that the institution might typically rely on may be delayed or unavailable because they are being employed in the broader community.

Being overwhelmed is a frightening and dismaying condition that can lead to paralysis of action. The problem is so large that the enormity of it cannot be grasped and the flood of visual and emotional stimuli causes an inability to discriminate. Where does one start to pick up the pieces, both literally and figuratively? Although extremely rare—so rare, in fact, that they usually have names attached to them, such as Hurricane Andrew, 9/11, the Northridge earthquake, or the Chicago fire—they are so devastating that they overwhelm even the most sophisticated and highly functioning systems and institutions. Perhaps the most obvious example is Hurricane Katrina, which overwhelmed the response capabilities of FEMA itself. In such disasters the first responders, caregivers, and management tasked with response and recovery may be as affected as the individual victims, or in extreme cases, unavailable because of injury or death. Virtually every institutional function on the campus and in the community is compromised and functioning at less than full capacity. Outside resources, if available, must be brought in as soon as possible to assist the physical and emotional healing that will have to occur for the community to move forward.

Events that become classified as disasters forever mark the lives of those who witnessed or lived through the experience. The institution is never free from the legacy of the disaster, although over time there is a lessening of the intensity of the response. Memorials on the anniversary of the event, or similar incidents differing in scale, will keep the experience of the disaster in the consciousness of the community for many years.

Type of Crisis

The second dimension in the crisis matrix is type of crisis. *Type of crisis* refers to the different kinds of crises an organization prepares for or could experience. Researchers (Clement & Rickard, 1992; Koovor-Misra, 1995; Meyers, 1986; Mitroff, Pauchant, & Shrivastava, 1988a, 1988b; Shrivastava, 1987) suggest that the different types of crises group together in relatively distinct sets or clusters, often referred to as *typologies*. The crisis management literature offers a variety of crisis typologies. These typologies can range from as few as five different clusters of crisis types (Ogrizek & Guillery, 1999) to as many as eleven (Mitroff, Pearson, & Harrington, 1996). In the crisis matrix we identify three types of crises that are common to institutions of higher education: environmental, facility, and human.

Environmental Crises

An *environmental crisis* is any event or situation that originates with the environment or nature. Typical weather-related crises such as hurricanes, earthquakes, and floods fall into this category.

Our natural environment provides different opportunities for possible crises to occur. Communities on the Gulf Coast or the Atlantic seaboard must contend with the inevitability of hurricanes and their corollary events, while the West Coast is always conscious of the threat of earthquakes or volcanic eruptions. Of course, the environment may affect us in a much more localized manner in the form of windstorms, lightning strikes, floods, or other localized weather conditions. Regardless of how widespread the crisis or its cause, the overriding power of the forces of nature dictates a response that must take place in a variety of conditions. The ability, or lack thereof, to control the operating conditions will have to be addressed as a campus responds.

Facility Crises

A *facility crisis* is any event or situation that originates in a facility or structure. Examples of such crises include building fires, power outages, and the like. All institutions must be prepared to respond to changes in the condition of their facilities. The possibility of structural weaknesses, fires, chemical spills, and a vast array of safety concerns bring the focus of a crisis into a localized area for first responders. Resources can be allocated depending on the size of the structure or the number of structures affected. The changing conditions of the structure or structures as the incident unfolds, and their potential loss to the institution, provide the need for contingency plans for activities and functions that normally take place there. Dealing with the destruction of a major classroom building or a campus's main computer center requires the development of a business continuity plan (described in more detail in Chapter Twelve), if the institution wishes to continue to function after the most extreme situation. Facility concerns may be one factor to address in a much larger problem, but some resources will have to be marshaled to ensure the safety of the community and to protect and repair the campus infrastructure.

Human Crises

A *human crisis* is any event or situation that originates with or is initiated by human beings, whether through human error or conscious act. They include criminal acts, traffic accidents, mental health issues, and the like.

As already noted, responses to all crises must address the impact on individuals and groups in the campus community. It is the impact on people that makes an event a crisis. If a Class Five tornado touches down in a prairie fifty miles from the nearest person, there is no crisis. No one may even know it occurred. What forces us to prepare to respond is the human factor. The starting point for any crisis, no matter how minor or severe, is a person who needs attention. Injuries, victimization, illness, death, mental illness, and grief enter our communities daily and require us to help each other cope. In many ways, colleges and universities already provide this type of support through existing institutions on their campuses and in their communities. Seeing how these services and support systems relate to crisis response in the matrix can be helpful in planning a flexible response to changing circumstances and conditions.

Intentionality of Crisis

The third dimension of the crisis matrix is intentionality. A concept originally introduced by Newsom, Turk, and Kruckeberg (2000), it distinguishes between unintentional and intentional crises.

Unintentional Crises

As the term implies, an *unintentional crisis* occurs by accident. No deliberate act initiates it. Accidents are not a new or unique phenomenon to anyone familiar with normal institutional operations. Workplace injuries, automobile and bicycle crashes, sports injuries, falls, and unanticipated illnesses are typical events that can be characterized as unintentional. They are unexpected or the result of an unanticipated action, and there is a clear absence of any purposeful behavior by an individual or group as a contributing factor. The ubiquity of this type of occurrence in everyday life can lead us to dismiss such minor incidents as routine, but when viewed in relation to the entire matrix they become another point of contact inside the whole of an institution's response capabilities.

Intentional Crises

Intentional crises occur as a result of a deliberate act. An individual or group of individuals purposefully takes steps to cause the event that has an impact on others. The daily interaction between students, staff, faculty, and visitors on college campuses provides the opportunity for acts that occur in our society as a whole to occur within our confines. Workplace violence, domestic violence, sexual assault, vandalism, and arson may happen on any day of the week, and sometimes without warning, while campus demonstrations, riots at sporting events, or murder can quickly change the character of a community as it struggles to respond. The possibility that a criminal act has occurred shifts the focus in this type of incident so that now multiple responses are required to address the concerns. The response to an unintentional incident may focus on only one individual, but in an intentional incident there will be at least one victim and one perpetrator, and the differences between them may be difficult to discern. By its very nature, the intentional nature of the incident complicates the matter and requires additional resources.

In the third part of this volume, "Lessons from Crisis Management," campus administrators from across the country share their insights and experiences in dealing with all three types of crises depicted in the matrix.

How Crises Evolve

Every event, no matter how it concludes, starts as a critical incident. The scale, scope, and impact are what expand the incident through the matrix, absorbing new constituencies, requiring additional resources, and affecting the ability to respond. If we note where the three axes meet, it establishes an end point for response. An *unintentional critical incident affecting an individual* may be the basis on which an institution builds an entire portfolio of services.

As we follows the vectors that proceed from the end point, additional services are needed. A lightning strike (unintentional, environmental) that damages the electronics in a lab (facility) that in turn destroys the data of a graduate student (human) is a critical incident. This set of circumstances requires a certain response from a specific set of resources. However, this can change, sometimes dramatically. A lightning strike (unintentional, environmental) that starts a fire (facility) that destroys a building and causes injuries and loss of life (human) quickly becomes a crisis and requires a significantly different response. It can appear to be a different type of event because of the personal tragedy that ensues. However, although the vector of response may now have a different slope, the end point remains at the intersection of the three axes *unintentional critical incident affecting an individual*. We begin our response with the same set of resources and add supports and services as needed.

We can address intentional acts here in comparison. Campuses need to develop a different set of resources to address them, because with intentional acts it is possible that university rules have been violated, or worse, that a criminal act has occurred. If an individual managing a small fire loses control of it (environmental), causing damage to a structure (facility) and receiving minor burns trying to contain the blaze before calling for assistance (human), that is an example of an *unintentional critical incident affecting an individual*. Once again, the end point in the matrix is at the intersection of the three axes, but it has shifted to the other corner of the cube to reflect the change in causative factors. The end point now begins at unintentional and includes additional factors that could affect the response after the fire is extinguished. In the human dimension there may be the need for disciplinary action in addition to medical care. In the facility dimension, the problem will differ significantly depending on the degree of destruction and the ability to replace the facility.

As the vector of response proceeds from the human dimension through the matrix, regardless of where it ends, the continuum of services will expand or contract as needed. Over time, an institution can begin to see patterns of need and easily scale its responses more efficiently. Even in a larger-scale campus emergency or disaster, where multiple vectors of response may extend from the end point along the intentional and unintentional axes and there are damages to facilities, pollution of the environment, and forever-changed lives, the vector of response can provide a guide for an institution's measured and planned response. For campuses that have not had a history of large-scale critical incidents or campus emergencies, the matrix can be used as a tool to hypothesize potential problem areas and develop protocols for response. In addition, gaps in service can become apparent during a case study experience rather than during an actual crisis and plans can be made to address the shortcomings.

Thus, the crisis matrix can be used as a guide to help conceptualize the need for specific resources and the scale appropriate for efficient response. As a planning tool, it serves as a template to use for the deployment of resources and the development of additional resources. We suggest that the matrix become part of the overall assessment process of a campus's readiness to respond to critical incidents, campus emergencies, and disasters.

A Phased Approach to Crisis Management

Although the crisis matrix provides a good framework through which to assess a crisis, determine its impact on the campus community, and identify considerations for responding, a sound crisis management system must also be in place. It is important to distinguish between managing crisis situations and simply responding to them. All too often, crisis management is considered a singular set of actions taken in response to a particular event or incident. Instead, crisis management should be seen as a process that includes a series of stages or phases in which administrators take certain actions. To effectively manage crises, administrators need to take action well before a crisis hits, as well as long after the crisis subsides. A good crisis management system needs to address not only the response phase but the pre- and postphases as well.

This phased approach to crisis management is frequently discussed in the crisis management literature (Abent, 1999; Coombs, 1999; Federal Emergency Management Agency, 1996; Koovor-Misra, 1995; Mitroff et al., 1996; Ogrizek & Guillery, 1999; Pauchant & Mitroff, 1992). The most common crisis management system is described by three phases: precrisis, crisis, and postcrisis (Birch, 1994; Coombs, 1999; Guth, 1995; Koovor-Misra, 1995; Meyers, 1986; Mitchell, 1986; Ogrizek & Guillery, 1999). The descriptions of each of these phases are relatively straightforward. The precrisis phase encompasses actions taken prior to the onset of a crisis. The crisis phase encompasses actions taken during a crisis. The postcrisis phase encompasses actions taken after a crisis. The importance of this concept is that it acknowledges that effective crisis management means more than simply responding or reacting to a crisis event. Instead, it involves administrators taking thoughtful, planned, and deliberate actions before, during, and after a crisis event.

Another approach that readers may be familiar with is provided by the Federal Emergency Management Agency (FEMA, 1996). Used by federal, state, and local emergency management professionals across the country, this approach describes crisis management in four phases: mitigation, preparedness, response, and recovery. The significance of this approach is that it adds the mitigation stage. The crisis management system proposed by FEMA acknowledges that we should not only make deliberate plans and preparations before a crisis occurs but also take specific actions to prevent or reduce the likelihood of a crisis occurring.

Building on these crisis management systems and borrowing from a third (Pauchant & Mitroff, 1992) we offer a five-phase crisis management cycle: planning, prevention, response, recovery, and learning (see Figure 2.2).

Figure 2.2. Crisis Management Cycle

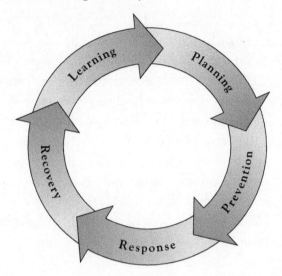

Planning

The institution must give deliberate thought to crisis management planning. In the middle of the event it is not the time to begin wondering how to go about resolving the issue or identifying key stakeholders who can respond in a coordinated fashion. An office (or at minimum, an individual) should be designated to develop and coordinate planning for crisis response. The office of crisis planning (or the coordinator of crisis planning) can allocate the resources to ongoing review of the plan, updating resources, and distributing the plan to the campus. As an added bonus, it becomes a starting point for training efforts to begin to gather allies who will need to work closely under pressure when the need arises. As staff and resources are brought together to learn about the plan, new issues will be identified that will require further training efforts. As this occurs, the ownership of the plan extends farther into the campus and enhances the institution's ability to respond.

Prevention

Consciousness of crisis issues and working toward avoidance of crisis situations are goals that must be shared by many campus partners. Knowing the types of incidents that a campus is likely to experience, such as large-scale events, weather incidents, and the possibility of exterior threats—a nuclear power plant located near a campus, for example, would require that campus to develop specific plans in the event of an emergency at that facility—can provide opportunities to avoid serious incidents from happening or at least mitigate their impact. Administrators need to carefully consider what actions can be taken inside the campus community to reduce the likelihood of a crisis occurring or at least reduce the impact of a crisis should one occur.

Response

When an event actually occurs that requires an institutional response, the plan, in whatever form it has been developed, begins to operate in real time. Teams form that have practice in case study format, and other individuals and entities appear. Turf issues and lines of responsibility are tested under pressure, and personal relationships that have been developed become important links among services provided to the affected community. The larger the scope of the necessary response, the more likely that there will be conflict between responders. It is important that, during the planning stage, clear expectations are communicated about who will respond, when they will respond, and where they will respond. A well-crafted plan with clear working relations established between the various players will allow for a coordinated response that uses the campus energy and resources to respond to the crisis, rather than to work out its own inner conflicts.

Recovery

The time it takes for a community to recover from an incident varies depending on the relationship of resources and stressors that are brought to bear. In incidents where the stressors far outweigh the resources and abilities of the community to respond, outside entities may need to be called on to assist, and the time needed to return to normal functions may be significant. In smaller incidents with less widespread implications—such as an incident that affects a living unit or student organization—a campus can focus considerable resources in the small area and possibly resume normal functions quickly. Individual responses will vary in communities, no matter how well the institution has recovered, and they must be addressed on a case-by-case basis. Closure events, memorials, permanent recognitions, and other ceremonial events provide wonderful opportunities to share healing processes and bring communities back together with the purpose of moving forward and putting the tragedy behind them. This is also a time for the institution to look to helping those who have been instrumental in serving the community as responders and service providers during the crisis. Crisis counselors, first responders, and other caregivers will need some attention paid to them now. With the crisis over and a return to normal life, the caregivers need some care themselves, so that they can be ready to respond when called on again in the future.

Learning

Each incident provides opportunities for us to learn from our successes and failures in responding adequately. Either as a special and targeted process or as part of a regular meeting, incidents of all sizes and scope should be reviewed by the responsible parties to gather information that will assist them during the next crisis. Out of this process come updates to existing plans and revisions of protocols. Staff is identified for further development based on perceived weakness or other traits, conflict points are noted and targeted for special attention, and new allies are discovered to include in future planning.

It is also important for the institution to debrief the crisis responders after significant events or series of events. The emotional toll on those who serve others is recognized as a potentially debilitating burden if left unresolved over time. Degradation of abilities and ultimately burnout can occur if their needs are ignored. Although much is learned about incidents during debriefings, their primary purpose should be to provide support and care to those we rely on most during crises.

All debriefing activities and incident reviews offer the opportunity to generate new and improved plans and topics and scenarios for staff training. This process helps us learn from mistakes, identify strengths of individuals and working relationships, and acquire and practice skills that will assist in the planning and prevention phases of crisis response. (See the Appendix for a checklist for conducting debriefings.) Failure to take the time for this last step in the process is a missed opportunity for growth among individual staff and the institution as a whole. It is imperative that the managers of the crisis response group ensure that the debriefing occurs.

Conclusion

The purpose of this chapter has been to present readers with a general theoretical and conceptual framework from which to understand crisis management. With this background we can now begin to fill in the details of individual crisis management systems. How do we form a crisis management team and who should be on it? How do we put together a crisis management plan and who do we include in the planning and implementation of a crisis response program? How do we coordinate our efforts with various community resources? How and where do we begin? The following chapters provide examples and resources that will allow readers to begin the process of development on their campuses more effectively.

References

Abent, R. (1999). Managing in time of crisis. *NASPA NetResults*. Retrieved November 30, 1999, from http://www.naspa.org/Results/pubrelat/managing.html.

Birch, J. (1994). New factors in crisis planning and response. *Public Relations Quarterly, 39*, 31–34.

Clement, L. M., & Rickard, S. T. (1992). Managing crises. In L. M. Clement & S. T. Rickard (Eds.), *Effective leadership in student services: Voices from the field* (pp. 145–164). San Francisco: Jossey-Bass.

Coombs, W. T. (1999). *Ongoing crisis communication: Planning, managing, and responding* (Vol. 2). Thousand Oaks, CA: Sage.

Federal Emergency Management Agency. (1996). *State and local guide (SLG 101): Guide for all-hazard emergency operations planning.* Retrieved June 16, 2006, from http://www.fema.gov/plan/gaheop.htm.

Guth, D. W. (1995). Organizational crisis experience and public relations roles. *Public Relations Review, 21*(2), 123–136.

Koovor-Misra, S. (1995). A multidimensional approach to crisis preparation for technical organizations: Some critical factors. *Technological Forecasting and Social Change, 48*, 143–160.

Meyers, G. C. (1986). *When it hits the fan: Managing the nine crises of business.* New York: Mentor.

Mitchell, T. H. (1986). Coping with a corporate crisis. *Canadian Business Review, 13*(3), 17–20.

Mitroff, I. I., Pauchant, T. C., & Shrivastava, P. (1988a). Conceptual and empirical issues in development of a general theory of crisis management. *Technological Forecasting and Social Change, 33*, 83–107.

Mitroff, I. I., Pauchant, T. C., & Shrivastava, P. (1988b). Forming a crisis portfolio. *Security Management, 33*, 101–108.

Mitroff, I. I., Pearson, C. M., & Harrington, L. K. (1996). *The essential guide to managing corporate crisis: A step-by-step handbook for surviving major catastrophes.* New York: Oxford University Press.

Newsom, D., Turk, J. V., & Kruckeberg, D. (2000). *This is PR: The realities of public relations* (7th ed.). Belmont, CA: Wadsworth/Thomson Learning.

Ogrizek, M., & Guillery, J.-M. (1999). *Communicating in crisis: A theoretical and practical guide to crisis management* (H. Kimball-Brooke & R. Z. Brooke, Trans.). Hawthorne, NY: Aldine de Gruyter.

Pauchant, T. C., & Mitroff, I. I. (1992). *Transforming the crisis-prone organization: Preventing individual, organizational, and environmental tragedies.* San Francisco: Jossey-Bass.

Shrivastava, P. (1987). *Bhopal: Anatomy of a crisis.* New York: Ballinger.

Part II

Crisis Management in Practice

3

Crisis Management Teams

Grant P. Sherwood and David McKelfresh

The key to successful crisis management is forming a team to deal with crises before they occur. According to Spillan (2003), "There are very convincing arguments supporting the formation of crisis management teams which can take charge of planning for a crisis before it occurs, as well as managing the problems that emerge during a crisis" (p. 162). Spillan goes on to say that a crisis can occur with little or no warning and cites examples of recent major crises:

- In 1993, twenty-three people were shot during an incident on the Long Island Railroad.

- In 1995, domestic terrorists bombed the Murrah Federal Building in Oklahoma City.

- In 2000, three students perished in the Seton Hall University residence hall fire (Barton, 2001).

Crisis Management Teams

Crisis management is the umbrella term that encompasses all activities when an organization prepares for and responds to a significant event. A definition of crisis was provided in Chapter One of this volume: "An event, which is often sudden or unexpected, that disrupts the normal operations of the institution or its educational mission and threatens the well-being of personnel, property, financial resources, and/or reputation of the institution." According to Crisis Management International ("Integrated Crisis Management Defined," 2004), an effective crisis management program should be consistent with the organizational mission and integrate plans such as emergency response, business continuity, crisis communications, disaster recovery, and humanitarian assistance.

An important part of the crisis management strategy is the creation of a team of people who are charged with the task of handling the response in an actual crisis situation. This crisis management team (CMT) must be able to work well together under pressure and should have clearly delineated responsibilities and authority. According to Blythe (2001), it is the role of CMTs to protect core assets—people, finances, and reputation—during times of risk.

Many higher education institutions have created CMTs and found success and peace of mind in doing so. In fact, many campuses have created teams with expanded roles. For example, Georgia State University (2006, p. iii) has charged its CMT with very broad responsibilities:

Mitigation: Activities which eliminate or reduce the probability of a disaster's occurrence.

Preparedness: Activities which focus on essential disaster response capabilities through development of plans and procedures, organization and management of resources, and training/education of people.

Response: Activities which provide emergency assistance for casualties and help reduce further damage or help to speed recovery operations.

Recovery: Activities, both short and long term, which help to return conditions to normal or improved levels. During the recovery operations, actions are taken to minimize recurrence of the disaster, or lessen its effects if prevention is not possible.

This model has obviously enlarged the responsibilities of the CMT far beyond mere crisis response. There is a proactive expectation that the team will engage in educational programs focused on risk management and prevention and have strong responsibilities in the areas of assessment and evaluation after the incident.

Forming a Crisis Management Team

We mention the breadth of the CMT's possible responsibilities early in this chapter because these responsibilities are directly related to the team's role and functions. In all cases, however, crisis management teams will find themselves best able to respond to a range of possibilities if four issues are carefully addressed: team membership, team leadership, team operations, and team training.

Team Membership

Several criteria will influence membership on the team.

Institutional Criteria

Institutional size and setting will influence membership. Smaller institutions probably will not have campus resources and services to draw from to form a comprehensive team and thus may need to partner with community resources outside the campus. Mental health professionals and emergency response personnel from the local community may play important roles on the team in these situations. Community colleges too may have limited resources to draw on. Urban campuses may have a greater need for security planning, and colleges and universities located in regions of the country that are at higher environmental risk (such as from earthquakes and floods) may want to add team members who can provide this kind of specific knowledge and expertise.

Typically, crisis management teams deal with public safety, facility issues, communication issues, risk management, people issues, legal issues, and financial issues.

With these concerns in mind, campuses that have formed CRT teams have built them around these personnel: chief business officer, chief administrative officer, chief student affairs officer, legal counsel, human resources officer, chief of police or security, information technology officer, director of housing and residence life, director of health and counseling, director of public relations, and director of environmental health.

At the University of Memphis, the CMT is actually composed of two subgroups: Policy and Operations. The Policy Group defines crisis policy, approves overall priorities and strategies, issues public information reports and instructions, determines program closures and resumptions, and plans and prioritizes long-term recovery. The Operations Group determines the scope and impact of the incident, prioritizes emergency actions, deploys and coordinates resources and equipment, communicates critical information and instructions, monitors and reevaluates conditions, and coordinates with government agencies.

Membership in each group varies based on function and purpose. Obviously, because of the nature of their responsibilities, some staff serve on both groups.

There exist many iterations of this basic model across campuses nationwide. Team membership is generally guided by core values that are well articulated to all stakeholders. In order to be effective, teams must be provided with the proper authority, funding, and human resources.

Skills and Competencies

Effective team members need certain skills or competencies.

Availability. Team members must be available to respond to a crisis in a timely manner. A number of institutions designate backup personnel as part of their contingency planning.

Knowledge of resources. Team members need to understand what support resources are available and how to employ them if necessary. It is particularly helpful to include members who have extended work experience on the campus and understand organizational structures both on the campus and in the community.

Team player mindset. Team members need to appreciate that group consensus is needed to resolve crises successfully. Individual egos should take a backseat to creative intervention. Team cohesion will always improve the members' performance under stress. Team members who know each other well, and in particular, appreciate and value one another's roles, will operate most efficiently.

Trainability. Team members need to dedicate time to go through orientation and training. They also need to view training as a form of continuing education and commit the time and energy to update themselves on current issues and protocols.

Diversity-communication skills. Different perspectives are valued as long as this diversity does not lead to unmanageable conflict. The goal is to create an opportunity to explore a variety of solutions, yet make decisions in a timely manner. Organizational structure and campus politics can hinder timely decision making. Trust is important to team success. Many of the team members might not routinely work with each other, so creating opportunities to build relationships is critical. Many authors (Brooking, 2000; Power, 2001) suggest that trying to build such relationships during a crisis can be a disaster in itself.

Good communications policy and practice will accomplish the following goals:

- Assist in the actual management of a crisis

- Provide direction to faculty, staff, and students

- Reduce rumors and uncertainty

- Ensure that clear and accurate information is disseminated to interested constituencies and the public at large

- Maintain the institution's credibility and minimize damage to its reputation

Assessment skills. Team members must also have good assessment skills, for two reasons. First, each team member must be able to assess the crisis and help determine a strategic response. Because each member represents an area of expertise or functional service, this diverse input is critical in pursuing viable response options. Second, after the crisis has been mitigated, assessment skills play an important role in determining how team members responded, what outcomes occurred, and how strategies can be improved for dealing with future issues.

Other Important Factors

When making appointments to crisis management teams, other factors that might interfere with team success should also be considered.

Motivation to serve. A critical element of team success is the individual motivation of team members. Some will serve out of passion and concern, others will serve only as a result of duty or assignment. It is important to find individuals who are committed to the cause and truly are concerned about the welfare of the campus community. In some cases, it may be appropriate for other senior-level administrators to serve on the team because of their specific skills and commitment.

Current job responsibilities. Specific departments might have individuals whose assigned job responsibilities include crisis intervention. Some of these same staff might have regular connections to other team members, which would facilitate communication and rapport. Sometimes job titles are misleading. For example, on some campuses being the housing director may mean only facility management; on another, the title might imply a more comprehensive student life responsibility. The key question is how one's role relates to decision making and communication with the rest of the campus.

Personality type. Stable, extroverted individuals are better suited to crisis response work. Good listening and processing skills are also important to being an effective team member. Decisions need to be made expeditiously, and having team members who are self-confident is a plus.

Territorial issues. College campuses are generally large, complex organizations that are home to many offices and departments with overlapping responsibilities. In some cases, the issues of funding and politics interfere with productive resolution of issues. Crisis management might be seen as the responsibility of a number of campus leaders, so it is critical that the president or chancellor designate who is officially in charge.

Flexible Teams

A number of institutions that have recognized the potential breadth and scope of issues that might arise on their campuses have developed smaller core crisis management teams that can add members as needed based on the circumstances. For example, the team dealing with a natural disaster might include different members than the team dealing with a major student disturbance. Most campuses recommend, however, that the core leadership remain the same during all crisis situations in order to bring predictability, continuity, and accountability to the planning and response process.

Why Good Teamwork Is Important

There are three main reasons why CMTs stumble in crisis:

- *Team roles are not clearly defined*. Tasks can fall through the cracks if responsibilities are allocated ineffectively or explained inappropriately.

- *There is a lack of coordination*. The goals are poorly defined. For example, some people may believe that a successful outcome is to control the emergency, whereas others may believe that their priority is to control the PR fallout.

- *There are communication problems.* This is a major stumbling block for any team trying to successfully negotiate a crisis. Communication problems may be caused by a number of things, including poor leadership, a subject discussed in the next paragraph.

Team Leadership

One of the most critical choices the campus CEO or president (or COO or chancellor) will make when it comes to crisis management is that of the individual who will lead this effort. The importance of leadership was clearly evident at Colorado State University during two recent natural disasters: the Pingree Park fire in 1993 and the main campus flood in 1997. In each case lives were at risk, core business operations were dramatically affected, building and property damage exceeded $135 million, and recovery involved significant planning that included negotiated insurance settlements. In both incidents the vice president for administration led a team effort that responded to the initial emergencies, helped stabilize the situation, and created a recovery plan that minimized loss of revenue and service. Leadership in this case was able to provide the authority, resources, and funding to accomplish effective management of the crisis from start to finish.

Key to effective leadership is the relationship of the team to the campus CEO or president. The latter must value the team's formation, support the team with a charge, and be ready to provide resources to assist the team's work. The CEO or president typically appoints a key subordinate to lead the group based on competency and authority in the campus community. Most often this is the chief administrative officer or chief student affairs officer.

Peter Power (2001) suggests that the team leader must always keep in balance three key considerations to make the team effective:

- *Team needs:* What does the group require, as a whole, to work?

- *Task needs:* What exactly is the job to be done?

- *Individual needs:* What does each individual require to give his or her best performance?

Power (2001, n.p.) goes on to state: "I guess it's all about CMT Leadership, which, like swimming, cannot be learned just by reading about it. It is best done with good advice and actually trying it out—before you are thrown into the deep end."

The CMT leader should also be aware that certain circumstances can affect team cohesion, productivity, and success. Anne Brooking (2000) suggests that the following circumstances can put extra demands on team members during times of crisis:

- Intense media interest or public scrutiny

- Physical and time pressures created by the nature of the incident

- Higher than usual or expected responsibility

- Uncertain or prolonged duration of the situation

- Possibility of recurrence

- Amount of contact with victims or their relatives

- Inappropriate leadership practices

- Coordination problems

- Poor role definition

- Conflict between those involved in the incident response

- Mission failure

The leader of the team thus has a unique duty not only to focus on the task but also to focus on the health and welfare of team members during and after the crisis. Team leadership also implies an important communication function, which is discussed in more depth later in this chapter.

A final comment on leadership is that crisis management work can engender positive outcomes as well as stressors. Brooking (2000) suggests that working in crisis situations enables people to employ their skills in a manner that can be intensely meaningful. So although it is really challenging, working in a response role (as a team member) has its positive aspects, including these:

- Enhancement and reinforcement of the team members' ability to cope with adversity

- Self-discipline

- Appreciation of the value of life and well-being

- A sense of accomplishment, competence, assertiveness, and resilience

A good leader will constantly remind team members that their work is valued and that there are personal benefits to serving in this important capacity.

Team Operations

Crisis management team operations have entered a new era. With an uncertain external environment, organizational fluctuations, and a changing student population at colleges and universities, crisis management teams cannot neglect any aspect of their operations. Careful and thoughtful operations are imperative.

The CMT should be able to work well together and have clearly defined responsibilities and authority. To achieve these goals, team members need a clear understanding of their jurisdiction and authority, the protocol for activating the team, and the initial activities involved in managing any crisis. Effective team operations also require the establishment of regular meetings and crisis plan development, maintenance, and dissemination.

Jurisdiction and Authority

The crisis management team includes university personnel who have the authority and resources to do whatever is necessary to resolve a crisis. As noted earlier, often the CMT is led by the chief administrative officer or chief student affairs officer. Generally, as previously stated, this person should be responsible for choosing team members. It is important that the team members be familiar with each other and fully aware of their responsibilities. Basic responsibilities may include the following:

- Developing precrisis contingency guidelines

- Gathering critical incident information

- Analyzing crisis information

- Developing crisis management strategies

- Making crisis management decisions

- Communicating with campus and community

- Reporting to the president

The CMT will be more effective and efficient if, as a crisis develops, it is clear to the members the extent to which they can make decisions about any campus crisis.

In addition, the crisis management plan (discussed in detail in the next chapter) should describe the order of succession for team members in case one or more of them is unable to be present or perform assigned duties as a result of the crisis.

One assumption should be in writing: in any situation where outside emergency agencies (for example, the police or fire department) are involved, they will secure the situation and take jurisdiction of all activities. The crisis management team will act as a support team to represent the interests of the institution.

Once the CMT is established and its structure and authority are clear, the team can focus its attention on developing the institution's crisis response procedures, including the protocol for activating the CMT, initial activities of the CMT, and the development and implementation of an action plan.

Protocol for Activating the Crisis Management Team

The CMT is generally activated by the president or the administrative vice president of the institution. The CMT may also be activated by the leader of the team. For example, Ball State University has a protocol authorizing the leader of the team (its "coordinator") to activate it. The university's crisis management plan (Ball State University, 2001) states:

> The crisis management team may be convened at any time at the discretion of the coordinator. Any member of the team is independently authorized to begin carrying [out] the duties of his or her role on the team should the crisis situation prevent the team [from] convening or communicating effectively with one another. Each member of the team is equipped with cell phones and contact information to expedite immediate communication.

In addition, all communications regarding the crisis will be coordinated through the university's public relations department, including those communications with the media. Any required university notifications or cancellations should be cleared by public relations.

Initial Activities and First Response

Initial CMT activities are important, and an effective first response may help shorten the duration of the crisis. The following is a set of basic first response activities:

- Campus security will contact the crisis management team.

- If necessary, campus security will contact the local police department or health officials.

- The CMT will set up a command center, if necessary.

- The CMT will arrange for relocations and temporary accommodations.

- The CMT will prepare to initiate the communications plan, coordinate media communications, arrange for a hot line for students and parents if necessary, and prepare a press release, if necessary.

- The CMT will arrange for counseling or appropriate services for victims and other affected individuals.

- The CMT will notify family, if required.

An example of the CMT's initial activities is provided in Ball State University's crisis management plan (Ball State University, 2001, n.p.):

Once convened, the crisis management team will:

- Immediately consider which other individuals may need to be added to the team to manage the crisis at hand.

- Review details of the crisis.

- Determine further/ongoing crisis management and response activities.

- Identify target audiences and determine communications strategy.

- Specify communication procedures to internal and external constituencies.

- Brief senior staff.

Crisis management teams are becoming more active in their planning and in their initial response to campus crises. Many are developing first response checklists for a variety of crises, including medical emergencies, violent crime or behavior, riots and demonstrations, environmental and natural disasters, and bomb threats. According to Murphy (2003, p. 37): "In any crisis situation, your institution will be judged more on its conduct than the cause of the crisis itself. Being prepared means your response will be swift, effective, measured, and complete."

Being prepared means developing an action plan.

Developing an Action Plan

One of the responsibilities of the crisis management team is to develop a written action plan with clear operating protocols. To be effective, Murphy (2003, p. 37) asserts that the plan should address six critical areas:

1. *A definition of crisis characteristics, specific to your institution.* Crises might be either real or perceived, come with no warning or with some form of prior alert, result from either controlled or uncontrolled events, or take place as a consequence of media involvement.
2. *Clear objectives of the crisis plan,* which should be to articulate an organizational policy for managing crises, identify the individuals who will comprise the crisis team, and designate those responsible for communicating with all stakeholders and the news media.
3. *Detailed crisis alert procedures,* which should include instructions for notifying members of the crisis team.
4. *External communication protocols,* including the timing for response or disclosure; spokesperson des-

ignation; a "push-button" media delivery and monitoring system; a system for correcting and following up on media reports; and consideration of "controlled" message delivery options such as advertising or direct mail (or e-mail).

5. *A crisis management game plan,* which should provide guidance in evaluating the scope and severity of the situation; gathering available facts and data; and projecting potential scenarios and responses.

6. *Tactical operations,* e.g., developing a public statement/release, conducting a press conference, and mobilizing supporters.

Crisis management plans are discussed in detail in Chapter Four.

Communicating with the Campus and Community

According to Blythe (2001), communications must flow efficiently to and from the CMT in the heat of a crisis. The CMT needs to identify *what* needs to be communicated, *when* it needs to be communicated, and *who* needs to be notified. During a declared crisis, communications should be under the direction of the senior officer of the university in cooperation with the crisis management team. Campus and community members want to know if there is "someone up there who is awake, present, and thinking." Campus and community members want to know that the leadership is engaged.

Campus Education Efforts

Educating the campus community may be one of the CMT's roles. If so, the crisis management team will be responsible for educating the campus community about its own role in the event of a crisis as well as what students, faculty, and staff can and should do.

Education efforts to be undertaken by the CMT at Ball State (Ball State University, 2001) include these:

- Posting the crisis management protocol and information about what to do in the event of a crisis on a special Web site

- Developing and disseminating a brochure to members of the campus community outlining the university's crisis management protocol and referring individuals to the Web for more information

- Developing and disseminating a user-friendly "emergency guide" with basic guidelines for the types of crisis handled by the crisis management team

- Conducting information sessions with appropriate groups around campus to familiarize them with the university's crisis management protocol

Team Training

Proper training is essential if the team is to operate effectively in times of crisis. According to Blythe (2001, p. 17), training is necessary for everyone involved in the CMT and should "inform the staff of the various procedures and programs necessary to implement the crisis response plans." It is critical not to overlook the significance of proper team training, which must include all aspects of crisis management. Because of the importance that proper training plays in the crisis management process, Chapter Eight is devoted to addressing the subject in depth.

Conclusion

Campus crisis team operations have entered a revolutionary new period, when the crisis management landscape is changing rapidly. With astute planning and implementation, crisis management teams can operate in this kind of volatile and uncertain environment.

When comprehensive teams are assembled, and there is effective team leadership, team operations are clearly defined, and there is team training, crisis management teams can effectively manage any campus crisis.

References

Ball State University. (2001, September). *Crisis management protocol*. Retrieved December 15, 2004, from http://www.bsu.edu/web/ur/crisisprotocol/crisisprotocol.pdf.

Barton, L. (2001). *Crisis in organizations II*. Cincinnati: South-Western.

Blythe, B. T. (2001, July 2001). Creating your school's crisis management team. *School Business Affairs*, pp. 16–18.

Brooking, A. (2000). *Handling stress in crisis management*. Retrieved December 15, 2004, from http://www.aip.com.auamosc/papers/brooking_a.doc.

Georgia State University. (2006, March 7). *Crisis management plan*. Retrieved October 9, 2006, from http://www2.gsu.edu/~wwwsaf/hs/GSU%20Crisis%20Management%20Plan.pdf.

Integrated crisis management defined. (2004). *Disaster Resource Guide*. Atlanta: Crisis Management International. Retrieved December 15, 2004, from http://www.cmiatl.com/news_article61.html.

Murphy, S. K. (2003, February). Crisis management demystified: Here's how to prevent a crisis from ruining your institution's reputation. *University Business*.

Power, P. (2001). *Crisis management teams: Who needs them?* Retrieved December 15, 2004, from http://www.globalcontinuity.com/article/articleview/1898/1/45.

Spillan, J. E. (2003). An exploratory model for evaluating crisis events and managers' concerns in nonprofit organizations. *Journal of Contingencies and Crisis Management, 11*(4), 160–169.

4

Developing a Crisis Management Plan

J. Michael Rollo and Eugene L. Zdziarski II

Crisis management requires an ongoing process of planning, prevention, response, recovery, and learning in a never-ending cycle. When new to a campus, some staff will set out immediately to organize and stratify the various components of the institution and community, whereas others may observe from a distance, gathering information and forming perceptions before getting down to the task of planning. How administrators go about doing this has as much to do with their personal style as the culture of the campus on which they work and reside. Preexisting plans that have been gathering dust or have been tested repeatedly, impending seasonal concerns about weather, recent incidents at an institution or similar institutions, or new leadership at an institution are all factors that affect how quickly this issue is addressed and when the planning phase of the cycle can begin.

As varied as people can be, the cultures of campuses are also distinct and unique and will dictate both how administrators begin to plan and what form the final product will take. Small campuses with stable staff and relatively minimal variations in facilities and programs may function with a greater informality due to the scope of the plan. In contrast, the institutional leadership or staff in key positions may have a high need for formal structure and require detailed and sophisticated protocols that guide what appears to be every conceivable incident. Larger institutions may have a history of large-scale planning and have the ubiquitous three-ring note-books to prove it, or they may be so large and complex that they have been unable to focus their energy into a comprehensive plan and instead function with a series of protocols developed by departments and programs, linked by an informal structure that relies heavily on personal expertise and contact between key individuals.

There is no fill-in-the-blank crisis management plan outline or turnkey software solution that can adequately address the characteristics and culture of the campus community. When arriving at a new institution or when beginning the crisis management cycle, it is important to have a clear understanding of the culture of the campus and how it both plans and uses plans. Knowing "who" you are as a campus is a critical first step in determining "what" you will become as the planning process proceeds. Where you end up on the formal-informal continuum may change the format of the plan or the sense of urgency felt, but it does not affect the overriding need for each institution to have a plan in place and in a usable form.

In studies of campus preparedness to respond to crises (Scott, 1999; Zdziarski, 2001), approximately 85 percent of the institutions indicated that they had some type of written crisis management plan. Although this bodes well in general for higher education, it still means that about 15 percent of institutions have no plan for responding to a campus crisis. The existence of a written crisis management plan is perhaps the single most important crisis management tool a campus can have. It is the foundation and framework from which a campus will operate. Having a written plan establishes a level of clarity and consistency in how the campus addresses a crisis and avoids confusion or debate on key issues that might arise in the heat of the moment. Standing in the midst of a crisis is obviously not the time to debate key response procedures or even develop a plan. When in the middle of a crisis, it is the moment to implement whatever plan the institution has taken the time to establish. Without even a modicum of planning, a campus's ability to respond will be limited and handicapped.

Gathering Information for the Plan

Development of any crisis management plan begins with an assessment or audit of the types of crisis events a campus might face and therefore the need to address them in its plan. In this process, campus administrators systematically consider the threats and risks in both the internal and external campus environments (Littleton, 1983). The objective is not only to identify the types of crises a campus is likely to face but also to consider the impact a crisis might have on the campus if it were to occur. Because there is no realistic way a crisis plan can address every conceivable type of crisis event a campus might face, this audit helps focus planning efforts on the events that have the highest likelihood of occurring and the greatest potential impact on the campus community.

Key campus stakeholders should be involved in conducting the crisis audit. If there is an existing crisis management team, these team members are a good group to initiate this process. If there is no existing team, representatives from campus law enforcement, health care services, academic affairs, and the physical plant, as well as the dean of students, may be enlisted. Involving individuals external to the institution may also be helpful, because they will add another perspective and avoid the insider's tendency to overlook some threats or risks (Mitroff, Pearson, & Harrington, 1996; Stubbart, 1987).

To begin the audit process, it is helpful to consider the three dimensions of the crisis matrix (see Chapter Two). First, all the different crisis events that might occur in each of the types of crises (environmental, facility, and human) should be considered, as well as the likelihood of each occurring on the campus. Second, the level of crisis for each of the events identified should be considered. Although the likelihood of a particular crisis event affecting the campus might be pretty low, if the level of this crisis is *disaster*, its impact would be so great that it should be included in the crisis plan. Third, like the level of the crisis event, the intentionality of the crisis event might have a similarly significant impact on the campus, so such events too should probably be considered in the crisis plan.

The crisis audit will identify what will likely be a fairly extensive list of events and provide a good understanding of how they might affect the campus if they were to occur. Although the goal is not to develop a specific protocol or set of procedures for responding to each crisis event on the list, some priorities for creating these protocols will be developed and will provide a comprehensive picture of the issues and considerations that will need to be addressed in the plan.

After a list of potential crisis events is created, the next step is to assess the availability of essential resources (human, physical, and fiscal) that may be needed in responding to these various crisis events. If a crisis were to occur, which campus personnel would need to be contacted, and how would they be contacted? If a disaster occurred in the local community, how would the campus generate power, obtain steam for heating or chilled water for cooling, or restore telephone communications? How would the institution access financial resources during a crisis and how would it fund the recovery efforts after a crisis? These are significant questions and issues to address as the crisis management plan is being developed.

Perhaps the most challenging aspect is keeping track of the constant personnel changes that occur. People are the means to accessing most resources. If you know the right person to call, that person can obtain the resources you need. The list of people identified in the plan is the path to all of the resources that will need to be used to respond to a crisis. Unless key individuals and resources can be contacted, response capability will be severely hampered. This array of human resources provides the knowledge base of the campus and community. Who can be counted on, where they can be contacted, who the key decision makers are, and which stakeholders must be given updates or final reports—all these must be acknowledged during the development of a crisis plan.

Although conducting an audit of crisis events and resources available to respond to them are important in the development of any crisis plan, it is even more important to review existing plans and protocols in place at the institution. Different organizational units in the college or university may have their own crisis management plans. In creating or reviewing a campuswide crisis plan it is important to make sure that these separate unit plans supplement and support the larger unit or institutional plan, creating an integrated system for managing a crisis across the organization. Ideally, the institution should be guided by an institutional crisis management plan that addresses the broad campuswide crisis management issues. As already noted, this plan should be implemented by an institutional crisis management team that is directed by the team leader, who is appointed by the university president or chief operating officer. (See Chapter Three for more on crisis management teams.)

Below the institutional plan are divisional plans—division of academic affairs, student affairs, finance, administration, and so on. Divisional crisis management plans address the roles and functions assigned to them by the institutional plan. Thus, academic affairs might be responsible for implementing plans and protocols to respond to aspects of campus crisis that affect faculty, whereas student affairs may be responsible for implementing plans and protocols to respond to those aspects that affect students. These plans are often implemented by a divisional crisis management team that is directed by the vice president or other key division administrator.

Similarly, below the divisional plans are departmental or college plans. In the same manner as the divisional plans, these address the crisis management roles or functions assigned to the departments or colleges. These plans are implemented by a department head or college dean.

A review of these separate unit plans may reveal that there is little coordination between them. The goal of any campuswide crisis management plan is to provide overall coordination and direction to these individual units and identify clear roles and expectations for each. Meetings with some of the key unit directors can begin this process of integrating the various plans into a coordinated and consistent institutional plan. Later, these meetings can be expanded to include additional services and administrative units that are identified as potential areas of concern.

Components of the Plan

While we have noted that there is no fill-in-the-blank template or turnkey software solution to develop a campus crisis management plan that is appropriate for every institution, we can offer a general outline with some key components that are typically included in well-designed plans. A good crisis management plan includes two fundamental parts: a basic plan and a set of crisis protocols.

Basic Plan

A basic plan outlines the general process and procedures for how a campus will respond in the event of a crisis, regardless of its nature. The basic plan explains the purpose of the plan, how the plan is activated, who has authority to implement the plan, and what the fundamental actions steps will be in the plan's implementation.

Purpose

The cornerstone of any crisis plan is its purpose. In the purpose the concept of crisis is defined. As noted in Chapter One, how an institution or organizational unit defines crisis will have a significant impact on the crisis management system it develops. It affects who will determine when and how a crisis management plan is activated, who will be part of the crisis management team, and what the specific protocols and procedures for responding to a crisis will be. In developing a crisis management plan it is important for the staff tasked with this effort to create a definition of crisis that emphasizes the characteristics and attributes that are meaningful and appropriate to the needs of their organizational unit and the campus community. Examples of how some campuses and organizational unit plans define crisis are given in Chapter One.

Plan Activation

Once the plan's purpose is determined, it is necessary to communicate how the plan will be activated. Should an event occur that meets the definition of crisis, how will the plan be put into motion and who will have responsibility for doing this? For most campuswide or institutional crisis management plans it will be the president who will have responsibility to declare that a crisis exists. This decision then sets in motion a series of other actions, including gathering the university crisis management team members in the appropriate operations or command center to direct the university's response. For other organizational unit plans, it might be the appropriate vice president, a college dean, or department head who puts the plan in motion.

Some crisis management plans might be activated by a set of specific circumstances or conditions that, once triggered, set the plan in motion. For example, a division of student affairs could have a crisis plan designed to respond to serious or life-threatening situations involving university students, and the plan could be activated by a call received by university police dispatch. This scenario would require coordination of response plans between university police and student affairs. Police procedures would include a list of crisis events or situations in which student affairs should be contacted or notified. Once the police dispatcher has dispatched the appropriate emergency personnel to the incident (police, fire, medical, and so on), the operator would then notify the appropriate student affairs crisis team member through a uniform contact number or paging system. Upon notification of the student affairs crisis team member, the student affairs crisis plan would be activated.

Whether based on the declaration of a particular university official or triggered by a set of specific circumstances, a good crisis management plan identifies how the plan will be activated.

Lines of Authority

Because crises can escalate and potentially engulf the campus, any plan must establish clear lines of authority that ultimately lead to the president or chancellor of the institution. Lines of authority provide direction for the appropriate role of the senior administrative officer in the process at critical junctures, and also provide the staff tasked with developing and implementing the plan at lower levels with the authority to act with the voice of the entire institution and minimize cross-departmental conflict. Direct oversight of a plan must be clearly established at all levels if it is to be maintained in a workable form and be useful during implementation.

A coordinator of crisis planning can coordinate the institution's response planning and have oversight and narrow authority over the various unit-specific plans developed by auxiliary enterprises, administrative units, and facilities. Acting under the authority of the institution's senior administrative officer, this individual may establish expectations for the scope and depth of unit-specific plans. The outcomes and focus of interest may vary widely in the context of the campus structure and culture. A staff member serving as the coordinator of crisis planning who receives direction from a campus safety director may have a very different point of view from a staff member reporting to the physical plant director or health center director. Depending on the campus history in responding to crises, individual units may need to invite themselves to become participants in the beginning stages of planning, or upon seeing early drafts of plans, note the absence of plans for their particular interest areas. Counseling services, food services, recreation facilities, and staff with specific skill sets may not immediately be included in plans developed by other staff who do not have a history of interacting with these groups.

Ultimately, the plan's path must lead back to the institution's senior administrative officer. Depending on the size of the institution, this individual may only be cognizant of the details of the plan when briefed during a crisis by the coordinator of crisis planning and other senior administrative staff. Which decisions reside at the various levels of crisis impact can be established in the plan to avoid unnecessary discussions in the midst of a crisis. Such items may include when and if to suspend normal operations, when to cancel and resume classes, who the key media spokesperson should be, who will determine if a state of emergency exists and what implications this has for decision making during this time period, among other things. Failure to establish directions for decision makers at critical moments during a crisis can complicate response abilities and limit the institution's ability to adapt to conditions as they unfold. Interfering administrators who arrive at the last minute without direct knowledge or experience and have no clear role in the approved plan can cause problems for the responders. This can be avoided if a plan approved by the senior administrative officer is created prior to the crisis.

Action Steps

Finally, the plan should outline the significant action steps that will be taken in a crisis. These action steps should be broad in scope and applicable in almost any crisis situation that can arise; actions unique to a specific crisis event should be reserved for the crisis protocols, discussed in the next section, rather than the basic plan. An action step to include in the basic plan could be how to notify the campus community that a crisis exists. Perhaps there will be a public address by the president, or perhaps an electronic communication will be sent to the campus community. Basic action steps might also include how institutional resources or various response personnel will be deployed in the event of a crisis. Where is the crisis management team to be assembled? For example, where is the Emergency Operations Center (EOC) to be located and who is designated to staff it? The basic plan might also identify actions steps for securing campus facilities and initiating a campus closure.

Depending on the complexity of the plan, the actions steps might be differentiated by level of crisis, as identified in the crisis matrix. For example, in a *critical incident* it may not be necessary to notify the campus community or assemble the entire crisis management team. However, in a *campus emergency*, the campus community as a whole would likely be notified and the team would be assembled. In a *disaster*, action steps might include not only some of those listed under the emergency level but also steps related to closing the campus and securing facilities.

Crisis Protocols

While the basic plan describes the broad response procedures a campus will take when a crisis event occurs, crisis protocols offer a more refined series of measures tailored to very specific types of events. These protocols denote the who, what, when, and where of institutional response efforts to these particular events.

Because of their level of detail and specificity, such protocols generally take the form of checklists rather than narrative descriptions. These checklists provide just enough information to trigger the responder's memory about the necessary actions to take, without being overly verbose or wordy. With proper training beforehand, crisis team members will not need a detailed narrative, but instead a quick reference list to make sure essential steps have been taken.

As already noted, it is not realistic to expect a crisis plan to address every conceivable type of event. Instead, crisis protocols should address the crisis events that have the greatest probability of occurring on a campus or that would have the greatest impact on the campus, as determined by the crisis audit. At the very least, a campus crisis management plan should include a crisis protocol for each crisis type outlined in the crisis matrix: environmental, facility, and human. For example, a campus might initially develop crisis protocols for hurricanes, building fires, and student deaths. These protocols could be further refined by incorporating the other dimensions of the crisis matrix: level and intentionality. This way, a campus can develop a crisis portfolio (Mitroff et al., 1996) that better equips it to respond to many kinds of crisis events. With a well-developed crisis portfolio that addresses all the dimensions of the crisis matrix, even if a campus does not have a specific protocol for every possible crisis event, it can apply the action steps from the crisis protocols it does have that match the dimensional characteristics of the event currently being faced. For example, although a campus may not have a specific protocol to address a bomb explosion in a campus building, its existing protocols for handling building fires and student deaths will provide a solid foundation from which to respond. The response efforts will be assisted further if the protocols identify particular action steps unique to *campus emergency* level, *intentional* act.

An effective campus crisis management plan includes a solid basic plan supported by a portfolio of relevant crisis protocols that address the types of crisis events a campus is most likely to encounter or will have the greatest impact should they occur. Somewhere in the planning process, the task of committing the plans and protocols to written form has to take place. What form these take varies and can be dictated by campus tradition, style of the administrator responsible, or mandates from governing agencies. The old standby, the three-ring notebook, always seems to have a place because it is easily copied and distributed, can be highly visible depending on its cover, and can expand and contract as needed to address the size and scope of the plan. Its shortcomings, however, are evident to anyone who has ever produced documents in this format. They are expensive to produce, they are static and cumbersome to update— depending on all users to add updates as released—they tend to gather dust on most people's bookshelves, and worst of all, they may be hard to locate during a crisis. Yet they serve a good purpose by providing a plan foundation in hard copy form for reference.

More recently, the same data can be produced on removable media (CD-ROM) or as files that can be shared with staff quickly and easily and stored on home computers, laptops, and even PDAs. Electronic formats allow for wider and less expensive distribution of the plan, and searchable text features add utility to find relevant data or protocols. With handheld devices, the actual plan can be brought on-site at incidents. The downside, however, is that multiple copies may proliferate, as newly distributed versions may not replace the older versions but just get added to hard drives all over campus. Variations in the staff's ability to use technology may make it unusable for those who are not as adept with electronic platforms. In a worst case scenario, if a natural disaster affects electric power for any length of time there may be no access to the plan at all. This is especially true if the master copy of the plan is stored on the campus's Web server. In sum, although electronic formats offer many advantages over others (no multiple copies, ease of distribution, searchability, flexibility of scale, ability to add images and graphics and updates on the fly), the issue of connectivity during loss of power or the Internet or both severely hampers them as standalone sources. Electronic files also enable significant breaches for portions of plans that address security or the security force's response to violence. Indeed, a crisis management plan should never be shared in its totality if a Web site is used as the primary or master source for the document.

After the plan is developed, the task of maintaining the plan as a consistent, accurate data source becomes a critical role for those leading the crisis planning effort. Format, timing of updates, regular distribution, accuracy of data, and security of the plan are ongoing responsibilities that require constant attention. For example, a crisis in a building or an administrative unit that has not been addressed in a plan because it has just recently been added to the campus results in a gap in service response. Although many skills are transferable to a new situation, surprises are always in store for the underprepared.

Other Considerations

A number of other points must be taken into consideration when the crisis management plan is being developed. With each of these considerations, the campus must begin to outline and then fill in the details that provide a complete picture of a response to events ranging from critical incidents to disasters.

Establish the Scope of the Plan

As the planning process begins, clear directions to the responsible staff are necessary to establish the scope of the plan. How wide and how deep does the plan go to provide direction to the staff? If major units exist on campus, such as a comprehensive health center, or there are off-site locations with resident staff, should they be included in the plan or encouraged to make their own plans to address their unique needs and situation? Ultimately, if they report to the senior administrative officer of the institution, they will have to be addressed in some fashion in a plan, but how and where they fit in the plan should be decided during its development.

Identify Key Response Modes

As the plan unfolds and is put to paper, the opportunity presents itself for the campus to limit what it will do as much as expand what it will do in any given crisis. Establishing response modalities based on staff capabilities and resource limits, usually already identified by existing administrative structures, can assist in identifying reasonable responses to different situations. Crisis management teams, first responders, emergency response staff, victim advocates, campus ministry support, fire and safety liaison, twenty-four-hour services, and other modes of response can be addressed systematically and added or excluded from a plan as conditions dictate. Expectations by the community and various constituencies will provide guidance, as will the relative ease with which certain resources can be provided by the community rather than the institution. Colleges and universities in remote locations may need to take on more of the responsibility internally than institutions that are closer to or surrounded by urban centers.

Most institutions will have some sort of response mechanism already established for residence halls or other living units, with a variety of protocols in place. If the plan expands response capabilities to provide faculty and staff with similar support (especially in the area of counseling services), additional resources and staff commitments will be required. An Employee Assistance Program (EAP) may be in place to provide these types of services, or campus counseling staff may be already offering them on an informal basis. In the latter case, it would be appropriate to codify expected responses to avoid overdependence on a service that may not be prepared to provide a large-scale response in the event of a full-blown crisis.

Establish Communication Methods

During the crisis is not the time to begin to collect e-mail and telephone numbers of important staff. Nor is it the time to wish you had approved the purchase of two-way radios that offer secure channels for sensitive discussions. Whom to communicate with and how this communication will actually take place in different types of crises must be established and understood by all participants and responders included in the plan. When cell towers are overloaded, land lines are tied up with incoming calls, Web servers are swamped, or e-mail in-boxes are flooded, a staff's ability to communicate internally and to respond to requests for information are limited. Technical staff, especially if the institution relies on Web and e-mail services to provide information, must review infrastructure concerns and address redundancies and load capabilities. Weather incidents and other types of damage to systems must also be considered, depending on the location and conditions prevalent in the area.

Establish an Emergency Operations Center

Depending on the severity of a crisis, it may be appropriate to establish a command center or Emergency Operations Center (EOC) to coordinate a campus's response efforts. Relying on the expertise of police and fire safety staff, the EOC provides a way for decisions to be made quickly with adequate input from key participants and communicate these decisions to others as soon as they are made.

Weather-related crises may require "hardened" shelters, while campus unrest or incidents involving public safety may require that command centers be established in close proximity to the event. Models for command centers exist in public security forces, such as the police, and tend to be highly structured and hierarchical. Determining who should participate and establishing a clear understanding among participants of the decision-making hierarchy is necessary to avoid conflict during incidents. Location, communication methods, decision-making authority, and identified participants must all be clarified in the crisis management plan.

Ensure Redundancy of Critical Staff and Facilities

No one likes to believe they are dispensable. However, during a crisis, all of the decision makers and all of the tools and facilities usually relied on may not be available. A well-crafted plan builds in redundancy to address such possibilities. Business travel, illness, injury, incapacitation, or even death of a key decision maker can affect how a decision is made during a crisis. Damage to facilities or loss of resources like power or communication tools require a plan to be flexible; decision makers must know how to operate with agility. Holding training sessions with key variables removed or key individuals not allowed to participate gives the institution the ability to simulate a worst-case scenario in this manner and establish potential solutions that can be added to the plan for contingency response. If, instead, a plan is rigidly designed and does not provide for such possibilities, it will fail if conditions change in unexpected ways.

Clarify Media Relation Responsibilities

Staff responsible for media relations on a campus will likely have a plan for distributing information and working closely with local, state, and national media outlets. Web-based publications are yet another outlet for media staff to be conscious of. At a minimum, media staff usually provide oversight of the institution's homepage to ensure that it is consistent with other media releases. The final crisis management plan will most likely only need to reference this preexisting "crisis communication plan." Crucial to this, however, is the understanding by all participants of their role in releasing information to the media in either written form or through interviews. Media plans that have not addressed crisis response will need to be reviewed by appropriate staff to bring them in line. Issues such as identifying the university spokesperson, the role of the senior administrative officer, the need for potential press conferences, onsite media management, and use of available facilities in the community will all be addressed and should be referenced in the full crisis management plan. (For a more detailed discussion of communication plans, see Chapter Five, "Crisis Communication.")

Specify the Role of Campus Security and the Role of Outside Agencies

One of the most important decision points in a crisis management plan is when to change campus security operations from a *campus service* to the entity that is *in control of the campus*. Who makes this decision, what conditions need to exist for this to happen, what authority they have during this time period, who provides oversight, what conditions need to exist for the campus to return to normal, and who makes that decision should all be clearly established in the crisis management plan. Campuses that traditionally rely on a collegial model for decision making may need to transition to a highly structured hierarchical model during a crisis. Preparing all concerned for this possibility will minimize hurt feelings when individuals who normally have substantial decision-making authority are excluded from these roles.

In critical incidents, when the standard decision-making models are still in place on campus, the role of security must still be addressed. What issues and aspects of an incident are reserved for security, and where are the conflict points with other services provided by staff in residence halls, counseling centers, campus ministries, and the like? Although it may be difficult to describe the nuances of these relationships in a crisis management plan, it is helpful to all participants to require this discussion to take place. Placing a reference to these potential conflicts in the plan will encourage dialogue and training opportunities for all identified parties.

Planning for outside agencies to interact with on-campus services also requires some attention. Good interaction and planning with local agencies will allow staff to prepare for outside contributions during a crisis event. Relationships with local off-campus entities, such as police or fire departments, should be developed over time through meetings and agreements. Interpersonal relationships between key leaders provide for smoother interactions during a crisis. This may not be the case with state or national entities that become part of a disaster response. The command structure models used in disaster response tend to overwhelm local entities and leave them out of key decisions at times. On-campus training should address how different outside agencies will use local resources and how to interface with multiple organizations. Effective plans must address critical incidents, emergencies, and disasters and allow for outside agencies to work closely or in parallel with campus resources. Understanding that coordination and communication during an incident are critical to a successful response, plans must establish the framework for this to occur as well as contingency plans if these entities fail to communicate well. The role of campus security and other emergency personnel is explored further in Chapter Six, "Working with Emergency Personnel and Outside Agencies."

Plan for Business Resumption

When it comes to the issue of business resumption, it is common to focus only on the replacement of equipment or responding to damage or destruction of facilities. But returning operations to normal after a crisis requires some planning to address the impact on both facilities and staff. The emotional toll on a staff can complicate an institution's ability to replace equipment, move operations in a timely manner, and adequately staff an office or even an entire campus. So much attention is usually paid to preparing for a crisis and working through a crisis that the recovery phase is given short shrift. Facilities issues that must be quickly addressed include having an inventory of appropriate alternative work sites to use if necessary to move operations; gaining easy access to replacement technology (computers, servers, fax machines, copiers, and so on) and reinstalling backup files; purchasing or using temporary furniture; having a clear supply chain for materials necessary to continue to work in offices, classrooms, and physical plant shops; getting telephone and data lines in working order; and purchasing or leasing services and supplies.

Even with all of these issues addressed, the impact of a crisis may limit a staff's ability to assist in the recovery. Some may be unable to work for a period of time; some may never return if the incident was traumatic enough (a terrorist act or a violent act in the workplace, for example). Providing counseling support for the staff to help them get through their experience assists in the human side of business resumption. The staff's reactions to the event, their relationships with coworkers who may have responded differently to it, and the stress on the system that comes from working in unusual conditions and perhaps with less than a full staff are some areas of immediate concern. A well-planned move to a new facility or reopening of a facility simply will not happen unless the staff is functioning effectively, and expecting staff to resume normal operations without some attention to them as people will be an obvious gap in the recovery plan. For more information on caring for staff affected by a crisis event see Chapter Seven, "Psychological First Aid in the Aftermath of Crisis." For more information on business resumption, and in particular, business continuity plans, see Chapter Twelve, "Contemporary Issues in Campus Crisis Management."

Delineating Responsibility for the Plan

If it is not to be left on a shelf to simply gather dust, a plan must have an author and a manager. Clear authority must be given to an entity on campus to develop the plan but also to maintain the plan as a viable document through regular reviews, training, and updates.

Managing a large and complex physical plant on even the smallest campus usually results in the plan administrator being connected in some way to the administrative division of the institution as opposed to academic or student affairs divisions. Ready access to information about the existing physical plant allows the plan to use this knowledge to build out response mechanisms to address probable concerns. Where the facility is, what is housed in it, who is affected on that site, and what implications it has for other facilities and populations provide a way to connect the necessary resources for a response to occur. Using this model, the plan would be built out in an ever-increasing web until the entire campus is covered by it.

In other models, where campus security or student affairs serve as the center for the plan, different starting points should be used. Student affairs might focus on populations and how best to serve them, giving more attention to the affective side of the crisis management plan. Campus security, in contrast, may start by identifying high-risk sites and develop the plan with a priority schema established for high-risk sites to low-risk sites and responses tailored to each as needed. Planning with a clear definition of triage assessment may occur with this model. Limited resources are focused in key response areas based on available data. Regardless of the starting point, any plan will ultimately cover the entire campus.

Some thought should be given to creating an office of crisis planning when establishing responsibility for the plan. If this is not possible, an individual should be assigned as coordinator of crisis planning. But as we have seen, although one office may be responsible for coordination, all offices and perspectives should be included in the process and evident in the results.

Maintaining the Plan

An important and unending aspect of a campus crisis plan is the process of maintaining it. Unless there is constant vigilance, there may be a failure to note the departure of key staff mentioned in the plan (both on and off campus) or a failure to take into account their historical perspective on dealing with a crisis, or there may be a change in philosophy of key services identified in the plan, a reorganization of reporting lines on the campus, and new services and facilities on the campus and in the community. Such omissions can damage the utility of a plan on virtually a daily basis. Possibly most problematic is the unending task of updating staff and key administrator contact information. When a crisis strikes, will you easily be able to put your hands on a contact list of crisis team members and the deans and department heads of your institution? Do you have multiple and redundant ways to contact and communicate with staff effectively? How current is your list and when was it last updated? There is nothing more frustrating during a crisis than to be disconnected from other resources, especially when that is due to something that could easily have been avoided by monitoring the plan and its components.

The central crisis planning office's scope can be established early in the process to avoid duplicating existing directory projects. Security operations and residence hall staff contact information tends to be well maintained and should be easy to access at most institutions. Home addresses and telephone numbers of staff, such as academic department chairs, and current e-mail and phone numbers of support staff can be more difficult to maintain unless a concerted and regular effort is made to check contacts. Regular reviews of contact information to identify areas of the plan that need to be updated should be made at least on a quarterly basis.

Emergency contact information can serve two purposes. In most instances, it is used to inform staff or request their assistance during an incident. However, in extreme cases, it allows for checking on the well-being of staff who may have been affected by an incident. In these extreme situations, staff and faculty will appreciate this added level of concern on the part of the institution and may also provide added resources to assist with recovery. These contact lists of key staff and faculty do not need to be widely circulated and may not delve deeply into the institutional structure. The central administration needs to know information only to the departmental level, leaving a broader list collection of staff to each unit. If key planning meetings are held during an incident or impending event, these lists can be circulated to provide a quick review and to ensure accuracy. It is understandable that some staff will not want this information to be available to the public, so some care should be taken to note unpublished telephone numbers or private office telephones or cell phones that should be restricted to limited access by key staff.

Distributing the Plan

Who should see the plan in its entirety? What sort of security problems will be caused by widespread distribution? How is data security addressed in the plan and to what specificity? As the plan unfolds in its development phase and evolves through review and use, discussion by the key planning forces on campus must address how much specificity to include. Protocols for special high-risk units (that is, hazardous materials, data centers, research labs, animal management, and the like) will exist and need to be referenced, but most likely will not be detailed in the actual plan. Regular review of the plan will require an ongoing check of the links to these various protocols to ensure that all units continue to remain current in their planning and are connected to the larger institutional crisis management plan. The coordinator of crisis planning (or the office of crisis planning) will become the keeper of the plan and its web of protocols, special focus plans, and contact information. How much bureaucracy an institution is willing to assign to this task will dictate how comprehensive the plan can become and how current it will be when needed.

Conclusion

A campus crisis plan is not one document. It is a basic plan, a set of crisis protocols, contact information, mutual aid agreements, and other annexes woven together to provide a complete response mechanism for an institution. Even on the smallest campus, it is unlikely that a comprehensive plan can be developed, written, and maintained in all of its necessary aspects by one office. There are just too many variables to consider. At a large, complex institution that may include multiple campuses, international travel, teaching hospitals, and clinics or an array of professional schools and distance learning sites, there are probably not enough three-ring notebooks or shelf space available to house a plan in one location. A master document will suffice as the "homepage" of this web of plans and documents. The coordinator of crisis planning, or the office of crisis planning, will serve as the monitor, guide, and regulator of all the various aspects of the plan to ensure that the campus is ready to respond as needed. The ability of this critical office or staff member to establish a model for the plan that can be easily cloned by the various units for consistency, present clear guidelines and expectations for maintenance of the plan, ensure coordination of contact information updates, and provide coordination and support for training exercises is key.

A model plan developed as an outline can be provided to campus units to ensure that each entity addresses the key issues that have been identified. An effective campus crisis management plan that includes a basic plan and a set of crisis protocols provides an institution with an adequate portfolio from which to base a response to crisis events that either have a high probability of occurring, or if they did occur, would have a significant impact on the campus. In summary, a comprehensive campus crisis management plan should:

- Establish the scope of the plan

- Identify key response modes

- Determine the communication methods

- Establish an emergency operations center

- Address redundancy of critical staff and facilities

- Determine media relations responsibilities

- Identify the role of campus security

- Acknowledge the role of outside agencies

- Address the business resumption process

- Identify who is responsible for the plan

- Address the maintenance of the plan

- Describe how the plan should be distributed

Based on this outline, a campus can begin to prepare itself for critical incidents, campus emergencies, and disasters in a thoughtful manner so that surprises and unexpected events will be minimized. Although responsibility for the campus crisis plan may be designated to a single person or office, an effective plan will be a shared responsibility among the many entities that the college campus comprises. Bringing all of the components together into a workable and flexible plan, and keeping it in the forefront of a campus although it is rarely used, will require diligence and perseverance.

References

Littleton, R. F. (1983). *Crisis management: A team approach*. New York: American Management Association.

Mitroff, I. I., Pearson, C. M., & Harrington, L. K. (1996). *The essential guide to managing corporate crisis: A step-by-step handbook for surviving major catastrophes*. New York: Oxford University Press.

Scott, J. E. (1999). [Crisis management survey]. Unpublished raw data.

Stubbart, C. I. (1987). Improving the quality of crisis thinking. *Columbia Journal of World Business, 22*, 89–99.

Zdziarski, E. L. (2001). Institutional preparedness to respond to campus crises as perceived by student affairs administrators in selected NASPA member institutions. *Dissertation Abstracts International, 62*, 3714.

5

Crisis Communication

Cynthia J. Lawson

To say that the communications function can make or break an institution, particularly in a time of crisis, is an understatement. Indeed, the speed with which an institution responds to a crisis by disseminating critical information to its various target audiences can become the primary factor in whether or not the institution is perceived as managing the crisis well. If target audiences *think* there is no response to a particular crisis, then perceptually, there is no response. The result is likely to be a loss of confidence in the institution. It is therefore imperative that administrators at all levels understand the important role communication will play throughout the duration of a campus crisis and that the institutional crisis management plan include a well-thought-out strategy—a *crisis communication plan*—for communicating quickly and adequately with the institution's various target audiences.

Target Audiences

Because communication is a two-way process between the communicator and the persons receiving the messages, it is important that administrators take time to understand how each target audience

---

Note: Some of the information provided in this chapter was adapted, with permission, from *Effective Crisis Communication*, published by the National Emergency Response and Recovery Training Center of the Texas Engineering Extension Service, College Station, Texas, 2004.

can affect the communication process. This process includes identifying an institution's target audiences and understanding the specific characteristics of each one of them, including their needs and the best communication approaches for reaching them.

Target audiences generally fall into two distinct categories: internal and external. And although one could debate the definitions of these two categories (for example, whether parents of existing students or alumni are internal or external audiences), there are, nevertheless, a number of key constituents with whom a university will likely want to communicate during a crisis:

- Students (current, former, and prospective) and their parents

- Staff

- Faculty

- Legislators (civic leaders, city council members, judges, and so on, as well as state and federal legislators)

- Donors (current and prospective)

- Community constituents where the institution is located (chamber of commerce, convention and visitors bureau, key business leaders, emergency workers, the fire and police departments, EMS, hospitals and clinics, and so on)

- Relatives and friends of victims

- Media (print, radio, television, and Web, including bloggers)

- Partners and stakeholders (those entities—educational, corporate, foundations, and so on—with whom an institution has a partnership, contract, or some other significant relationship that could be affected adversely by a crisis)

- Funding and granting agencies and organizations

- The general public

Making a conscientious and consistent effort to reach out to all of these groups is an arduous task. And trying to develop systems for communicating with each one of them as the crisis unfolds is particularly difficult, given the intense demands on an institution's communication processes. Therefore, it is important that communication processes be developed, in advance of the crisis, to ensure the quick, systematic, and efficient dissemination of information.

Unfortunately, administrators usually assume that internal audiences are either less important or are already somehow "in the know," and as a result, internal audiences may be forgotten. This absence of information, however, will leave a vacuum, which, in turn, will result in speculation—speculation that frequently will lead to erroneous information being inadvertently disseminated, or even rumors. This only adds to the communication burden. A special crisis link on the university's Web page, a hot line, or any number of the other communication methods described in the following paragraphs can be employed to effectively inform internal audiences.

Developing fast and reliable channels for communicating directly with external constituencies and community leaders will help ensure that they receive the facts they need before their own constituents begin asking them questions. A special "community" intranet site is one communication channel administrators may want to consider deploying. Another is a special telephone hot line specifically designated for the institution's partners and community leaders. And of course, if resources are available, administrators may want to designate one or more people on the crisis management team with sole responsibility for maintaining continuous contact with the institution's community partners and leaders.

Because each target audience is unique, it stands to reason that each of them will be looking for specific messages that resonate with them. There will likely be some basic demographic issues to consider when crafting specific messages that address the needs of each target audience, including these:

- Educational level

- Familiarity with or uniqueness of the particular crisis

- Expertise

- Background and experience

- Age

- Language spoken and read

- Cultural norms

- Geographic location

- Social groups or other influencers

Furthermore, each target audience may prefer different channels of communication. Therefore, administrators will want to:

- Prioritize the development of messages for each audience based on its needs and potential involvement

- Concentrate on those target audiences that have the greatest impact on the institution's ability to accomplish what needs to get done

- Use multiple methods for communicating the institution's messages to its various target audiences

- Repeat those messages that are particularly critical

During a crisis, an institution's target audiences may become disenfranchised quickly if they do not feel they are getting the appropriate information when they need it, when they want it, and in the manner in which they want to receive it. Indeed, a great message delivered after a particular target audience has moved on to another issue is a message that is not really delivered at all. This was evident on several occasions during the Katrina hurricane, when the media quickly moved from reporting about the hurricane's devastation to reporting about the federal government's lack of response. The public had become disillusioned with the federal government because of its failure to provide information about what was being done to assist the victims. By the time the information came out, the public was demanding an explanation of why the response took so long. The government's failure to communicate in a timely fashion kept it behind the eight ball during most of the rescue and recovery operation. Simply put, effective communication depends on selecting communication methods that are quick, efficient, and responsive to the needs of the target audiences.

Consistent messaging is also vital. To be sure, inconsistent messages can, and will, increase anxiety and quickly undermine the credibility of an institution's experts. Target audiences will be listening for factual information, and some will be expecting to hear a recommendation for action. It is important for the institution to get the facts right, repeat them consistently, and avoid speculation. Speaking with one voice—by ensuring that all credible sources share the same facts—is critical to ensuring that an institution's crisis communications are effective.

Communication Methods

Communication methods are as diverse as the target audiences they are designed to reach. They may include print, radio and television media, and special Web pages, intranet sites, and blogs. Ham and dispatch operators, posters and flyers, phone banks, "town-gown" meetings, beepers and pagers, and iPods may also be deployed. But there are some other communication methods administrators do not normally consider. Although the following communication methods may change from time to time, depending on the circumstances one or more of them might be warranted:

- *Public Web sites:* Most satellite trucks have access to Web sites, so putting information on a public Web site can save an institution a lot of time in responding to needless questions. If the crisis involves a disease, providing individuals with a direct link to the local health department or the Centers for Disease Control is especially helpful.

- *Toll-free phone service:* An 800 number is particularly effective for parents and alumni.

- *Public e-mail response service (PRS):* This is similar to a toll-free phone service, but incorporates the use of the Internet (e-mail) instead. PRS provides a rapid, turnkey toll-free hot line and interactive e-mail service with both local information specific to a health emergency (such as where to get shots) and CDC-approved background health and medical information. This service is available to help an institution manage its public information requirements during an emergency that involves the public health. In addition, this service is available for both Spanish- and English-speaking persons, as well as for the deaf and hearing impaired.

- *Reverse 911 automatic call system:* This system has the ability to send messages to all campus residents, instantly and simultaneously, over the telephone. Several vendors provide this kind of service, including ERMS (Emergency Response Management System) by AudienceCentral.

- *Emergency Alert System (EAS):* This was formerly called the Emergency Broadcast System. EAS information is disseminated to the public by way of "ticker tape" banners at the bottom of the television screen.

- *Siren systems:* Many communities that are subject to hurricanes and tornadoes, or that are within ten miles of a nuclear facility, have siren systems that enable different types of signals to be used to warn residents to take specific actions, depending on the nature of the crisis (tornado, hurricane, train spill, lightning in the area, and so on). Some of these siren systems are equipped with loudspeaker capabilities so that specific verbal messages also can be broadcast to residents. Campus administrators should inquire whether any sirens located in close proximity to their campus could be commandeered during an emergency to communicate with faculty, staff, and students.

- *PIER (Public Information and Emergency Response):* PIER is an online, on-demand communication management system for communicating with and responding to a variety of target audience inquiries, including those from the media. Used widely by government agencies, corporations, universities, and nonprofits for both public and internal communications, PIER is designed for communicators with all the tools they need in one application: content, contact and inquiry management, and the ability to push critical information to target audiences by phone, fax, or e-mail. With backup servers located strategically throughout the United States, PIER also provides for business continuity in the event the electrical infrastructure is malfunctioning or inoperable.

- *Loudspeakers*: Loudspeakers, such as bullhorns on squad cars, may be particularly useful when the communication infrastructure is disrupted.

- *Secure phone lines*: There are alternative systems for communicating, using secured lines obtained through the NEXTEL company.

- *802.11G communication system*: This wireless Internet communication system is especially useful when the electrical infrastructure is disrupted.

- *Portable transmission towers*: Many local wireless providers can bring portable transmission towers onto campus, thereby helping absorb or divert some of the telephone demand that frequently occurs in a crisis.

- *Amateur Radio Emergency Services (ARES)*: Ham operators are part of a larger network called ARES, which is an excellent resource for disseminating information. ARES has a "ResourceNet" that tracks the deployment of its people, provides status reports at each location, and so on.

- *Phone books*: Electric utility companies with nuclear power plant facilities frequently use community telephone books as an effective way to communicate evacuation procedures in the event of a nuclear accident. Campus phone books are an excellent method for disseminating information about evacuation routes, crisis Web sites, and other critical information that faculty, staff, and students may need during a crisis.

- *Backup cell phones*: Assuming that overusage of phones (cell phones or land lines or both) has not resulted in a

significant disruption of service, cell phones are probably the most valuable tool for a campuses crisis management team to have. Prior arrangements can be
made with local cell phone vendors to provide extra
phones and batteries, or even special relay towers (see
earlier item), in the event that a campus crisis warrants
their use.

- *CEO COM LINK*^{SM}*:* Developed by the Business
  Roundtable, this is a secure telecommunications bridge
  that enables senior federal officials and corporate CEOs
  to exchange timely information in case of a terrorist
  threat or crisis. CEO COM LINK^{SM} includes representatives from the banking, chemical, and water industry
  sectors. Administrators should determine whether any
  corporate leaders in nearby communities are part of
  this link and whether these CEOs can partner with the
  university in assisting the campus with its crisis management efforts.

- *Business Roundtable:* The Department of Homeland
  Security is including the Business Roundtable and
  member companies as part of its Crisis Action Team
  (CAT). Not only can various company experts be
  called upon by the government in the event of a terrorist attack, but the partnership enables workplace evacuation of thousands of employees to be coordinated
  with state officials and local responders who may need
  to use the same roadways. Extremely large research
  campuses might want to consider developing a similar
  CAT-type partnership with state and local responders.

In sum, which communication method to use depends, to a large
extent, on several criteria:

- The nature of the crisis

- The phase of the crisis (planning, prevention, response, recovery, or learning)

- Time constraints for disseminating a particular piece of information

- The resources (money and personnel) available for implementing a particular communication method

- The format preferred by any or all of the target audiences

- Whether the electrical infrastructure is operable to support a particular communication method requiring electricity

Regardless of the method selected, it is important to remember that the first message received on a subject typically sets the stage for comparison of all future messages. Indeed, first impressions are lasting impressions. This does not necessarily mean that administrators will have all the answers. Rather, it means that administrators must have an early presence so that students, faculty, staff, partners, and stakeholders, as well as the general public, know that the institution has systems in place to effectively respond to the crisis and that the emergency is being well managed.

The News Media

More than seventy-thousand media outlets operate news activities in the United States alone, and most are interested in breaking news. To be sure, a crisis event will instantly engage the media, especially if it is unusual, catastrophic, or the first of its kind. A workable crisis communication plan will cover how to respond to the surge of media inquiries that normally occur during a crisis.

Media need to know ahead of time how the flow of information will work in a crisis, whom they need to contact to get their questions answered, and what the university's media relations team (that is, crisis communication team) can or cannot do for them. Simply put, working with the media during a crisis is not an option, but a must.

Any resources allocated to the media response are well invested and will provide long-term returns. If news sources do not believe the institution is responding well to them during a crisis, they may not believe the institution is responding in good faith or at all. Indeed, during a crisis, the manner in which an institution responds to media inquiries may make a real difference in how the institution's responsiveness or professionalism is portrayed to each of its target audiences and the general public.

Anticipating the needs of the media will help an institution accomplish its communication goals in three ways: informing all of its target audiences simultaneously, helping the media understand the actions being taken by the university, and gaining media acceptance—and even support—for the institution's response and recovery efforts. One highly effective method for communicating with both the media and an institution's various target audiences is to provide equal access to information by posting vital information to the university's Web site at the same time that it is given to the media via a press release or press conference.

An institution can expect that as a crisis event unfolds there will be a widening gap between what it believes the media should be concentrating on (or not) and what the media wants to know. And because it is the media's job to look for varying perspectives on what is happening, journalists are likely to interview numerous individuals among the faculty, staff, and student body. Remember, controversies and crises sell! Therefore, an institution should expect only limited success in influencing that part of a crisis devoted to this debate, discussion, and speculation. It thus becomes all the more imperative that the institution clearly, consistently, and repetitively articulates its messages through as many credible sources and experts as it can deploy.

As with target audiences, a variety of methods can be used to communicate with the media. They include the following:

- Press statements and press releases, including fact sheets or backgrounders

- Press conferences

- Visuals, video news releases, and B-roll footage (video footage provided by the institution to illustrate or support the story)

- Photo opportunities

- Satellite media tours

- Telephone news conferences, Webcasts

- Commercial press release services (such PR Newswire, US Newswire, AP)

- E-mail listservs

- Broadcast faxes

- Web sites, blogs, iPods, and so on

- Streaming video

- Telephone calls (phone lines may become overloaded; make sure there is a backup, alternative plan!)

- Contracted vendors such as VOCUS, Newswise, AudienceCentral, and others

Since research has shown that the degree to which the general public believes an emergency response was effective directly correlates with the degree to which they had access to information during the crisis, speed and accuracy are especially important.

The Four-Step Crisis Communication Process

Like the phases of crisis management, crisis communication involves similar steps.

Step One: Prepare

The planning and preparation step is the most important, because it will have the greatest long-term impact on a university's image and reputation. Although an institution likely cannot foresee when a crisis will occur and what its nature will be, it can anticipate many of the various types of crises it may need to address. These can then be planned for well in advance. Reasonable questions can be anticipated and preliminary answers sought. Initial message templates can be drafted with blanks to be filled in as the crisis unfolds. Spokespeople, resources, and resource mechanisms can be identified. Training, refinements of the crisis communication plan, and specific messages for various crisis scenarios can be developed. Community and vendor partnerships can be fostered to ensure that everyone involved in the crisis is speaking with one voice. Expert lists for various types of crises can be created. Simply put, a well-written and well-practiced crisis communication plan goes a long way toward mitigating the many communication challenges that typically occur during a crisis. A number of actions can be taken to help develop this plan prior to a crisis.

Research the Various Types of Crises That Typically
Occur on University Campuses

The institution's public relations officer should conduct Internet searches of media coverage on various campus crises that have occurred at institutions across the United States. Among the questions to be asked and analyzed are these: *What went well? Why? What did the university do to preserve its reputation? What did not go so well? Why not? Did the university make key mistakes, particularly with respect to the way in which it communicated to its various publics? What were they? How could they have been avoided?*

Developing a reference file on these various types of campus crises, including news clippings and the key points that enabled a particular institution to communicate effectively with its target audiences during the crisis, can be most valuable. Including the name of that institution's media relations executive, along with his or her contact information, might be an additional resource. The institution might also consider consulting with another institution's professional communications executive—one who has experienced a similar crisis at his or her own institution.

Draw Up the Crisis Communication Plan

Although most public information officers are accustomed to working with little or no budget, during a crisis the public information officer must be able to acquire supplies, people, equipment, and space as needed. The crisis communication plan should name the various resources that are available, cost information, contact information, and any time constraints that may affect their deployment. Chancellors or presidents must give their public information officers the authority they need to do their jobs effectively. This is not the time to communicate on a shoestring.

Create a Crisis Communication Team with Clear Procedures

Emergencies are chaotic enough without one individual not knowing what the next member of the team is doing and when. Too often, the initial confusion and mixed messages that cripple an institution's credibility come from a lack of clear role and responsibility definitions, as well as undefined lines of authority. All members of the crisis management team, and especially the crisis communication team, must be familiar with all aspects of the crisis communication plan.

Human assets must be identified in advance. Furthermore, these assets must be identified by specialty areas, level of experience, and availability. If additional training is required, it is during the *preparation* stage that this training should be conducted. Although the composition of a crisis communication team may vary from institution to institution, there are some individuals who are especially helpful when having to communicate quickly during a crisis. They include the person in charge of media relations, the advancement director, the institution's legal counsel, the person in charge of governmental affairs, a student affairs officer, an academic officer, and the director of human relations. To expedite communications, it is helpful to include those individuals who must approve any communications prior to their being disseminated.

The quickest way for an institution to publicly fall flat on its face is to be unable to release accurate information quickly. Someone must be delegated the responsibility of being in charge of the release of information to the media, to the general public, and to the institution's partners. Ideally, three people should officially approve a document before it is released: the administrative leadership, the public relations officer, and a subject matter expert (when appropriate). If legal implications are involved, a fourth individual—legal counsel—should review the document. This does not mean that others cannot review and comment on the document; it simply means they cannot be allowed to delay its release. As a courtesy, institutions should have mechanisms in place for providing *courtesy checks* to those individuals and response agencies having a stake in the information the institution is releasing.

Have the Crisis Communication Plan Approved

Once the crisis communication plan is written, the university president or chancellor and other senior administrators should approve it. If the plan cannot be executed because of resistance or lack of understanding by the response leadership, the plan is subject to inevitable failure. To be sure, there is no guarantee that, even if a crisis communication plan does exist, it will be followed. Indeed, it is not uncommon "in the heat of battle" for well-intentioned university administrators to make communication decisions without first consulting their chief public relations officer about the possible implications of those decisions. Yet failing to do so can result in conflicting messages or in the public relations officer spending needless time "correcting" or adjusting messages that could have been crafted correctly in the first place.

Identify Key Spokespersons and Experts

Spokespersons bring a human face to a crisis. They are the conduits to various target audiences, communicating different types of information at different times during a crisis. How a spokesperson handles public and media inquiries, in addition to what he or she says, helps establish credibility for the university. Therefore, the public relations officer should insist that spokespersons be well trained in advance of the actual crisis. No person should represent the university during a crisis unless that person has invested the time and energy to develop the appropriate skills through adversary media training and practice.

Spokespersons do not just read a statement; perceptually, they *are* the statement. Therefore, if the spokesperson does not fully understand the purpose behind the messages or recommendations, he or she will have difficulty assuming a stance of confidence and conveying believability and trust. As such, spokespersons must be involved in the development of messages they are being asked to convey.

Build Relationships with the Media

It is virtually impossible to develop important media relationships in a crisis. Having good relationships with local media representatives is an asset an institution must cultivate long before any crisis takes place.

In addition, during the onslaught of crisis events, public relations officers will not have time to prepare press kits. Institutional press kits should be created and stored, ready for dissemination in a crisis. These press kits should include background information about the institution, contact information for experts, and other relevant information.

When the crisis does occur, the public relations officer must quickly decide where the media should be stationed in relation to the event so there is no interference with the rescue and recovery operation. This includes space for satellite trucks as well as for media to gather to receive the information being disseminated, to make phone calls, and to file their stories. When possible, this should be the same place where designated spokespersons will deliver statements and answer the media's questions about the crisis that is unfolding.

Identify Partners and Stakeholders

If and when a crisis occurs, it helps to be able to count on a university's friends for various types of support. Institutions should identify which local and state businesses can be of a special value to them during various types of crises. These may include the electric company, telecommunication vendors, and businesses capable of providing a variety of tools and other types of equipment.

These partners and stakeholders should not only be familiar with the institution's crisis management plan but should know the members of the public relations team. It may be that some of these partners will be more familiar, more trusted, and more influential with some of the institution's target audiences than with the institution itself. Thus, these partners and stakeholders can be valuable in gaining support for the institution's actions, distributing information, or helping the institution counter rumors.

Identify Key Communication Messages

It is important to have as much information on a topic prepared and preapproved as possible. Much of this information can be anticipated and developed. Most important, messages should answer the questions that are most likely to be asked.

Messages should be tested to ensure they are culturally and demographically valid. This allows all spokespersons and experts to speak with one voice and deliver messages that resonate with particular target audiences. In addition, the public relations officer should convey that there is a crisis communication process in place. He or she should describe the process, identify the roles various individuals will play, and explain how and when the crisis communication team will be disseminating information.

Practice the Crisis Communication Plan

Unfortunately, far too many institutions develop crisis plans, including crisis communication plans, only to put them on the shelf until such time as an unfolding crisis warrants the plan being dusted off and implemented. This breeds unfamiliarity with the plan and with the various roles to be played in executing it. Instead, simulating various crises and testing the effectiveness of the crisis communication plan are among the most critical steps an institution can take. Doing so enables institutions to evaluate how quickly its crisis communication operations can be mobilized, how the crisis communication team performed, and what aspects of the plan should be modified. The plan, including any contact information, also needs to be updated on a regular basis.

Step Two: Respond

The first hours of a crisis response are often the most important. The pressure to release information prematurely can be intense. Simplicity, credibility, verifiability, consistency, and speed matter when communicating with target audiences at the onset of a crisis. Depending on the nature, uniqueness, magnitude, and intensity of the crisis, some confusion and intense media interest can be expected. Initially, information may be incomplete, and for many, the speed at which information is disseminated may not be great enough. Furthermore, information from the media, from other organizations, and even from inside the institution itself might not be as accurate as the university would like. This is inevitable. The role of the public relations officer is to learn the facts about what happened, determine what the university's response to the crisis should be, and verify the true magnitude of the events as they occur as quickly as possible. As more accurate information becomes available, the public relations officer needs to disseminate that information—again, as quickly as possible.

How facts are learned and shared shape the opinions of an institution's target audiences. This is particularly evident as they form their opinion of the overall crisis response, leaving an indelible mark on an institution, either positive or negative. There is no second chance to get it right during this initial phase. An institution's reputation is clearly on the line.

Therefore, setting the proper communication course and then managing that course are the "make-or-break" variables in surviving the crisis event. Administrators should take several key initiatives in managing the institution's crisis communications:

1. Gather the facts; verify the situation.

2. Activate the crisis communication plan. Gather information; try to determine the severity of the situation and the potential impact it might have on communication operations, resources, and staffing requirements.

3. Activate the crisis communication team, organize assignments, and determine whether backup personnel will be required for a second or third shift if the crisis is expected to last more than ten to twelve hours.

4. Identify specific target audiences for this particular crisis. Predict the level of information that will need to be disseminated as well as the level of media interest to which the crisis communication team will need to respond.

5. Decide which communication tactics will be most effective with which target audiences, as well as with the media.

6. Contact partners and stakeholders. Remember that the quicker the channels of communication with support vendors and other partners are opened, the more smoothly and accurately the crisis communication operation likely will go.

7. Using the "experts" list, identify key spokespersons and experts for the particular crisis.

8. Plan the initial media response; share with the media the process being used to resolve the crisis.

9. Monitor and track all the information being disseminated. Monitoring should include phone inquiries as well as information being disseminated over television, radio, print media, and Web sites, and in chat rooms. Stay on top of the information flow. Unexpected developments, rumors, or misinformation may require additional press releases or press conferences.

10. Make sure that university staff members monitor their e-mails. These e-mails may be from individuals volunteering to help or may provide other in-kind resources to the crisis management operation.

11. Monitor the crisis communication team. It is important to understand that emotional reactions will vary. Bring in a psychologist or counselor to address some of the emotional or psychological responses staff members may be exhibiting.

Step Three: Recover

As the crisis resolves, there will be a return to normalcy, along with an increased understanding about the crisis. Once the crisis appears to be over, the institution will need to decide whether the types and frequencies of communications need to change. Individuals are usually most responsive to taking long-term corrective action immediately after a crisis, so it is important to capitalize on this mindset. Appropriate responses might include new procedures or regulations, changes to student rules, a public education campaign about safety or crisis management, changes to the university Web site, scheduling town-gown meetings in the community, and creating new positions or departments (such as risk management, for example) in the university, and so on.

Key communication initiatives that should be taken at this point include the following:

- Create and execute a strategic plan to get the message across that "everything has returned to normal." Determine which target audiences can help in communicating such messages: student government, faculty, staff, international programs, alumni, partners, stakeholders, and so on. Also determine which communication tactics will be most effective for reaching these target audiences in the immediate aftermath of the crisis: student newspaper, faculty and staff newsletters, campuswide e-mail, small group meetings, alumni magazine, local chamber of commerce communiqués, and so on.

- Communicate what initiatives the university is taking to ensure that a crisis of this type or severity never happens again.

- Inform target audiences about changes and improvements to the crisis communication plan. Communicate what additional resources will be purchased to address these changes and improvements.

- Consider a campuswide or communitywide thank-you letter. Consider placing thank-you advertisements in the student paper and in local community newspapers. And if the magnitude of the crisis warrants it, consider a thank-you advertisement in a statewide newspaper. Institutions may even want to consider hosting a thank-you luncheon for individuals who helped manage the crisis.

- Even after the crisis is no longer a front-page story, those who have been most severely affected will continue to have significant emotional needs. Emotional symptoms may present themselves as physical health symptoms such as sleep disturbances, indigestion, fatigue, or even difficulties with interpersonal relationships at home, at school, and at work. Indeed, these symptoms may be evident at all levels of faculty, staff, and students. Therefore, individuals affected by the crisis should be required or encouraged to visit a mental health counselor.

Even as the crisis is drawing to a close, intense media scrutiny will likely continue—not about the crisis itself but rather about how well it was handled or who was responsible for it happening in the first place. Press releases and photographs must focus on keeping the media informed about the aftermath—particularly on the results, and not on the crisis itself. Sharing the lessons learned and disseminating information about additional initiatives that were not in existence prior to the crisis (new equipment, security measures, and so on) will go a long way in helping focus media attention on the positive steps being taken by the university to prevent similar events from happening in the future.

Step Four: Learn

One of the most critical pieces of any crisis response process is to initiate a *lessons-learned session,* so that the crisis communication team can assess how well it handled the media and communication needs that evolved during the crisis. This assessment must include successes as well as analyzing mistakes, failures, and miscues. Valuable feedback information can be obtained from university staff, target audiences, partners, and the media through focus groups, surveys, and one-on-one discussions.

Therefore, a crisis communication assessment should be conducted as soon as possible after the crisis is over. The feedback should be used to make modifications to the crisis communication plan and even the crisis management plan. All of these efforts will be invaluable to the members of the crisis communication team the next time it faces a significant challenge.

Conclusion

When all is said and done, successful communication during a crisis is really a matter of good planning and preparation, anticipating the communication needs of a university's target audiences, communicating with speed, accuracy, and consistency, making good decisions, maintaining an appropriate balance of action and reaction, collaborating with an institution's partners, spokespersons, and experts, and—most of all—using common sense when making communication efforts.

6

Working with Emergency
Personnel and Outside Agencies

Norbert W. Dunkel and Linda J. Stump

The college or university campus does not stand alone. Any event occurring on a campus that can be categorized as a critical incident will involve emergency personnel from local off-campus agencies as among the first responders. Higher levels of crises will bring with them corresponding increases in the number of personnel and agencies and levels of government involvement in the response to and management of the situation.

It is essential that campus administrators appreciate the roles and responsibilities of emergency personnel and off-campus responders, as well as the protocol for determining command-and-control relationships. Jurisdictional "turf" issues can best be avoided if there is advance planning, including the development of formal or informal working agreements and the routine participation by key campus officials in noncrisis interactions with local and regional emergency managers. Emergency personnel and other outside agencies play a key role in crisis preparedness and response. Many campuses are able to provide crisis-related services through their own various agencies and departments. Due to their size, geographic location, public or private status, political position, or budget, other campuses may not be able to provide some of the basic emergency response services.

This chapter will present an overview of emergency personnel and outside agencies, the organizational structure of these agencies, how these personnel and agencies operate together with campuses, and how a positive working relationship can assist with campus crisis planning. An overview of the Incident Command System (ICS) will also be provided.

Emergency Response Roles

Life safety is the first priority of all emergency response personnel. Members of various agencies perform specific duties, such as security on the scene, rescue and treatment of those injured, suppression of fire, and containment of hazardous materials. As already noted, the degree to which campus personnel can carry out these first responder functions will vary with the size of the institution, its setting, and the level of sophistication of its in-house security or law enforcement, emergency management system and services, and occupational safety units.

Who's in Charge?

Whenever outside assistance is summoned to deal with a campus incident, questions can arise over "who's in charge." For routine events such as accidental injuries, minor fires, or nonviolent crimes, responses typically involve limited numbers of personnel from individual agencies, and they deal with the issues in their respective areas of responsibility without much debate. Campus security or law enforcement supervisors, as well as first-line officers, will frequently know local off-campus emergency responders on a first-name basis. But in times of crisis, the need for control on a larger scale quickly overwhelms the management capabilities that informal relationships provide.

The Incident Command System (ICS)

This section of the chapter describes the history, features, principles, and organizational structure of the Incident Command System (ICS). It also explains the relationship between ICS and the

National Interagency Incident Management System (NIMS; Emergency Management Institute, n.d.).

The Incident Command System was developed in the 1970s by the state of California in response to a series of major wildfires in Southern California. In 1980, federal officials transitioned ICS into a national program called the National Interagency Incident Management System (NIMS), which became the basis of a response management system for all federal agencies with wildfire management responsibilities. Since then, many federal agencies have endorsed the use of ICS, and several have mandated its use. For example, federal law requires the use of ICS in response to all hazardous materials incidents (U.S. Coast Guard, n.d.).

An Incident Command System/Unified Command (ICS/UC) is an efficient on-site tool that can be established by the campus leadership. It can help manage both emergency and nonemergency events. It can be used equally at small and large institutions. The system has considerable internal flexibility, allowing it to expand and contract to meet current needs. It gives responders an integrated organizational structure that meets the complexity of any incident or multiple incidents without being hindered by jurisdictional boundaries. It was originally created to address the following problems:

- Too many people reporting to one supervisor
- Different emergency response organizational structures
- Lack of reliable incident information
- Inadequate and incompatible communications
- Lack of structure for coordinated planning among agencies
- Unclear lines of authority
- Terminology differences among agencies
- Unclear or unspecified incident objectives

An ICS enables integrated communication and planning by establishing a manageable span of control. An ICS divides an emergency response into five manageable functions essential for such operations: command, operations, planning, logistics, and finance and administration.

- *Command:* Sets objectives and priorities. Has overall responsibility at the incident or event.

- *Operations:* Conducts tactical operations to carry out the plan. Develops the tactical objectives and organization, and directs all resources.

- *Planning:* Develops the action plan (recovery strategy) to accomplish the objectives, collects and evaluates information, maintains resource status.

- *Logistics:* Provides support to meet incident needs; provides resources and all other services needed to support the incident.

- *Finance and administration:* Monitors costs associated with the incident, provides accounting, procurement, time recording, and cost analysis.

NIMS notes that, if warranted by the situation, a sixth functional area—intelligence—may also be established.

The incident commander (IC) or the unified command (UC) is responsible for all aspects of the response, including developing incident objectives and managing all incident operations. The Incident Command Structure consists of a command staff, including a safety officer, information officer, and liaison officer, and a general staff, including the areas of operations, planning, logistics, and finance and administration (U.S. Department of Labor, n.d.). In a major disaster, the incident commanders of all the organizations involved are brought together to coordinate an effective overall response while each carries out his or her own jurisdictional responsibilities. Federal, state, and local lines of government may be involved. The UC structure provides a forum for consensus decision making and may result in the blending of various agencies into an integrated response team.

According to NIMS, the key elements and features of a unified command are as follows:

- *Preparedness.*Readiness to manage and conduct incident actions is significantly enhanced if professionals have worked together before an incident. NIMS recognizes this and defines advance preparedness measures such as planning, training, exercises, qualification and certification, equipment acquisition and certification, and publication management. Preparedness also incorporates mitigation activities such as public education, enforcement of building standards and codes, and preventive measures to deter or lessen the loss of life or property.

- *Communications and information management.* Standardized communications during an incident are essential, and NIMS prescribes interoperable communications systems for both incident and information management. Responders and managers across all agencies and jurisdictions must have a common operating picture for a more efficient and effective incident response.

- *Joint information system (JIS).* NIMS organizational measures further enhance the public communication effort. The joint information system provides the public with timely and accurate incident information and unified public messages. This system employs joint information centers and brings incident communicators together during an incident to develop, coordinate, and deliver a unified message. This ensures that federal, state, tribal, and local levels of government are releasing the same information during an incident.

- *NIMS integration center (NIC)*. To ensure that NIMS remains an accurate and effective management tool, the NIMS NIC will be established by the secretary of homeland security to assess proposed changes to NIMS, capture and evaluate lessons learned, and employ best practices. The NIC will provide strategic direction and oversight of the NIMS, supporting both routine maintenance and continuous refinement of the system and its components over the long term. The NIC will develop and facilitate national standards for NIMS education and training, first responder communications and equipment, typing of resources, qualification and credentialing of incident management and responder personnel, and standardization of equipment maintenance and resources. The NIC will continue to use the collaborative process of federal, state, tribal, local, multidiscipline, and private authorities to assess prospective changes and ensure continuity and accuracy ("Department of Homeland Security Secretary Tom Ridge," 2004).

Incident Action Plans

We highly recommend using an incident action plan when an ICS is developed on a campus. The incident action plan documents the actions outlined by the incident commander and general campus staff during the planning meeting. When all attachments are included, the plan specifies the control objectives, tactics to meet the objectives, resources, organization, communications plan, medical plan, and other appropriate information for use in tactical operations. An incident action plan is completed after each formal planning meeting conducted by the incident commander and the command and general campus staff. The plan must be approved by the incident commander before it is distributed. Sufficient copies of the plan can then be reproduced and provided to supervisory personnel at all levels. The plan has seven components:

- *Incident objectives*. This is the first page of the plan. It describes the basic incident strategy and control objectives, and provides weather information and safety considerations for use during the operational period. The objectives are developed by the incident commander based on the goals outlined by the agency administrator with the advice and consultation of the general campus staff.

- *Organization assignment list*. This provides information on the units that are currently activated and the names of personnel staffing each position or unit. It is used to complete the incident organization chart, which is posted on the incident command post display. The list is prepared and maintained by the resources unit under the direction of the planning section chief.

- *Incident map*. The incident map may be a print map, diagram, or sketch of the incident location and the surrounding structures and land. All descriptions of the incident are made using this map. The incident map is situational and may be prepared or adapted on-site.

- *Assignment list*. The assignment list is used to inform the operations section personnel of incident assignments. Once the assignments are agreed to by the incident commander and general campus staff, the assignment information is provided to the appropriate units and divisions via the communications center. The assignment list is normally created by the resources unit, with guidance provided by the incident objectives, operational planning worksheet, and operations section chief.

- *Incident radio communication plan.* This plan provides all radio frequency assignments for each operational period. The information on frequency assignments is normally placed on the appropriate assignment list. This radio communication plan is prepared by the communications unit leader.

- *Traffic plan.* The traffic plan is internal and external to the incident. It identifies all roads and traffic direction. A traffic plan may be prepared in advance or on-site. The key is for it to be functional and easily understood.

- *Medical plan.* The medical plan provides information on incident medical aid stations, transportation services, hospitals, and medical emergency procedures for incident personnel. The medical plan is prepared by the medical unit leader and reviewed by the safety officer.

Pre-event Cooperation

A major campus crisis or a disaster can involve agencies of the federal government as well as resources of the campus, local municipality, county, and state. When there is no crisis, however, interaction with representatives of federal and even state emergency response agencies is unlikely to occur with great frequency unless specific outreach efforts are made. And they should be. Local and regional emergency responders should be made familiar with, and welcomed by, the campus community. They should play an integral role in crisis management training exercises (see Chapter Eight for more on this) and encouraged to make use of campus-based scenarios and resources for their own in-service training and professional development programs.

Campuses that work with several emergency personnel and outside agencies during the course of the year will form closer working relationships. Such relationships are of tremendous value and benefit to campus administrators (that is, staff from housing, athletic association, student union, environmental health and safety, counseling center, dean of students offices, and so on). The likelihood is that only the campus security or law enforcement agency will work with federal or state agencies such as the Secret Service or Federal Bureau of Investigation, as well as with the Department of Homeland Security. Nonetheless, it is important for the greater campus to understand the organizational structure, services, and context of each of these agencies. The following sections provide a brief overview of mutual aid agreements that may be developed with these agencies and what each one involves.

Mutual Aid Agreements

Off-campus responders to a low-level campus crisis (a critical incident) are typically members of the local emergency service agencies within whose jurisdiction boundaries the institution lies. Once the level of crisis rises to a point where the services of personnel from neighboring (or even noncontiguous) jurisdictions are required, the legalities of mutual aid become important. Mutual aid agreements among fire departments are the norm, and they generally do not involve direct participation by the campus, because few institutions have in-house firefighters. However, educational institutions with sworn personnel may be permitted by state law to enter directly into mutual aid agreements with nonconcurrent jurisdictions. These agreements typically formalize assistance request procedures, establish command responsibility, confer appropriate enforcement authority upon extrajurisdictional officers, and specify financial obligations such as salary, benefits, and equipment maintenance ("Resource Management," n.d.).

Campus staff may work with a number of emergency personnel and outside agencies. Each one possesses its own organizational structure and reporting relationships to the others. It is incumbent upon campus staff not only to understand the basic organizational structures and reporting relationships of these agencies but also to establish relationships with these agencies. These different staff should aid in the development of campus protocols and also be involved during nonemergency meetings. In some cases these agencies have been formed since the September 11, 2001, terrorist attacks. In other cases, existing agencies, some over a hundred years old, were tasked with additional responsibilities or reporting relationships after September 11. An overview of pertinent agencies follows.

Campus Security and Police

Most college campuses have their own campus security or campus police agency. A campus security operation provides campus access services (such as entrance gate monitoring, information booth staffing, and so on), key control, building security, traffic monitoring, escort services, and the like. For higher-level services, the campus may enter into a mutual aid agreement with the city or county.

Campus police likely provide or coordinate the same services as a campus security operation, but they also may provide criminal investigations (evidentiary collection and analysis, reports, and so on), victim advocacy (twenty-four-hour care, work with hospitals, case adjudication, and so on), community services (bike safety, theft prevention, identification of possessions, and so on), critical incident response (injuries, medical illnesses, accidents), emergency operations center coordination (hurricane service coordination, large-scale critical incidents), and the like. Many campus police operations employ certified law enforcement officers who are fully trained in all aspects of law enforcement, including the use of weapons. Campus police may use cars, ATVs, snowmobiles, motorcycles, bicycles, and more to operate in various campus environments and situations.

The structure of a campus security or campus police operation is likely quite familiar to readers. The chief (director) is generally selected for the position by the campus senior administration and reports to a senior administrator. Chiefs oversee the operation and may have colonels or majors (associate directors or assistant directors) reporting to them. These direct reports oversee the various divisions of the operation, such as investigations, patrol, community service, administration, and so on. The military-style organizational structure includes captains, lieutenants, sergeants, and corporals. Police service technicians provide civilian support for dispatching, parking patrol, and the like. In addition, many full-time support staff and hourly staff work to support the various functions of the operation.

The jurisdiction of campus security or police includes the lands and buildings owned and operated by the campus. For large land-grant campuses that operate agricultural outreach offices in each of the state's counties, this jurisdiction may be statewide.

City Police

City police may provide the primary campus police services, fulfilling such campus security functions as information booth services, access, building and parking patrol, and the like.

Like the campus police, the city police also work in a military-style organizational structure, with the chief of police overseeing the operation. The chief is generally selected by the city commission/council or city manager for the position and generally reports to the city manager. Most city police operations can provide full police services, unless the operation is low level, such as in a smaller city that has a small number of staff, limited resources, and so on. City police on lower-level operations may call on the county sheriff or state police. The jurisdiction of the city police includes lands and buildings within the city boundaries; it may also include campus property if there are appropriate aid agreements.

County Sheriff

The county sheriff may provide a higher level of services if campus or city operations are unable to carry out these services. The county sheriff also works in a paramilitary organizational structure, with the sheriff overseeing the operation. The sheriff is generally elected by the county citizens and may work in conjunction with a county commission for budget and policy issues.

Services provided by county sheriffs include patrol (using cars, ATVs, snowmobiles, horses, bicycles, and so on), investigations (evidentiary collection and analysis, reports), jail services (jail management, transportation), crime prevention (computer crime, community education), juvenile programs where officers are assigned to local schools (that is, they may support Explorer programs, accompany spring break trips, operate teen courts, and so on), and victim advocacy (twenty-four-hour crisis counseling, assistance in filing for crime victim compensation, information and victims' rights during the judicial process, and so on).

The county sheriff's jurisdiction covers the lands and buildings in the county boundaries and may include city and campus property, if there are appropriate aid agreements.

State Police

The state police are infrequently used on campus, although campuses that host large-scale events such as sports functions, concerts, speakers, and the like may utilize the services of the state police for security purposes.

The state police generally work in a military-style organizational structure, with the commander (director) overseeing the operation. Large states may be divided into districts, with deputy commanders overseeing their individual districts. A campus may work with the respective district deputy commander to coordinate services.

The state police provide full services for patrol (enforcement of traffic laws, and so on), conduct investigations over which they have jurisdiction (evidentiary collecting and analysis, reports, and so on), victim advocacy (assistance during judicial proceedings, and so on), contraband interdiction (drug seizure, apprehension of drug traffickers), and the like.

The state police are generally funded through an appropriation from the state legislature. The state police's jurisdiction includes the lands and buildings in the boundaries of the state, including county, city, and campus property, if there are appropriate aid agreements.

Fire and Rescue Services

Only a few campuses operate their own fire and rescue services. For most, these services are provided by the city or county fire and rescue departments. A fire and rescue operation may include the following services:

- Emergency management, including mitigation, preparedness, response, and recovery from natural and manmade threats

- 911 services, including the coordination and development of the emergency 911 system

- Fire protection services, including fire suppression, prevention, life safety, fire investigation, and coordination of contracted fire services

- Emergency medical services, including advanced life support, rescue, and ambulance transportation

Fire and rescue may also specifically coordinate and oversee hazardous materials–related issues and community fire education programs. Campuses generally handle some form of hazardous material, from paint supplies to pool chemicals to nuclear materials. Protocols for the handling and storage of these campus materials should be developed in concert with the fire and rescue operation staff.

The two main areas of service to campuses generally provided by fire and rescue operations are fire protection services and emergency medical services.

One of the greatest challenges that fire and rescue operations face in providing fire protection to a campus is accessing a facility twenty-four hours per day, seven days per week. Generally, when facilities are occupied, day or night, access is not so much an issue. But when an academic building, sports facility, ancillary facility, and the like are empty and locked, then it is an issue. A few approaches have successfully been implemented by campuses. First, building fire alarms that not only go off at fire rescue but also at the campus security or law enforcement office provide the police with notice to proceed to the building in alarm. Campus security and law enforcement operations possess master keys that can access the buildings and provide entrance for fire rescue. Second, on campuses where campus security or law enforcement do not carry master keys, vaultlike key boxes have been employed. These boxes are small and "vandalproof," set flush against the exterior of the building at least eight feet above the ground. The fire rescue operation, generally a district chief or ladder truck, has the key to open the box and gain access to the key. The fire station must first send an electronic signal to the vehicle to release the key before it can be used to open the box. Third—and this generally involves campus housing—the housing staff provide on-duty campus coverage and in the event of a fire alarm, a staff member is on-site to provide full access to the facility. Campus security or law enforcement is intimately involved in most fires on campus. Their relationship with fire and rescue has developed from years of working collaboratively on training, procedures, and events.

The second main responsibility of fire and rescue operations is emergency medical services. Ambulance service to sick or injured students, faculty, or staff must be a coordinated effort between the campus security or law enforcement and fire and rescue operations. A similar access issue arises when emergency medical services receive a call for assistance. If campus security or law enforcement can be notified of a 911 emergency call from fire and rescue or serves as a 911 agency, then the security or police can be on-site to assist with building access, crowd control, traffic control, and the like. These routine types of medical service responses can be handled quickly if there is proper coordination.

Finally, in many local communities the fire chief is the highest-ranking local official and will serve as the incident commander in a local emergency. It is important to distinguish the person who will be identified as the incident commander in the local community, because this person may also serve as incident commander during an emergency on the campus.

County Emergency Coordination

Emergency coordination for counties generally exists in a dedicated office funded by the county. This office may be an Emergency Operations Center or County Emergency Coordination Office, but its responsibilities remain the same, including coordination of training for Community Emergency Response Team (CERT) members, natural disaster preparedness, coordination with the state emergency coordination office, coordination with city, campus, private, and other local entities, and oversight of a county emergency operations center in case of a catastrophic event. It also helps coordinate training for CERT members, who are community individuals trained in basic disaster response skills such as life safety, light search and rescue, team organization, and disaster medical operations. Campuses have elected to send campus staff to the CERT training program in order to possess ample staff in the event of a campus large-scale disaster. CERT-trained staff can assist with both emergency and non-emergency tasks such as passing out water, providing services at special events, or passing out disaster educational materials ("Federal Emergency Management Agency," n.d.).

Campuses should work closely with the county office in planning protocols, nonemergency meetings, mock exercise coordination, and shelter management. It is important to include the county coordinator for emergency services on any campus disaster planning committee. A good working relationship and coordinated county and campus efforts in emergency preparedness will benefit all parties when an emergency affecting the campus or the county occurs.

American Red Cross

Clara Barton successfully organized the American Association of the Red Cross in Washington, D.C., on May 21, 1881. The Red Cross provides relief to victims of disasters and helps people prevent, prepare for, and respond to emergencies.

The Red Cross provides numerous community services for citizens: senior services—friendly visitors, caregiver support; hospital and nursing home volunteers; electronic personal emergency response service; transportation to doctor appointments and other essential trips; food pantry and hot lunch programs; homeless shelters and transitional housing services; school clubs and community service learning programs and projects; youth programs—violence and substance abuse prevention, peer education and mentoring, leadership development camps; food and rental assistance; language banks (lists of individuals who speak languages other than English); and community information and referral (American Red Cross, n.d.).

Red Cross disaster relief focuses on meeting the needs of individuals and families affected by the disaster. When a disaster threatens or strikes, the Red Cross provides shelter, food, and health and mental health services that address basic human needs (American Red Cross, n.d.). Campuses may choose to designate qualified buildings as Red Cross shelters in times of natural disaster or disaster relief. These buildings are then managed by trained Red Cross shelter managers. Campuses that possess designated Red Cross shelters may qualify for federal funds to upgrade those buildings with hurricane- or tornado-tempered windows, windscreens, and the like. Campuses possessing designated Red Cross shelters should check with their local Red Cross Office to determine the availability of upgrade funding.

The Red Cross also feeds disaster victims and emergency workers, handles inquiries from concerned immediate family members outside the disaster-affected area, provides blood and blood products to disaster victims, and links disaster victims to other available resources. The Red Cross may also help persons needing long-term recovery assistance when all other available resources, including insurance and government, private, and community assistance, are either unavailable or inadequate to meet the needs. All assistance is based on verified disaster-caused needs and is free—literally a gift as a result of the generous support of the American people (American Red Cross, n.d.).

When developing an overall campus disaster plan, consideration should be given to the potential involvement of the Red Cross and shelter management. It is a good idea to include the community Red Cross representative on a crisis management team campus disaster committee.

Federal Bureau of Investigation (FBI)

The Federal Bureau of Investigation (FBI) was formed on July 26, 1908, when Attorney General Charles Bonaparte ordered new staff to take on investigative assignments in areas such as antitrust, espionage, and land fraud (Federal Bureau of Investigation, n.d.).

The FBI is headed by a director appointed by the president and confirmed by the U.S. Senate. FBI field offices are located in major cities throughout the United States and in San Juan, Puerto Rico. In addition, resident agencies are maintained in smaller cities and towns across the country. The locations are selected according to crime trends, the need for regional geographic centralization, and the need to efficiently manage resources.

Each field office is overseen by a special agent in charge (SAC), except those in Los Angeles, New York City, and Washington, D.C. Due to their large size, these offices are managed by an assistant director in charge (ADIC). The ADICs are assisted by SACs responsible for specific programs. It is the special agent in the field who looks for clues, tracks down leads, and works with local and campus law enforcement to apprehend criminals.

The FBI priorities are as follows (Federal Bureau of Investigation, n.d.):

- Protect the United States from terrorist attacks

- Protect the United States against foreign intelligence operations and espionage

- Protect the United States against cyberattacks and high-technology crimes

- Combat public corruption at all levels

- Protect civil rights

- Combat transnational and national criminal organizations and enterprises

- Combat major white-collar crime

- Combat significant violent crime

- Support federal, state, county, municipal, and international partners

- Upgrade technology to successfully perform the FBI's mission

Campus staff may have limited experience with the FBI, although campuses do have occasion to provide the FBI with the paperwork or information on individual students. It is prudent for staff to be trained in how to respond when an FBI agent approaches them for information; agents must identify themselves with their badge and ID, but the staff member must also contact the campus general counsel's office for verification of paperwork before handing over any student information.

Campus security or campus law enforcement may work more frequently with the FBI on specific cases that warrant their involvement.

Department of Homeland Security

The National Strategy for Homeland Security (*National Strategy for Homeland Security*, 2002) and the Homeland Security Act of 2002 (House of Representatives, 2002) provided the impetus to organize and secure the United States from terrorist attacks. The Department of Homeland Security was established to unify the numerous organizations and institutions involved in providing national security. There are over 180,000 employees in the Department of Homeland Security, which includes twenty-two major components (Department of Homeland Security, n.d.). Several of the major Department of Homeland Security components that campus staff may work with are as follows:

- *The Federal Emergency Management Agency.* This office prepares the nation for response and recovery following a national incident.

- *The Transportation and Security Administration.* This office protects the nation's transportation systems.

- *U.S. Customs and Border Protection.* This office secures the nation's borders.

- *U.S. Immigration and Customs Enforcement.* This office is responsible for investigating vulnerabilities to the nation's border and infrastructure.

- *The Science and Technology Directorate.* Covers catastrophic terrorism that could result in large-scale loss of life or economic impact at the local, state, and federal levels.

- *U.S. Coast Guard.* Protects the nation's waterways to support national security.

- *U.S. Secret Service.* Protects the president, nation's leaders, and nation's infrastructure and carries out investigations.

A campus that hosts large events, speakers, and political visits may work with the Secret Service, but relationships with other Homeland Security offices will likely involve single events only. For instance, a campus that lies along a major waterfront will have a developed protocol for waterfront events such as a chemical or oil spill. That campus security or law enforcement agency may work with local agencies as well as the local United States Coast Guard on the development of such a protocol. Similarly, campuses that operate student flight schools will likely work with local agencies as well as the Border and Transportation Security or the Federal Aviation Administration in developing policies and procedures. Each campus needs to assess its vulnerabilities and develop protocols using the appropriate agencies given its circumstances of academic program, geography, and the like.

Federal Emergency Management Agency (FEMA)

FEMA is an organization now housed inside the Department of Homeland Security. FEMA provides response and recovery to natural disasters and terrorist attacks. FEMA traces its history back to the Congressional Act of 1803, when assistance was provided to a New Hampshire town following an extensive fire. Over the subsequent years, over a hundred pieces of legislation have been passed to provide assistance to communities that have experienced devastating hurricanes, earthquakes, floods, and other natural disasters (Federal Emergency Management Agency, n.d.).

Campuses developing natural disaster plans can find excellent resources through FEMA for flood hazard mapping and floodplain management, dam safety, earthquakes, fires, hurricanes, multihazards, and terrorism prevention.

Campuses involved in a natural disaster will likely work directly with a FEMA representative during response and recovery. Once a county or state has been declared a federal disaster site, it is eligible to receive disaster relief. Immediately after the disaster, it is important to assess the damages, document the damages with photographs, videotape, and any supporting materials regarding pricing, and contact the FEMA office. A FEMA representative will assist campus staff in identifying damaged buildings and items for potential financial assistance, assist in the processing of paperwork to support the claim, and assist in the follow-up recovery.

It was FEMA that developed the Community Emergency Response Team (CERT) national program; it did so because communities had difficulty identifying individuals who can provide large-scale emergency response.

Secret Service

The Secret Service is also housed in the Department of Homeland Security. It was developed on July 5, 1865, in Washington, D.C., to suppress counterfeit currency. Over the years since its founding, the U.S. Secret Service has expanded its role to now include protecting the president, national leaders, and visiting foreign dignitaries; investigating to safeguard the nation's financial system; and designing and planning national security special events.

Campuses that host events involving national or foreign leaders will likely work with the U.S. Secret Service. Campus security or law enforcement will serve as the point of contact with the U.S. Secret Service advance team and on-site team leader. Campuses that have worked with the U.S. Secret Service understand that their role is to provide the information, materials, and resources that the U.S. Secret Service requires to develop the event plan (U.S. Secret Service, n.d.).

Conclusion

Outlining how to work with emergency personnel and outside agencies is a vital aspect in developing a comprehensive campus crisis management plan. Most campus staff do not work with these outside agencies, except, perhaps, on occasions when emergency medical services or fire services are needed. Yet understanding the organizational structures and method of operation of these outside agencies allows everyone to better relate to the approach, personnel, and services these agencies can ultimately provide.

Communicating and meeting with individual agencies provide campus staff the opportunity to establish and strengthen working relationships. In times of crisis, issues of authority and command will have already been worked through, so that assistance can be provided without confusion. When multiple agencies become involved in a crisis, there will be methods and command structures in place to minimize confusion and maximize efficiency. Campus staff who understand these overarching command structures will be able to train other staff in working with emergency personnel and outside agencies. In sum, campuses that involve these emergency personnel and outside agencies in developing and refining their crisis management plan will experience the benefits of a coordinated plan in a time of crisis.

References

American Red Cross. (n.d.). Retrieved August 18, 2005, from http://www.redcross.org/.

Department of Homeland Security. (n.d.). Retrieved October 12, 2006, from http://www.dhs.gov/.

Department of Homeland Security Secretary Tom Ridge approves national incident management system (NIMS). (2004, March 1). Retrieved August 18, 2005, from http://www.dhs.gov/.

Emergency Management Institute (n.d.). Retrieved October 12, 2006, from http://www.training.fema.gov/index.asp.

Federal Bureau of Investigation. (n.d.). Retrieved August 18, 2005, from http://www.fbi.gov/.

Federal Emergency Management Agency. (n.d.). Retrieved August 16, 2005, from http://www.fema.gov/.

House of Representatives (2002). *Homeland Security Act: HR 5005.* Washington, DC: Author.

National Strategy for Homeland Security. (2002, July). Washington, DC: Department of Homeland Security. Retrieved November 7, 2006, from http://www.dhs.gov/xlibrary/assets/nat_strat_hls.pdf.

Resource management and mutual aid. (n.d.). Retrieved October 3, 2006, from http://www.fema.gov/emergency/nims/mutual_aid.shtm.

U.S. Coast Guard. *Incident Command System.* (n.d.). Retrieved October 3, 2006, from http://www.uscg.mil/hq/g-m/mor/Articles/ICS.htm.

U.S. Department of Labor. (n.d.). Retrieved October 12, 2006, from http://www.osha.gov/SLTC/etools/ics/whatisics.html.

U.S. *Secret Service.* (n.d.). Retrieved August 16, 2005, from http://www.secret service.gov.

7

Psychological First Aid in the Aftermath of Crisis

Wayne Griffin

A first-year debate team student dies in an auto crash while on a university trip, leaving the faculty adviser and other members of the team in shock. Students in a residence hall are distraught that a roommate is the victim of sexual assault. A graduate student on the eve of his graduation is discovered by a peer, dead from an overdose of cyanide. A student loses control in a residence hall and confronts his peers and police with a knife. A faculty member and an academic adviser, concerned about a student who has written disturbing e-mails, go to his off-campus apartment and find him unconscious, the victim of a drug overdose. An off-campus student is transported to an emergency room, where she dies from a communicable disease; her roommates and others at the apartment complex fear for their own health. A fraternity member is accidentally shot to death by another member.

All these are tragic but too-familiar examples of crises that occur on our college and university campuses. A number of questions arise as colleges and universities increasingly face the challenge of providing care during these critical incidents. How does the campus community respond effectively to such crises? What factors expose colleges and universities to increased demands for emergency psychological services? And how are crisis intervention services integrated into the college's comprehensive provision of psychological support for the campus community?

The goal of this chapter is to provide a framework for psychological services as an integral component of a college or university crisis intervention program. A rationale for *psychological first aid* as a component of campus crisis intervention services will be discussed. Types of crises will be conceptualized based on the crisis matrix promoted in this book. Underlying principles of effective crisis intervention and application to various types of crises will be described, and a typology of several forms of individual and group response will be examined. Several issues salient to emergency services will also be examined, including relevant ethical and legal considerations, responder training, use of interpreters, awareness of multicultural concerns, and care for the caregivers.

The Need for Crisis Intervention

Colleges and universities increasingly reflect the complexities of life in general society. Campus communities are hit by natural and human-made disasters, campus emergencies, and critical incidents. Several factors may be contributing to the emergence of these crises on campus, including the growing number of students who come to college with existing vulnerabilities.

Rising Student Concerns

Over the past decade, research has indicated that students are presenting to campus counseling services with more severe issues (Benton et al., 2003; Gallagher, Sysko, & Zhang, 2001; Gallagher, Gill, & Sysko, 2000; Pledge, Lapan, Heppner, & Roehlke, 1998; O'Malley, Wheeler, Murphey, & O'Connell, 1990; Robbins, May, & Corazini, 1985; Stone & Archer, 1990). Summaries of this research indicate a higher percentage of students are presenting with problems related to suicidality, substance abuse, depression, anxiety, eating disorders, and a history of psychiatric treatment (Gallagher et al., 2001; Pledge et al., 1998). Though there is hopeful evidence suggesting that young people who attend college are less likely to commit suicide than their nonstudent peers, suicide is now reported to be the third leading cause of death in persons ages fifteen to twenty-four (Ellen, 2002; "In Harm's Way," 2005; National Center for Health Statistics, 2002). The 2004 American College Health Association (ACHA) survey of over forty-thousand students reported that approximately 9.2 percent responded that they had seriously considered suicide. Sixty-three percent indicated they felt hopeless at times, and 45 percent described themselves as feeling depressed to the point of having trouble functioning. Although these statistics are alarming, of most significant import is the finding that the behavioral continuum related to unintentional harm from accidents and homicide—the first and second causes of death among college students—is often related to thoughts of suicide (Barrios, Everett, Simon, & Brener, 2000).

Besides having increasingly severe psychological issues that they bring with them to campus, while in school students are also subject to a range of developmental transitions and situational crises. These include the breakup of family systems, interpersonal violence, sexual assault, death of significant others, impairment of physical health, and injuries from accidents. Since the terrorist attacks of September 11, 2001, students are also more sensitive to the possible recurrence of similar incidents and their impact on the larger social order. In reviewing research on the first-year college student experience, Bartlett (2002) notes the important challenges of these concerns and their potential to increase stress on students' physical and emotional health and affect their concentration and academic progress.

Reaction by Campus Emergency Services

Faced with the prevalence of more severe concerns presented by students, college and university counseling services are adjusting to a paradigm shift—from treatment for what have been viewed traditionally as developmental and personal identity concerns to clinical intervention and support for chronic illnesses (Kitzrow, 2003). The severe nature of such issues as substance abuse, chronic depression, history of psychiatric care, self-injury and harm, and disorders associated with decreased impulse control also increases the likelihood of students experiencing a crisis during their time in school. During an acute period of distress, often characterized by confusion and the erosion of adaptive skills, students may require more intense and frequent forms of intervention, possibly including hospitalization.

Evidence emerging from the psychological literature and risk management fields suggests the importance for campuses to have in place resources and personnel to efficiently identify and implement emergency services to support students. In addressing the risk management factors associated with student suicide and self-inflicted injury, Bickel and Lake (1999) advocate for campuses to adopt a "facilitator model." They argue that although colleges and universities cannot place students in custodial control sufficient to prevent suicide, they must strive to create learning environments that are supportive of students with mental health concerns. Moreover, a facilitative institution needs to take reasonable steps to protect the physical safety of their students and other individuals.

The response of campuses to the increase in both number and types of personal crises is reflected in the call for timely access to initial assessment, supportive counseling, and provision of emergency psychological services (Blom & Beckley, 2005; Kadison, 2004; Kitzrow, 2003). The International Association of Counseling Services standards (Boyd et al., 2000, p. B2) states that counseling centers "must provide crisis intervention and emergency coverage either directly or through cooperative arrangements with other resources on campus and in the surrounding area." In Coulter, Offutt, and Mascher's (2003) survey of 192 campuses ranging in size from two thousand to ten thousand–plus students, 56 percent of the responding counseling centers reported having staff formally on call after hours, 35 percent assigned staff on an informal call basis, while only 9 percent of the campuses offered no on-call emergency service. The provision of crisis intervention services is rapidly becoming a reflection of the college or university *ethic of care* for the campus community and the idea that effective prevention and crisis management are the responsibility of all members of the campus community (Lerner, Volper, & Lindell, 2004).

In summary, the need for campuses to develop and implement emergency psychological intervention services is supported by several factors. First, college students are presenting with increasingly severe psychological concerns, including previous psychiatric care. Along with these more serious mental health concerns there are the normal needs for adjustment to college, including meeting new academic demands and creating a social support system. For students who already struggle with existing mental health concerns, these tasks may become overwhelming and leave them more vulnerable to crisis states. Second, colleges and universities must be prepared to address the significant threat of suicidal ideation and self-harm. Because suicide is the third leading cause of death among traditional-age college students, significant and coordinated steps are warranted to provide education and intervention ("In Harm's Way," 2005). Suicide threats, attempts, and successful completions affect large numbers of persons in students' study, social, and living environments. Third, campuses also experience unpredictable tragedies that result in injury or death of students, faculty, and staff. These incidents may exacerbate existing mental and physical health problems and further affect students' ability to function. Early psychological intervention can provide initial assessments needed to promote safety and security, facilitate referrals to appropriate campus and community resources, provide support and education for affected members in students' study, social, and living environments, and assist in providing and coordinating aftercare.

Psychological First Aid in Crisis Intervention

Crisis, as defined by James and Gilliland (2005), involves the experience of an event in such a way that it is perceived to be intolerably difficult and exceeding one's available resources and capacities to adapt. If crisis goes unresolved, the person can potentially experience further distress and more severe affective, behavioral, and cognitive malfunctioning. Crisis can be experienced as a danger further exacerbating deficiencies in coping, or with proper resources, can be integrated as a growth experience (Hoff, 1995).

Defining the Basis of Need

Some crises involve highly traumatic events. These life events are often unpredictable, involve being exposed to horrible scenes, and are associated with terror and helplessness. Persons are suddenly swept into an event over which they feel they have no control and which they think they may not survive. In the aftermath of such events, they are left to repair their assumptions about the world and implement their capacities for adaptation. Results of population studies suggest approximately five out of ten individuals will experience some form of major stressor or significant life event or trauma during the course of their lifetime (Breslau et al., 1998; Kessler et al., 1995). Though these events are influential, by and large people are resilient and adapt in ways that allow them to function quite effectively. Results of studies indicate approximately 8 to 9 percent are likely to develop chronic mental health problems related to all forms of trauma (Breslau et al., 1998; Kessler et al., 1995). Some individuals, after a period of adjustment, use the event as an occasion for personal growth, developing adaptive assumptions about life, enhancing coping skills, and acquiring support in novel ways (Bonanno, 2004; Frazier, Conlon, & Glaser, 2001; Tedeschi, 1999).

Events that precipitate crises exist on a continuum. Some are severe and more likely to result in post-trauma complications. McFarlane and DeGirolamo (1996) suggest the intensity and duration of exposure to traumatic events often mediate the effects and degree of complications. For example, seeing death or surviving by freak circumstances is likely to offer more potential for complications in the aftermath than simply being aware of destruction or loss. At the other end of the crisis continuum are events that do not include life-threatening or intense experiences yet are perceived as highly stressful. For the student who does not make the final grade in a course required to continue in her academic major or who fails to pay enrollment fees on time, forgets a deadline, or experiences the breakup of a dating relationship, life may temporarily feel overwhelming. Lacking a sense of options, adequate coping skills, or awareness of resources, the student may feel paralyzed to know what course of action to take. When associated with other problems, such as chronic depression, uncontrolled anxiety, or other mental disorder, this student may experience a more intense and debilitating period of acute crisis.

Goals of Early Psychological Intervention

Early psychological intervention in the aftermath of crisis has been valued as a compelling component of survivor welfare since World War I (Everly, 2002). After the attacks on the World Trade Center in 2001 interest in research on what constitutes effective evidence-based crisis interventions and who should receive such services increased. Public safety, military, and community relief agencies, such as the American Red Cross and National Organization of Victim Assistance, have expressed interest in crisis intervention as a means of attenuating the impact of trauma on victims and service personnel. Because most people adapt to traumatic events and crisis on their own, it is important to avoid implementing services based on assumptions of need that may impede the resilience and healing process rather than serve its best interest (Bonanno, 2004; Litz & Gray, 2004). The core concept behind providing early crisis intervention services following trauma is to enhance the affected persons' abilities to stabilize their physical and emotional reactions, access adaptive behaviors, and develop meaning from their experience, thereby promoting effective coping and psychological healing.

Benefits to the Campus Community

The goals of crisis intervention in the college and university setting are threefold. First, to the degree possible, crisis intervention seeks the timely restoration of physical safety and emotional security for those most severely affected. This goal is often achieved by public safety personnel such as police, fire, and emergency medical personnel. First responders to crisis events are primarily focused on assessing for and containing threats to safety and security. Persons in crisis need to perceive a basic level of physical and emotional safety in order to process information in ways that promote cognitive adaptation and reduce their stress reaction. According to Abraham Maslow's (1954) theory on human growth and achievement, meeting the basic need for safe shelter, adequate sustenance, and reduction in threat are the foundation for a person's capacities for higher-order thinking, problem solving, and efforts at self-actualization.

A second goal of psychological intervention is to help people in crisis cope and adapt to their experience. This includes their ability to respond cognitively, affectively, and behaviorally in ways that promote healing and meaning. This occurs through the supportive presence of others, validation of experience, nurturing of resilience, education, and preparation related to the normal reactions to stress and trauma, and where appropriate, referral to resources for post-trauma counseling. The focus of psychological first aid, a concept first utilized by Beverly Raphael (1977, 1986), as a component of crisis intervention, is to help persons recognize and correct temporary affective, behavioral, and cognitive distortions that are associated with the crisis event and interfere with their ability to function healthfully (James & Gilliland, 2005). Helping people regain their precrisis equilibrium, to the degree possible given the severity of the crisis event, enhances their potential for constructing meaning and thus better prepare to adapt to future stressors (Young, 2002).

The third goal of crisis intervention in the college or university setting is to respond effectively to the incident in the context of the larger community. A comprehensive approach to understanding crisis incorporates the interrelationships that exist between persons and the environments in which they live, work, study, and socialize. For students in crisis this may include the classroom, student organizations, on- or off-campus residence areas, work site, and other settings in which they interact. For example, the death of a student may have implications for all of the preceding settings in the way the loss is perceived, bereavement is facilitated, and level of personal vulnerability is understood. A facilitative institution (Bickel & Lake, 1999) will understand the larger scope and impact of crisis and view the incident as an important opportunity to exercise its ethic of care, express concern through compassionate outreach, and provide support to those directly and indirectly affected.

Characteristics of Effective Intervention

Effective psychological first aid during crisis intervention assesses four dimensions of individual and community well-being. According to Young (2002), the presence of ongoing danger, threats to physical safety, persistent mental and emotional vulnerability, and risk to community integrity may further complicate initial reactions to crisis. A person's physical integrity is related to the level of felt or perceived bodily threat, including extensions to the person such as significant others, pets, and sentimental property. Mental integrity is represented in the person's capacity to conceptualize, problem-solve, understand context, and implement adaptive behaviors. Emotional integrity is reflected in one's ability to maintain a meaningful sense of control and support perspective. Community integrity is characterized by the resilience of the social fabric, the stress related to interpersonal and group agreements, and the ongoing plausibility of connection. Meaningful intervention requires an initial assessment of all these dimensions and distinguishing between persons or groups who appear to be coping effectively and those exhibiting more complicated responses.

At this point, an important distinction should be made between initial efforts at crisis intervention and post-trauma counseling. Psychological first aid in the aftermath of crisis is aimed at reducing the temporary effects of distortions in the cognitive, affective, and behavioral domains. The support and education provided during the initial response are geared toward helping students or a community regain, to the degree possible, their precrisis equilibrium. Following the initial assessment and stabilization, persons who are demonstrating more complex or persistent reactions are appropriately referred to counseling and medical resources. Where threats to engage in self-harm or threatening and disruptive behaviors exist, timely assessment and transportation for evaluation by medical and psychiatric personnel may be warranted. In rare instances, to protect the person from self-harm or injuring others, it may become necessary to involuntarily transport the person for help. Advance planning to prepare for these critical assessments needs to be integrated into the institution's response protocols and training exercises.

Guidelines for Psychological First Aid

Several recommendations have emerged as best practice strategies for psychological first aid in the aftermath of crisis. The National Institute of Mental Health (NIMH, 2002) published the following recommendations for early intervention programs based on a workshop to identify best practices for crisis intervention in the aftermath of mass violence:

- Population studies indicate most persons experience a normal recovery from a traumatic incident or disaster. An overriding goal of crisis intervention is to facilitate adaptation and avoid impeding the normal pathway to recovery.

- It is important to meet basic needs first, such as shelter, nurture, safety from continued threat, triage, need for

information to promote a sense of control and validation/
normalization of experience through psychological
first aid.

- Services are provided on an as-needed and voluntary
  basis. Subjecting persons to mandatory interventions
  may interfere with their resilience and normal efforts
  to restore their equilibrium.

- Response programs should be sensitive to the ethnic
  and cultural characteristics of the person and community affected.

- Emergency mental health interventions are part of the
  larger program of support and are integrated into the
  comprehensive planning and response efforts of the
  institution.

- Psychological first aid comprises a multidisciplinary,
  multiphasic, and integrated program that includes incident preplanning, responder training, access to services, triage and assessment, stabilization, and referral
  for follow-up treatment services.

Foa and Meadows (1997) recommend that crisis intervention
programs seek to enhance the victim's or survivor's use of natural
support systems. Talking with persons with whom they are comfortable may increase self-disclosure at a pace and in an atmosphere
of safety that promotes integration and meaning making. Persons
in crisis should be encouraged to understand the potential value of
reflection, but to do so while meeting their needs for physical and
emotional security. For persons who wish to speak with a professional, responders should be trained in effective helping skills,
including active listening and supportive techniques, while avoiding
probing that may be perceived to be invasive and untimely. An
important goal for the interventionist is to promote normalization

of reactions, encourage hopefulness in recovery, and be available to provide appropriate postintervention referrals as needed.

In the aftermath of a traumatic experience, Litz and Gray (2004) recommend that the following steps be taken to provide effective psychological first aid. First, seek to empower the person to describe what may be most helpful to him or her at this time. Second, provide soothing, respectful, and well-timed comfort (hand-holding or a hug). Third, seek to accurately communicate the person's response while remaining nonjudgmental and validating the person's experience. Fourth, remind the person that he or she is not alone and resources are available for support through this difficult time. Fifth, seek to provide education on the cognitive, affective, and behavioral reactions the person may experience subsequent to the crisis and suggest methods to attenuate the escalation of those symptoms (stress reduction, exercise, nutrition, and professional help). Sixth, work to reduce any stigma associated with the experience and avoid suggesting the person self-disclose in any way unless he or she feels it necessary to do so.

In summary, crisis intervention in the higher education setting benefits from guidelines based on current research and practice, addresses the salient needs of students and others affected by the event, and models the institution's mission and ethic of care.

A Phase Model for Intervention Services

Early psychological intervention services are more effective when responders function within a model in which they have trained and practiced. Campus crisis intervention systems often include multi-disciplinary teams, with members functioning in different roles to mitigate the impact of the crisis (Scott et al., 1992; Griffin, 1998; Griffin & Lewis, 1995). Thus, the need to communicate and act collaboratively across various disciplines becomes an important aspect of the intervention. For example, a responding team to a student death may consist of members from student affairs, public safety, health care, and mental services. A campus crisis team may also include mental health providers from differing disciplines, including psychologists, counselors, social workers, psychiatric nurses, and psychiatrists. In some cases, smaller institutions may employ community personnel to augment the campus response to crises. It is very helpful if all mental health personnel responding on behalf of the institution be familiar with, and to the degree possible, work in the same intervention model.

Everly (2002) recommends that early crisis intervention be grounded in a plan detailing how to approach, assess, and implement resources appropriate to the nature and severity of the incident. This form of preplanning helps teams define the extent of need for psychological first aid and types of interventions best suited for the affected population. It also provides a mechanism for clarifying which campus and community resources may be needed and in what time frame various interventions are appropriate.

Everly's (2002) plan includes the following steps:

1. Assess and define the level of existing "threat"—that is, the nature, severity, and potential for harm inherent in the incident.

2. Develop an understanding of which persons are appropriate recipients of intervention based on the identification of the various threats to safety and security.

3. Define the types of psychological first aid needed, such as individual, group, or larger multiphasic interventions.

4. Ascertain a time line for the interventions that takes into consideration level of need, availability of identified recipients, and access to trained resources.

5. Clarify current access to trained personnel to respond within the scope of need and the time frame determined in the preceding steps. Delineate referral and follow-up resources as needed.

The literature on crisis intervention is rich with information on models of practice (Aguilera, 1998; Everly, 2002; James & Gilliland, 2005; Kanel, 2003; Lerner et al., 2004; Greenstone & Leviton, 2002; Roberts, 1990; Young, 2002). Many of these models have commonalities, including establishing safety and security, determining the nature and scope of the event, assessing the impact on cognitive, affective, and behavioral responses, deescalating and stabilizing the acute crisis reaction, educating about and normalizing potential reactions, pairing the identification of severe reactions with appropriate referrals, and providing follow-up resources.

Greenstone and Leviton (2002) provide a crisis intervention model that lends itself well to a variety of settings and severity of incidents. The six-step model includes concerns for immediate triage, provision of stability, assessment of potentials for harm, action steps to distribute resources, and referral and follow-up.

The first step, termed *immediacy*, is to act as quickly as possible to stop what the authors refer to as *emotional bleeding*. The goal is to relieve anxiety, minimize potential for further disintegration and disorientation, and make sure persons will pose no additional threat of harm to themselves or others. It is important to assess for factors that may contribute to the perception of threatened safety and security and stimulus cues in the environment that may trigger reactivity (such as smoke or sirens following a serious fire), and provide a physical and emotional space that will promote deescalation.

The second step is to establish a level of *control* in what may be a chaotic situation. Carefully establishing control and creating structure for persons in crisis can provide an increased sense of physical safety and emotional security. The goal is not to take away from persons in crisis their autonomy but to provide enough structure for them to exercise their power of control and decision making safely. Crisis responders are encouraged to be aware of what is going on in the immediate environment, create a supportive alliance, and be sensitive to dynamics that may be influenced by cultural practices. It may be necessary to remove persons in crisis from an environment that continues to pose a perceived threat. Generally, persons in crisis will respond to interventions perceived to be trustworthy, genuinely grounded in concern, and put forward by responders who are calm and knowledgeable.

Assessment is the key function of the third step. Although immediate triage around safety and security has taken place in Steps One and Two, additional triage is needed to begin clarifying and prioritizing the type and timing of further interventions. It is important to try to determine what is most troubling at this time and what prior history of trauma exists that may exacerbate the current reaction. In addition, it is important to establish and rank intervention priorities and identify complicating variables that could impair problem solving. According to recent research and recommendations (Epstein, 2004; Foa & Meadows, 1997; Litz & Gray, 2004), effective assessment is necessary to develop interventions that are clinically appropriate to the affected populations. This is especially true when considering single debriefing interventions for either individuals or groups where actively soliciting reflection and self-disclosure carries the potential for intense expression of emotions and reactions associated with prior traumatic experiences.

Although it may be difficult to assess while in the field, doing so is increasingly viewed as a critical component in psychological first aid. Creative measures may need to be taken by the interventionist to take oral histories, or when possible, to administer quick self-report instruments such as the Stressful Life Experiences Screening Short Form (Stamm et al., 1996), which can provide a quick assessment of stress history. Crisis responders also need to possess a practiced competency for assessing lethality for suicide or homicide, a skill that merits periodic training, including simulations in the field. This second phase of assessment identifies which persons are being affected, clarifies what needs are present, helps design interventions that fit the needs of the various levels of impact, and defines the associated follow-up referrals.

The fourth step in the model is what Greenstone and Leviton (2002) describe as *disposition*. This is the process of determining what actions will be recommended and undertaken by the crisis responder as part of psychological first aid. Using information gained from the persons affected, professional judgment, and knowledge of existing resources, the responder will develop a plan for providing appropriate support. This may call for a range of actions, from immediate transportation of a person for medical evaluation to psychoeducation of an individual or group of persons in order to predict and prepare for normal reactions to the short-term crisis response. The individuals providing psychological first aid solicit the collaboration of the person in crisis to help develop the plan of assistance. The involvement and cooperation of those directly affected by the crisis can contribute to their likelihood of compliance and successful implementation of the plan.

Providing information and developing options are important considerations in resolving crisis. One of the recommendations for early psychological interventions is to exchange information that helps victims understand the normal reactions to traumatic incidents, prepares them for what may be experienced, and equips them with basic skills to reduce the intensity of those experiences. For instance, possessing information on how crisis and increased stress may disrupt eating, sleeping, and patterns of concentration, paired with suggestions on good nutrition, an increase in fluid consumption, exercise, stress reduction, and avoidance of self-medication with alcohol and other drugs may create or support the resilience necessary to avoid complications. Generally, psychological first aid will help decide what actions should be taken next and may include the use of safety plans to provide support. Local support systems, family resources, and institutional resources are identified to assist in deescalating the crisis and providing inspiration for a hopeful outcome.

The last two steps in Greenstone and Leviton's (2002) model for crisis intervention, *referral* and *follow-up*, are closely related. The decision to refer for further consultation is based on a confluence of factors, including information gathered from the person in crisis, the clinical knowledge and intuition of the responder, and environmental factors that will affect continued care. Persons who experience severe trauma, have a prior history of traumatic reactions, exhibit impaired stabilization during the initial psychological first aid, or are isolated may benefit from consultation services beyond the initial crisis intervention (Bisson, McFarlane, & Rose, 2000; Litz & Gray, 2004). These persons may be referred to campus or community counseling and medical resources that provide specialized services.

Decisions to schedule group interventions are likewise based on the type of need represented in the affected populations. Best practice, as noted earlier in this chapter, recommends group interventions when limited to supportive and psychoeducational information. Attendance is voluntary and not a mandatory requirement for continuance in either the academic or residence life settings. However, where ongoing physical safety issues are of significant concern, students and staff can be strongly encouraged to attend, and information on the purpose of the meeting can be clearly stated in meeting announcements.

To summarize, in this section crisis intervention has been conceptualized as a multiphasic process designed to provide supportive resources over a period of time, sometimes referred to as the *recovery trajectory* (Bonanno, 2004). Efforts at psychological first aid in the initial or what Litz and Gray refer to as the immediate phase of crisis are focused on defining the scope of impact and mobilizing resources to attenuate the initial suffering and reduce the escalation of risks that may result in post-trauma complications. Secondary or formal interventions are more appropriate during the acute phase or follow-up to the initial intervention. Follow-up activities examine the ability of persons in crisis to participate in the process of reframing and learning from their experience. At this time more comprehensive plans can be made to examine interpersonal, academic, and occupational dimensions of the crisis. This is also the time to assess whether the initial steps taken to support and enhance a victim's native resilience are proving to be robust. Eventually, issues may change and personal development and additive stress may precipitate postcrisis concerns. Follow-up activities reflect not only the institution's ethic of care but also the need to ensure that conditions and resources that promote well-being are in place and accessible to the victim during the extended period of recovery.

Suggested Interventions

Psychological first aid can be provided in a variety of contexts and diverse settings, and to varied populations. The decision about what types of interventions to provide is based on a number of different but interrelated factors, including the nature and severity of the event, assessed needs of those in crisis, available resource personnel, and advance preparation. In Everly's (2002) discussion of core competencies for early crisis intervention, three basic types of interventions are described: individual (including phone and personal), small group, and a larger cohort or community gathering. The typology offered by the author is provided as a framework for conceptualizing the types of services most often encountered in the college and university setting. The three types discussed are services to individuals, group psychoeducational interventions, and services of remembrance.

Services to Individuals

Perhaps one of the capstones of serving the individual during crisis intervention is to understand how rare it is that a person suffers alone. It is important that responders to crisis consider secondary victims who may also need services. Roommates, classmates, fellow employees, instructors, and dating partners are often affected by the crisis. What begins as an individual intervention can quickly become fertile ground for additional individual or group work. Initial assessment with the primary affected person may yield rich information on the scope of additional needs.

During the immediate phase of intervention, psychological first aid to the individual is focused on providing physical safety and emotional security, creating a helping alliance, promoting structure, and assessing for appropriate services. As noted earlier, efforts to promote cathartic self-disclosure, particularly when the person in crisis is reluctant to do so, are counterproductive and may impair the person's natural recovery process. The primary focus for the intervention is minimizing the cognitive, behavioral, affective, and somatic effects of the short-term crisis reaction. This includes deescalating anxiety and fear while promoting effective coping skills. Management of physical complaints includes assessment of bodily injuries, sleep disruption, and joint and muscle ache from the stress related to exposure to the source of the crisis.

Establishing a caring presence goes a long way toward facilitating a reduction in the chaos experienced by the victim. While providing support and assurance, it is prudent to avoid making promises that cannot be kept or offering unrealistic solutions to complex life events. Individuals can often be served well through the use of basic helping skills, effective history taking and assessment, education to help prepare them to cope with anticipated stressors (including basic stress management skills), and as needed, referral for follow-up care at campus or community resources.

When responding to a crisis where there are concerns for lethality, responders need to be competent in assessing for potential self-harm and threat to others. Given their exposure to severe crises, responders need a working knowledge of the warning signs and risk behaviors associated with suicidal and homicidal persons, a framework for lethality assessment, and plans for coordinated intervention with public safety personnel (Hoff, 1995; James & Gilliland, 2005). In addition, responders must be familiar with institutional protocols for transport of voluntary and involuntary persons, and the available resources for psychiatric and medical assessment. Mental health laws in states differ on the criteria that establish the threshold for involuntary transport and hospitalization, the professionals given statutory powers to institute the action, and the extent to which a person can be detained for assessment. However, given the prevalence of suicide—as noted, the third leading cause of death in the college-age cohort ("In Harm's Way," 2005)—college and university personnel need to be trained in relevant law, institutional policies, and the clinical skills necessary to address these concerns.

Perhaps one of the most difficult tasks in working with an individual is to provide a death notification. In his 1982 study of 2,049 college students, LaGrand reported that 28.4 percent of the respondents had experienced the death of a loved one or a sudden death. Seventy-three percent of the students in the study reported having experienced some form of significant loss, including death, the end of a love relationship or friendship, or separation from a loved one.

Traditional-age college students (eighteen to twenty-five years old) are typically engaged in developmental tasks that promote an increased sense of autonomy, use of social support systems, clarification in sense of purpose, and construction of a meaningful worldview (Chickering, 1981). The death of a family member, friend, or close peer can affect their ability to focus on their academic and personal development. In a study of bereaved college students, Balk and Vesta (1998) identified the presence of intrusive and avoidant thoughts, trouble concentrating, and disruption in the use of support systems. Unaddressed, these symptoms may become a distraction or impairment to students' well-being and ability to successfully accomplish their academic goals.

Persons responsible for the notification of students or others on campus about the death of significant others need training and practice in this skill. It is important to exercise knowledge and sensitivity to the psychological, cultural, and spiritual experiences around loss. Several agencies, including the National Organization of Victim Assistance and American Red Cross, provide training for crisis responders to assist in this process. Not every crisis responder will wish to participate in this service. It is recommended that death notification be made by a pair of trained responders. A comprehensive campus crisis intervention plan will include the selection and training of persons willing to provide this important service.

Group Psychoeducational Interventions

A crisis may be of such magnitude that it affects groups of students, faculty, and staff. Many small groups exist in a student community, both on and off campus. Examples of on-campus groups are residence life floors, student organizations, Greek organizations, athletic teams, classrooms, and faculty and staff who provide support to the overall academic mission. Off-campus groups may include student apartment complexes, campus ministries, campus annexes, training sites, and distance education programs.

Crisis affects groups in varying ways. Much like a pebble dropped into a pond, its influence washes over those closest to the center of familiarity and outward toward those with less intense but meaningful relationships. One of the first tasks in working with groups is to identify all parties affected by the event. In this process it is important not to overlook persons who may normally be in less direct contact with the most affected persons—for example, custodial, facility, and secretarial personnel. Although the latter groups may differ somewhat in the type of information they need, including them in the process helps provide institutional connection and concern for their well-being.

When implementing outreach services to a group, several administrative concerns must be addressed. One of these is for administrators to convey their support and impart important information. Administrative concerns may include the communication of information related to academic issues like class absences, missed exams, notification of instructors, and procedures for withdrawal under special circumstances. Additional administrative concerns may relate to access for specialized health information and services, public safety and police investigative issues, the relevance of student conduct code or judicial processes, and the likelihood of media coverage. In instances where there is an ongoing threat to public safety, meetings may be made mandatory. During the immediate crisis phase, the information provided can often provide the institutional support necessary for structure and direction. The administrative group meeting is one component of early crisis intervention and a complement to psychological first aid in helping to deescalate crisis.

Attention also must be paid to the emotional impact a crisis has on a group's membership and identity. Early psychological intervention for the small group can provide education on the expected reactions to crisis, promote the use of social supports, encourage utilization of campus resources, and identify persons for whom more specialized follow-up may be appropriate. A key task in doing small group work is the timely and efficient identification of group members. Use of group leadership, membership roles, faculty advisers, and mentors can facilitate this process. Attendance at group interventions can be encouraged by effective advertising that enumerates the purpose of the meeting. Litz and Gray (2004) recommend that participation in group interventions be on a voluntary basis to avoid prematurely exposing vulnerable persons to information from the trauma. The purpose of the group meeting is to model support and educate students on ways to successfully adapt to the event, provide support for the group's identity, and advertise additional campus resources. It is helpful to include an opportunity for questions and answers.

Leadership for psychoeducational group interventions requires competence in effective communication with groups in stressful circumstances, a basic knowledge of the short- and long-term reactions to crisis, familiarity with constructive adaptation and stress management skills, and awareness of campus and community resources. A well-trained leader will also possess a knowledge of and ability to recognize signs of more serious post-trauma symptoms that merit additional assessment and referral to specialized resources.

Some campuses follow formalized psychological debriefing (PD) protocols as a component in their crisis intervention. Critical Incident Stress Debriefing (CISD; Mitchell, 1983) is an example of a popular PD protocol used on some campuses. CISD was popularized through its application to first responder groups and theorized as a method for attenuating the impact of highly traumatic work and a mechanism for reducing post-traumatic symptoms. More recently, similar PD models have been developed that emphasize various components of the CISD protocol. These models focus on aspects of the cognitive, affective, and behavioral dimensions of experience, the necessity of self-disclosure as a factor in resolving traumatic experience, and an emphasis on psychoeducation, skills development, and referral (Dyregrov, 1989, 1998; Raphael, 1986; Rose, 1997; Young, 2002). Typically, PD models explore the factual details of what has occurred, initial thoughts and impressions, and the emotional reactions to the event. A period of self-disclosure is followed by education, which normalizes the expected range of experiences following a traumatic event, prepares participants for future triggering events, and provides some basic training in coping skills and use of resources.

A review of current research suggests that some cautions are merited in the use of PD as a primary intervention during the immediate stage of crisis (Bisson et al., 2000; Epstein, 2004; Litz & Gray, 2004). Persons with prior histories of unresolved trauma, deficient precrisis coping skills, predisposition to hyperarousal and dissociation, or other psychiatric diagnosis that may become exacerbated by the trauma may become vulnerable and retraumatized during the exposure aspect of the PD (Litz & Gray, 2004). The timing and efficacy of a single PD to reduce symptoms is also questioned when compared with interventions that occur later and involve a series of therapeutic interventions (Shalev, 2002; Foa & Meadows, 1997).

In view of concerns about single-session PD implemented in the immediate phase of crisis recovery, the following guidelines for this type of intervention are suggested. First, leadership for the PD should be well trained in the procedure and also possess the knowledge and ability to recognize persons having strong reactions to the process. Second, timing of the PD should consider the ability of persons to effectively comprehend and communicate their experiences in the immediate aftermath of a traumatic experience. A waiting period may allow a victim's normal resilience enough time to manage and integrate the traumatic material that would be evoked in the PD. Third, a focus on the educational component that emphasizes the normalization of the crisis reaction and resilience, development of coping skills, and promotion of social support may more broadly benefit persons without unnecessarily exposing victims to retraumatization. Fourth, the PD should not be mandatory; rather, persons should participate voluntarily and at a level at which they feel safe. Fifth, where possible, screening should be provided to identify persons for whom more specialized resources and referral are merited. Last, a comprehensive intervention plan will include follow-up to the group session to ascertain the well-being of participants and need for ongoing services.

Services of Remembrance

Campus communities often experience the death of students, faculty, and staff. Some deaths occur because of tragic accidents or other traumas; some are more expected and developmental in nature. While recognizing that persons will grieve in ways particular to their culture, religious beliefs, and family history, it is helpful to recognize that communities too undergo a process of bereavement. Efforts by the college or university to recognize the loss helps the campus community remember and integrate the experience of loss into a meaningful and constructive basis for hope. The general purpose of institutional services of remembrance is to provide occasion for the personal and social expression of mourning, confirmation and use of social support, and emphasis on ongoing life. For some persons, services of remembrance will also contribute to integrating loss into a faith and spiritual paradigm that underpins the meaning of life and value of relationships.

Effective planning of a service of remembrance entails attention to several factors, including the following:

- The goal of the service of remembrance is to provide a forum for the campus community to remember the deceased in the context of a supportive environment. While family members of the deceased may be present and perhaps even participate in the service, it is aimed to serve the campus community. Services of remembrance reflect the institution's desire to facilitate remembering and healing in the context of its mission as an academic community.

- Services need to reflect the diversity of the campus community. The content of a service—its liturgy, music, readings, and personal statements—reflect on the inclusiveness of the college or university. Leadership for the service of remembrance needs to take special care to avoid statements or rituals that may be perceived as proselytizing or otherwise isolate members of the community.

- Thoughtful planning of the timing and location of a service encourages participation. Dates that conflict with key dates on the academic calendar should be avoided, and locations that are large enough to accommodate the number of possible attendees should be selected. Announcements for the service of remembrance need to target as many of the affected groups as possible.

- Collaboration with members of the print and broadcast media should be planned in advance. Particularly in crises that involve violence, a large number of persons injured, loss of life, or an ongoing threat, a greater demand for information exists. Advocacy for privacy and safeguarding the dignity of persons affected by the loss need to be discussed alongside the media's need for access to sources of information.

- As with other forms of individual and group crisis interventions, attendance at remembrance services should be voluntary. Persons grieve in ways specific to their personal history and experience with loss. Information on normal bereavement, effective use of social support, and access to campus counseling resources can be provided during the remembrance service.

- Certain types of crises, such as natural or human-made disasters or acts of violence that victimize a number of persons or identified group, can disrupt the community to such an extent that a long-term memory is created. It is not unusual in traumatic losses for anniversary events to trigger memories and reactions on the part of individuals and the community. Rituals that recognize the anniversary can be restorative and act as a reminder of the ongoing support offered to resolve and integrate the crisis. Advance planning that incorporates key persons who were involved in the initial crisis intervention can contribute to the service's timeliness, inclusiveness, and content. It is helpful to normalize the grief pattern of a community and provide a sense of hope and a trajectory of recovery.

In summary, services of remembrance can provide a meaningful way to assist affected groups through the initial stages of bereavement. Through thoughtful planning, a service reflects the facilitative institution's ethic of care, is inclusive and considerate of the diversity of participants, promotes use of social support, and provides information on access to campus and community resources.

Special Issues for Psychological First Aid in the Campus Setting

Some special issues particular to the campus setting are credentialing, legal and ethical concerns, and helping the helpers.

Competencies and Credentialing

It is recommended that campus psychological providers be well-trained, credentialed, and where required, licensed according to state standards (Blom & Beckley, 2005; Boyd et al., 2000). Crisis intervention shares some of the knowledge base and skills associated with formal training in the mental health field, including effective listening and helping skills and basic understanding of human development, and the emotional, affective, physical, and neurological domains and responses. More specific competencies and training are recommended for campus personnel when working with persons affected by trauma and the immediate phases of a crisis (Coulter et al., 2003; Pledge et al., 1998). These competencies include the knowledge and skills necessary to differentiate between benign and more harmful psychological symptoms, knowledge of trauma and loss, skills in individual and group crisis intervention, knowledge of short- and long-term crisis reactions, familiarity with psychobiological assessment, and ability to use effective referral skills (Everly, 2002; James & Gilliland, 2005; Young, 2002). Campus crisis responders need to be familiar with the impact of and protocols relevant to working with victims of relationship violence, assessment of self-injurious persons, sexual harassment and sexual assault, traumatic loss, and death notification.

Several personal attributes also characterize the effective crisis interventionist. These include the ability to reflect on personal life experience, remain poised under stress, be a creative and flexible problem-solver, be compassionate, have effective decision-making and team leadership skills, have multicultural competency, and show hardiness, resilience, perseverance, objectivity, and hopefulness (James & Gilliland, 2005). Several organizations provide formal programs in crisis intervention, including the American Association of Suicidology, National Organization for Victim Assistance, Federal Emergency Management Agency, and the American Red Cross.

Legal and Ethical Concerns

Several legal and ethical issues may emerge for responders providing psychological first aid.

Mandatory Reporting and Confidentiality

First, it is important that campus crisis responders be aware of state and institutional regulations on such issues as mandatory reporting requirements of child sexual abuse and neglect, sexual harassment and assault, confidentiality and duty to warn, rights of privileged communication, FERPA regulations on safety and security, and the provision of emergency services to minors and role of parental informed consent (Aguilera, 1998; Greenstone & Leviton, 2002; James & Gilliland, 2005; Kanel, 2003). Campus crisis interventionists need to routinely review the provisions of law and consult with college or university attorneys to clarify questions about their practice during emergencies. Use of case simulations in training may help clarify less obvious but important issues in these areas.

Language Interpreters

As the makeup of campus populations becomes more diversified and international, the need for and utilization of language interpreters and signers in crisis intervention increases. Persons in the immediate impact phase of trauma response may naturally revert to their native signing or oral language to describe their experiences. Training interpreters in the concepts, language, cultural awareness, and interpersonal helping skills associated with crisis intervention is important to ensure effective communication between responder, interpreter, and person in crisis. This becomes particularly important during death notification or when informing persons of legal restraints that are inconsistent with their culture of origin. Interpreters also need to understand and be adequately prepared for the possibility of postincident involvement during interrogation by public safety or judicial agencies.

Interagency Communication

Communication between psychological and medical providers and other campus agencies is an important aspect of coordinated crisis services. This is particularly cogent when working with students who have engaged in self-inflicted injury or returned to campus after an unanticipated, early release from a hospital (Kitzrow, 2003; Lake & Tribbensee, 2002). Campus interagency collaboration requires careful forethought about the limitations of what is permissible under both state regulations and professional codes of ethics. Ideally, the crisis responder should acquire an informed consent to permit communication with relevant campus agencies. In some cases, persons in crisis want to restrict information and the release of their identity. While it is important to respect and generally empower the person in crisis, it can be useful for the responder to revisit this issue and point out how campus agencies may be helpful as a source of support. On campuses that have both counseling and medical facilities present, initiating a provision that permits counselors and medical personnel from the different agencies to communicate is very helpful. On one campus this is achieved by having the student or parents of a minor authorize the student health service to provide treatment and communicate within and between its own agency and the campus counseling center.

During the immediate phase of crisis intervention, communication about the incident may include a general characterization of the response and recommendations for aftercare. In cases where public safety officers are present, communication between that agency and the campus administration may be less restricted, though there are times when crime-scene investigation restricts what law enforcement may share.

When multiple campus resources are involved or when the crisis reflects a chronic and dangerous pattern of behavior, a case management team with representatives from the relevant responding agencies on campus can be helpful in developing a coordinated follow-up plan. The goal of the case management process is to clarify concerns, identify and centralize resources, and prepare an action plan. Having a psychological provider present who is not a therapist of record can be instrumental in providing consultation to the campus team making recommendations on student welfare and ongoing matriculation.

Professional Standards and Codes of Ethics

Crisis interventionists are required to practice not only by their profession's code of conduct (National Association of Social Workers, American Counseling Association, American Psychological Association, National Association of School Psychologists, American College Personnel Association) but also by that of the organization that provided their specialized training in crisis intervention, such as the National Organization for Victim Assistance, American Association of Suicidology, or the American Red Cross. These ethical codes address the nature and scope of practicing psychological first aid in the aftermath of crisis. The scope of crisis intervention practice depends in great part on training, ongoing professional development, knowledge of limitations, and access to appropriate resources. Continued professional development is encouraged to help practitioners stay abreast of best practices and research inquiry in the field.

Helping the Helpers

The work of providing psychological first aid in the aftermath of crisis comes with its own set of stressors. Some practitioners appear to be equipped with a native resilience, such as described by Bonanno (2004), and can function effectively in the role. However, the risk of exposure to terrible life events requires ongoing attention to prevent burnout or the development of secondary stress disorder. Campus mental health providers responding to increasingly severe student problems with limited personnel and a heavier workload may be at increased risk for burnout (Rodolfa & Park, 1993; Stone & Archer, 1990). Coulter, Offutt, and Mascher (2003) reported that 24 percent of the respondents in their survey of counseling centers observed staff burnout resulting from overtaxed personnel answering afterhour emergencies. For the college or university that strives to emulate what Lake and Tribbensee (2002) refer to as a facilitative campus environment, routinely visiting the well-being of staff who respond to emergencies is important.

One definition of burnout is a pattern of symptoms that include emotional exhaustion, detachment from and depersonalization of others, and the overall perception of diminished personal effectiveness that results from repetitious involvement with persons during intense life experiences (Garden, 1989; Maslach & Jackson, 1979; Pines & Aronson, 1981). The progression and symptoms related to burnout are described by Edelwich and Brodsky (1980) as the increasing diminishment of enthusiasm for one's work, growing stagnation in professional development, emerging frustration in what can be accomplished and breadth of recognition, and last, the emergence of apathy—a detachment from those served and with whom one works. Aguilera (1998) adds a phase of hopelessness, which represents the lost sense of personal vitality and purpose.

Charles Figley (1995) states there is a cost to caring. He differentiates secondary stress disorder or compassion stress (CS) from burnout. CS is the product of natural behavioral and emotional responses that emerge from knowing about a traumatic event experienced by oneself or a significant other, or the stress that accumulates from helping or desiring to help a person who has been traumatized. In essence, what Figley terms *empathic induction* occurs when the helper begins to acquire and manifest the symptoms of the persons being helped. This phenomenon can over time become debilitating in much the same way that post-traumatic stress disorder (PTSD) affects the victim of trauma.

In order to avoid burnout or the development of CS among crisis responders, administrators of campus crisis intervention services need to take a number of preventative steps. First, they must provide opportunities for training and ongoing professional development in order to prepare staff for the intense nature and scope of crisis intervention services. Second, they should designate adequate personnel to meet the campus demand for services to avoid overutilization of a few staff members. Next, they need to provide appropriate monetary compensation and compensatory time for crisis services, with particular note of the demand required for afterhours on-call and on-site consultation. They need to develop standardized protocols that require the use of pairs or teams for responses to crises. These protocols should include provisions for postincident review and debriefing of the crisis team by a third party familiar with the work of crisis intervention. They should design assignment schedules that include down time and ensure periods of privacy for members of the team. Next, they should develop case management and accounting procedures that meet legal and ethical standards of accountability without requiring a surplus of paperwork and reporting. They need to foster a workplace in which healthy humor, creativity, and flexibility are valued. They should encourage crisis team members to refuse an assignment for reasons of personal or professional limitations and assure them there will be no repercussions. They should promote the use of professional consultation for crisis responders as a means to maintain well-being. Last, they should carry out periodic checks of crisis team members to assess and plan their professional development, ascertain their desire to continue this specialized work, and monitor their overall state of well-being.

Conclusion

Crisis intervention programs play an increasingly important role in college and university settings. These programs reflect an institutional ethic of care and also promote the cohesion and support needed for adaptation to crisis. A number of factors contribute to the increased need for these services, including the unpredictability of natural and human-made disasters, violent acts against self and others, and mental health issues that students currently bring to their college experience.

This chapter highlighted the value of early psychological intervention—or psychological first aid—as an important component in a comprehensive campus plan. Psychological first aid provides helpful recovery information, identifies persons who may be at risk for complicated reactions, enhances adaptation through supportive interventions at both individual and group levels, and refers appropriate persons for continued follow-up. A model for systemic crisis intervention, best practices for psychological first aid, and recommendations for several types of interventions were suggested. Based on the outcomes of current research, distinctions were made between several types of psychological debriefing and suggestions offered to create safe and effective interventions. Special concerns related to the legal and ethical practice of crisis intervention were discussed, including mandatory reporting, role of confidentiality, effective interagency communication, and professional standards and codes of ethics. Finally, suggestions were made for helping prevent job burnout and avoid development of secondary stress syndrome among the helping professionals.

References

Aguilera, D. (1998). *Crisis intervention: Theory and methodology* (8th ed.). St. Louis, MO: Mosby Year Book.

American College Health Association. (2004, June). *National college health assessment Web summary*. Retrieved November 8, 2006, from http://acha.org/projects_programs/assessment.cfm.

Balk, D. E., & Vesta, L. C. (1998). Psychological development during four years of bereavement: A longitudinal case study. *Death Studies, 22,* 23–41.

Barrios, L. C., Everett, S. A., Simon, T. R., & Brener, N. D. (2000, March). Suicide ideation among U.S. college students: Associations with other injury risk behaviors. *Journal of American College Health, 48,* 229.

Bartlett, T. (2002, February 1). Freshman pay, mentally and physically, as they adjust to life in college. *Chronicle of Higher Education,* p. A35. Retrieved January 16, 2005, from http://chronicle.com/prm/weekly/v48/i21/21a03501.htm.

Benton, S. A., Robertson, J. M., Tseng, W.-C., Newton, F. B., & Benton, S. L. (2003). Changes in counseling center client problems across 13 years. *Professional Psychology: Research and Practice, 34*(1), 66–72.

Bickel, R. D., & Lake, P. F. (1999). *The rights and responsibilities of the modern university: Who assumes the risk of college life?* Durham, NC: Carolina Academic Press.

Bisson, J. I., McFarlane, A. C., & Rose, S. R. (2000). Psychological debriefing. In E. Foa, T. Keane, & M. Friedman (Eds.), *Effective treatments for PTSD* (pp. 39–59). New York: Guilford Press.

Blom, S. D., & Beckley, S. L. (2005, January 28). Six major challenges facing student health programs. *Chronicle of Higher Education*, p. B25. Retrieved on February 1, 2005, from http://chronicle.com/prm/weekly/v51/i21/21b02501.htm.

Bonanno, G. A. (2004). Loss, trauma, and human resilience. *American Psychologist, 59*(1), 20–28.

Boyd, V., Hattauer, E., Spivack, J., Deaking, S., Hurley, G., Buckles, N., Ershine, C., Piorkowski, G., Brandel, I. W., Simono, R. B., Locher, L. L., Steel, C., & Davidshofer, C. (2000). *Accreditation standards for university and college counseling centers*. Retrieved January 16, 2005, from http://iacsinc.org/uccstand.htm.

Breslau, N., Kessler, R., Chilcoat, H., Schultz, L., Davis, G., & Andreski, P. (1998). Trauma and post-traumatic stress disorder in the community: The 1996 Detroit area survey of trauma. *Archives of General Psychiatry, 55,* 626–632.

Chickering, A. (1981). *Education and identity.* San Francisco: Jossey-Bass.

Coulter, L. P., Offutt, C. A., & Mascher, J. (2003). Counseling center management of after-hours crises: Practice and problems. *Journal of College Student Psychotherapy, 18*(1), 11–34.

Dyregrov, A. (1989). Caring for helpers in disaster situations: Psychological debriefing. *Disaster Management, 2,* 25–30.

Dyregrov, A. (1998). Psychological debriefing: An effective method. *Traumatology, 4*(2). Retrieved February 22, 2005, from http://www.fsu.edu/~trauma/art1v4i2.html.

Edelwich, J., & Brodsky, S. (1980). *Burnout: Stages of disillusionment in the helping professions.* New York: Human Sciences Press.

Ellen, E. F. (2002). Suicide prevention on campus. *Psychiatric Times, XIX,* 10.

Epstein, B. (2004, Winter). Crisis intervention on campus: Current and new approaches. *NASPA Journal, 41*(2), 294–316.

Everly, G. S. (2002, Fall). Early psychological intervention and college personnel services. *Commission on Counseling and Psychological Services Newsletter.* Retrieved January 16, 2005, from http://www.acpa.nche.edu/.

Figley, C. (Ed.). (1995). *Compassion fatigue: Coping with secondary traumatic stress disorder in those who treat the traumatized.* Bristol, PA: Brunner/Mazel.

Foa, E. B., & Meadows, E. A. (1997). Psychosocial treatments for posttraumatic stress disorder: A critical review. *Annual Review of Psychology, 48*, 449–480.

Frazier, P., Conlon, A., & Glaser, T. (2001). Positive and negative life changes following sexual assault. *Journal of Consulting and Clinical Psychology, 69*, 1048–1055.

Gallagher, R., Gill, A., & Sysko, H. (2000). *National survey of counseling center directors.* Alexandria, VA: International Association of Counseling Services.

Gallagher, R., Sysko, H., & Zhang, B. (2001). *National survey of counseling center directors.* Alexandria, VA: International Association of Counseling Services.

Garden, A. M. (1989). Burnout: The effect of psychological type on research findings. *Journal of Occupational Psychology, 62*, 223–225.

Greenstone, J. L., & Leviton, S. C. (2002). *Elements of crisis intervention: Crises and how to respond to them.* Pacific Grove, CA: Brooks/Cole.

Griffin, W. (1998). Crisis management in the higher education setting: A multidisciplinary approach. *Talking stick: Association of College and University Housing Officers International, 16*(2), 6–7.

Griffin, W., & Lewis, L. (1995). The trauma response team: An institutional response to crisis. *American College Personnel Association-Commission VII Counseling and Psychological Services Newsletter, 22*(2), 3–4.

Hoff, L. A. (1995). *People in crisis: Understanding and helping* (4th ed.). San Francisco: Jossey-Bass.

In harm's way: Suicide in America. Retrieved January 16, 2005, from http://www.nimh.nih.gov/publicat/harmaway.cfm?styleN=three.

James, R. K., & Gilliland, B. E. (2005). *Crisis intervention strategies* (5th ed.). Pacific Grove, CA: Brooks/Cole.

Kadison, R. D. (2004). The mental health crisis: What colleges must do. *Chronicle of Higher Education, 51*(16), B20. Retrieved January 17, 2005, from http://chronicle.com/prm/weekly/v51/i16/16b02001.htm.

Kanel, K. (2003). *A guide to crisis intervention* (2nd ed.). Pacific Grove, CA: Brooks/Cole.

Kessler, R. C., Sonnega, A., Bromet, E., Hughes, M., & Nelson, C. B. (1995). Posttraumatic stress disorder in the National Comorbidity Survey. *Archives of General Psychiatry, 52*, 1048–1060.

Kitzrow, M. A. (2003, Fall). The mental health needs of today's college students: Challenges and recommendations. *NASPA Journal, 41*(1), 167–181.

LaGrand, L. E. (1982). How college and university students cope with loss. In R. A. Pacholski & C. A. Corr (Eds.), *Priorities in death education and counseling* (pp. 85–97). Arlington, VA: Forum for Death Education and Counseling.

Lake, P., & Tribbensee, N. (2002, Fall). The emerging crisis of college student suicide: Law and policy response to serious forms of self-inflicted injury. *Stetson Law Review, 32,* 125.

Lerner, M. D., Volpe, J. S., & Lindell, B. (2004). *A practical guide for university crisis response.* New York: American Academy of Experts in Traumatic Stress.

Litz, B. T., & Gray, M. J. (2004). Early intervention for trauma in adults. In B. T. Litz (Ed.), *Early intervention and traumatic loss* (pp. 87–111). New York: Guilford Press.

Maslach, C., & Jackson, S. E. (1979). Burned-out cops and their families. *Psychology Today, 12,* 59.

Maslow, A. (1954). *Motivation and personality.* New York: HarperCollins.

McFarlane, A., & DeGirolamo, G. (1996). The nature of traumatic stressors and epidemiology of posttraumatic stress reactions. In B. van der Kolk, A. C. McFarlane, & L. Weisaeth (Eds.), *Traumatic stress: The effects of overwhelming experience on mind, body, and society* (pp. 129–155). New York: Guilford Press.

Mitchell, J. T. (1983). When disaster strikes: The critical incident stress debriefing process. *Journal of Emergency Services, 8,* 36–39.

National Center for Health Statistics. (2002). *Suicide rates.* Hyattsville, MD: National Center for Health Statistics, Division of Data Services.

National Institute of Mental Health. (2002). *Mental health and mass violence: Evidence-based early psychological intervention for victims/survivors of mass violence. A workshop to reach consensus on best practices.* NIH Publication No. 02–5138. Washington, DC: U.S. Government Printing Office.

O'Malley, K., Wheeler, I., Murphey, J., & O'Connell, J. (1990). Changes in level of psychopathology being treated at university and college counseling centers. *Journal of College Student Development, 31,* 464–465.

Pines, A. M., & Aronson, E. (1981). *Burnout.* New York: Free Press.

Pledge, D., Lapan, R., Heppner, P., & Roehlke, H. (1998). Stability and severity of presenting problems at a university counseling center: A 6 year analysis. *Professional Psychology: Research and Practice, 29*(4), 386–389.

Raphael, B. (1977). The Granville train disaster: Psychological needs and their management. *Medical Journal of Australia, 1,* 303–305.

Raphael, B. (1986). *When disaster strikes: How individuals cope and communities cope with disaster.* New York: Basic Books.

Robbins, S., May, T., & Corazini, J. (1985). Perceptions of client needs and counseling center staff roles and functions. *Journal of Counseling Psychology, 32*, 641–644.

Roberts, A. R. (1990). *Crisis intervention handbook: Assessment, treatment, and research.* Belmont, CA: Wadsworth.

Rodolfa, E., & Park, S. (1993). *Managing demands for counseling services: Seeking direction during change.* Paper presented at the 101st American Psychological Convention, Toronto, Canada.

Rose, S. (1997). Psychological debriefing: History and methods counseling. *Journal of the British Association of Counseling, 8*(1), 48–51.

Scott, J., Fukuyama, M., Dunkel, N., & Griffin, W. (1992). The trauma response team: Preparing staff to respond to student death. *Journal of the National Association of Student Personnel Administrators, 29*(3), 230–237.

Shalev, A. Y. (2002). Acute stress reactions in adults. *Biological Psychiatry, 51*, 532–543.

Stamm, B. H., Rudolph, J. M., Dewane, S., Gaines, N., Gorton, K., Paul, G., McNeil, F., Bowen, G., & Ercolano, M. (1996). Psychometric review of stressful life experience screening. In B. H. Stamm (Ed.), *Measurement of stress, trauma, and adaptation.* Lutherville, MD: Sidran Press. Retrieved January 30, 2005, from http://www.isu.edu/~bhstamm/tests/SLESref.htm.

Stone, G., & Archer, J. (1990). College and university counseling centers in the 1990s: Challenges and limits. *Counseling Psychologist, 18*, 539–607.

Tedeschi, R. G. (1999). Violence transformed: Posttraumatic growth in survivors and their societies. *Aggression and Violent Behaviors, 4*, 319–341.

Young, M. (2002). *Community crisis response training team manual* (3rd ed., pp. 1–17). Washington, DC: National Organization for Victim Assistance.

8

Crisis Training

Maureen E. Wilson

A residence hall student dies of bacterial meningitis and others have been exposed to the deadly disease. A fire in a campus apartment complex leaves fifty students homeless the week of final exams. A tornado causes extensive property damage on campus and in the surrounding community. Someone is holding hostages in a campus building. A key administrator is arrested after being found with child pornography on a campus computer. A long-standing campus tradition goes awry and several students are gravely injured. A bomb threat has been reported. A van carrying student athletes overturns, killing some and injuring others. A high-profile professor is charged with sexual harassment. A domestic dispute leaves one dead in a campus parking lot.

The list of potential crises is endless. What training needs to take place to ensure that a campus community can respond effectively to a crisis?

As is made clear throughout this book, it is imperative for colleges and universities to have a comprehensive plan to prevent critical incidents, campus emergencies, and disasters from occurring when it is possible to do so. Most crises follow a series of warning signs that were not heeded adequately. Astute administrators can prevent or minimize many traumatic events. When a crisis cannot be prevented or prevention efforts are unsuccessful, having an effective crisis management plan is crucial. One vital element of that plan is the crisis management team, described in detail in Chapter Three. For those teams to manage crises effectively, they need well-planned, ongoing training. The preceding chapters lay the foundation for developing a comprehensive crisis management training program on every campus. Training should involve all members of the crisis management response team and be based on the crisis management plan. Specific sessions should address crisis communication, working with emergency personnel and outside agencies, attending to psychological needs in the aftermath of a crisis, understanding contemporary issues in crisis management, and debriefing crises. (The last two issues are discussed in greater depth later in the volume.) This chapter addresses planning crisis management training, types of training activities, and sample training activities.

Planning Crisis Management Training

Comprehensive, regularly scheduled training for all members of the crisis management response team is necessary for staff to understand and be well prepared for their roles and responsibilities in responding to crises on campus. Although it is impossible to predict every detail that will need attention, team members must have strong foundational skills so they can manage a wide variety of situations. According to Duncan and Miser (2000), "The list of responses that are required at the time of crisis is almost endless, and the circumstances will dictate priorities. However, the complex responses that are necessary must often be accomplished almost simultaneously at a time of enormous emotional stress. As a result, staff involvement in thinking about responses to a crisis before they happen will be time well spent" (p. 456).

Since every conceivable crisis cannot be predicted, avoided, or planned for, efforts should be made to determine the key elements of an effective response to any situation (for example, caring for those involved, preventing further harm to persons and property, communicating with stakeholders) and ensuring that team members can meet those responsibilities.

In addition to possessing specific skills to fulfill assigned roles, crisis response team members are best when they are levelheaded, calm and calming, quick-thinking, assertive, and able to defuse tense situations. Individuals who are very excitable, nervous, argumentative, or panicky can make problematic situations worse. Qualitative skills such as flexibility, negotiation, and effective communication may be most important in facilitating crisis management (Borodzicz & van Haperen, 2002). Staff must be able to transfer their crisis training and experience to handle new, difficult, and complex situations as they arise. Training helps build a crisis repertoire or crisis portfolio on which to draw. In tense situations, decisions may need to be made quickly with little time for consultation. Effective team members have a strong set of skills, resources, and perspectives from which to make appropriate decisions in challenging situations. Furthermore, effective crisis management demands critical thinking. "Critical questions are at the heart of critical thinking" (Mitroff & Pearson, 1993, p. 8). Team members should be encouraged to think critically and to ask critical questions to improve procedures for managing crises.

Training Objectives

Objectives of training should be clearly stated and determined prior to training. Knowing what expertise is needed to address the range of situations identified through the crisis audit (see Chapter Four), what resources are available on campus, and what external resources are needed can help clarify training objectives and how to meet them. A therapist from the counseling center may be able to conduct training on grief processes. An external consultant might be hired to discuss risk management and legal liability.

Crisis responders need a job description that summarizes their tasks, duties, and responsibilities, and training should prepare them for their roles. Protecting life and property from harm, minimizing risk and damage to persons and facilities, and assisting in recovery from traumatic events are the primary goals of crisis management. Recovery may involve providing support to those affected by tragedy, facilitating healthy coping and grieving processes, and providing cleanup following natural disasters or fires. The training should address the knowledge, skills, and attitudes needed to respond effectively to crisis.

Knowledge objectives pertain to what staff members need to *know* or understand in order to fulfill their roles. For example, team members must know the important campus policies and procedures, organizational structures and reporting lines, and protocols in place for handling emergencies. Scott, Fukuyama, Dunkel, and Griffin (1992) developed training for their trauma response team that addressed several knowledge objectives. The team was trained on the nature and setting of crisis, long- and short-term needs of individuals and groups involved, and dealing with the media. Specific responsibilities of the person initiating the trauma response and of each team member were discussed. The crisis management flow chart and team member phone numbers were part of a set of resources provided to team members. Campus and city maps, the student handbook, campus phone book, and student affairs and residence life staff rosters can also be included.

Skill objectives focus on what team members *do* during a crisis. They must have the abilities necessary to fulfill their roles. A wide range of skills can enhance the ability of an organization to respond effectively to crisis. Strong skills in communicating verbally and in writing, planning, coordinating, organizing, confronting, and building relationships are important. Role-playing is one strategy that can be used to develop skills. Silberman (1998) argued that facilitators who demonstrate a skill without explanation encourage participants to be mentally alert. Participants can observe a demonstration, figure out and discuss what they saw, ask questions, and then practice the skill in pairs or groups. Participants with stronger skills can be enlisted to help others practice the skill.

In addition to knowledge and skills, training should address *attitudes* that facilitate effective crisis management. A variety of attitudes or characteristics, such as being caring, positive, calm, and helpful, are important. People are understandably tense in times of crisis or emergency. How they perceive the response of campus officials can influence how they cope with difficult circumstances. They expect staff to be attentive, communicative, empathetic, and helpful.

Preparing staff to *train others*, including support staff, student leaders, and student employees, for their roles in crisis prevention and response is another objective of training. For example, fraternity and sorority presidents play key roles in helping their chapters deal with the death of a member. A campus receptionist might be the first to receive a bomb threat. Resident assistants have a role in responding to a residence hall fire. Ensuring that all of these staff have the knowledge, skills, and attitudes they need to be successful in their roles is an important piece of the overall crisis management plan. Furthermore, if hot lines or e-mail accounts are set up to respond to crises, those who manage these systems must be trained as well. Even if dedicated phone numbers or e-mail addresses are not published, call volume can be significant, so staff need to be prepared to handle that.

Those trained for roles in crisis management may also help prevent crises by becoming better sensitized to spot potential problems. With heightened awareness of factors that can lead to a crisis, some may be avoided. Early warning signs can be detected and responded to in order to avert some crises. Well-trained staff may also be able to prevent a critical incident from becoming an emergency or a disaster by handling it effectively and not letting it spin out of control and negatively affect the broader community or result in more extensive harm to persons and property.

Media Training

An effective training program will include sessions on managing and responding to interview requests from print, radio, and television reporters, some of whom are sure to seem aggressive or adversarial in their pursuit of a major story or potential scoop. Spokespersons should be identified and trained, but support staff to key administrators, switchboard operators, and receptionists can also benefit from training to handle media because they may be the initial points of contact. West Virginia's Sago Mine disaster provides a powerful case study of what can happen to communications in times of tremendous stress. In that case, poor communication controls led to erroneous reports in the national media that twelve miners had survived, and even though officials knew that the facts were quite different (only one lived), the affected families did not learn the truth for several hours. Take profound media presence, combine it with extreme stress and ease of cell phone communications, and you have a very combustible mix.

If possible, internal public relations staff should be involved in planning and presenting this training, or an external agency may be hired. It is important to know the policies that cover media access to campus facilities. Can reporters legally enter any area of the campus, such as residence halls or classrooms, or do some restrictions apply? To whom should staff direct media requests for interviews? Actively attending to the media and media requests may curtail potential problems and assist in getting accurate information to the campus and the public.

The best time for key members of the crisis management team to develop positive relationships with the public relations staff on campus and the media is *before* a crisis strikes, not after. This can build goodwill that will be critical in tense times. Having a reputation for responding to media calls in a timely manner is helpful. Public relations representatives must understand the context of a crisis and any special circumstances involved. For instance, have threats been made that are putting others at risk? Are tensions especially high? Although PR staff may issue press releases, the media will want to speak with high-level administrators who are managing the crisis. Therefore, key administrators such as the directors of residence life, Greek life, and student activities, along with deans,

vice presidents, and presidents, should also have some media training prior to an actual crisis. The image of the campus and its administrators that will be portrayed by the media can help or harm crisis
management efforts. In sum, a wide variety of media issues must be
dealt with in training (Abent, 1999; Duncan & Miser, 2000).

Principles of Effective Training

Training is best when it is active and engaging, not lecture-based.
Participants should be extensively involved—thinking, talking,
practicing, revising, and evaluating. Silberman (1998) proposed
eight characteristics of active training programs. First, have a mod-
erate level of content. Focus on what is most critical. It is better to
do less well than do more poorly. Second, strike a balance between
cognitive, behavioral, and affective learning (knowledge, skills, and
attitudes). Third, use a variety of learning approaches. This helps
maintain interest and is consistent with principles of adult learning. Fourth, create opportunities for group participation. Active
engagement creates positive learning partnerships between trainers
and participants. Fifth, utilize participants' expertise. They bring a
great deal of experience and perspectives and will be actively
engaged when they can share with and teach others. Sixth, recycle
concepts and skills learned earlier. This provides review of material
and encourages its application to more complex situations. Seventh,
use real-life problem solving. Crisis management training can be
directly and immediately applied in practice, and drawing on those
situations enhances learning. Finally, allow for future planning.
Active training design considers the next steps for participants and
how what is learned will be applied.

Pfeiffer and Ballew (1988) described five elements of what they
call the *experiential learning cycle*. The process starts with *experiencing*
or doing an activity (for example, role-playing). Activities can be
done individually, in small groups, or with the whole group. *Publishing*, the second step, is sharing reactions and observations with those
who have participated in or observed the activity. Next, *processing* is

the exploration and discussion of patterns and dynamics that emerged in the activity. Although this is the step that is often compromised when time is short, it is perhaps the most critical component of the learning cycle. To ensure that key messages are learned, adequate time must be devoted to processing even if the activity needs to be stopped sooner than planned. Silberman (1998) agreed, stating, "Talking about what has just happened is important not only to bring the learning into focus but also to take advantage of peer pressure toward positive change" (p. 132). Fourth, *generalizing* helps participants clarify or elaborate on principles (or generalizations) to be applied in actual situations they may face. Finally, the cycle concludes with *applying or planning* more effective behavior. The learning cycle can then begin again.

Silberman (1998) argued that the "hallmark of active training programs is the variety of sequences employed to keep participants not only awake but also learning" (p. 175). To teach a procedure, trainers can begin with either the first or last step of the process. To train participants to do proper documentation, the process can be demonstrated step-by-step, or completed documentation can be presented and then the group can work backward to focus on the steps. An experiential activity can precede or follow a content presentation. For example, effective confrontation can be illustrated by discussing principles of confrontation and then role-playing a scenario, or the lesson could begin with the role-play and proceed to the discussion. Lessons can be taught from theory to practice or practice to theory. In training team members to manage potentially volatile students, relevant theories can be discussed and followed by practice, or the team can begin by practicing an approach and then focusing on the theory behind it.

Giving and receiving feedback are key to effective training sessions. To capitalize on the learning opportunities provided by role-plays, tabletop exercises, or simulations, participants need timely, clear, and developmental feedback. It is best to encourage participants to evaluate their own performance and solicit feedback on specific elements of it prior to providing feedback. This can feel less threatening to some, and it also encourages staff to think critically about their strengths and weaknesses and identify future training needs.

Feedback should be holistic, emphasizing what was done well and what might be improved. If mistakes were made, such as providing erroneous information or misinterpreting a policy, that should be clarified for the benefit of all. Feedback should be specific. Vague comments not linked to specific examples are not very helpful. Feedback should be descriptive, not evaluative. "You raised your voice and interrupted the student" is descriptive. "You were very aggressive" is evaluative. To ensure that feedback was heard and understood, participants can be asked to summarize the feedback that was given. Facilitators and group members have an obligation to provide constructive feedback and to listen to it nondefensively to enhance their ability to manage crises.

Types of Training Activities

A variety of activities can be used to train staff for their roles in preventing and responding to critical incidents, campus emergencies, and disasters. As part of the professional development plan, key administrators may be sent to conferences or workshops on crisis management. Those staff can then train others on campus. In addition, members of the crisis management team will have expertise that can be shared with other team members. The vice president for student affairs or dean of students is likely to have extensive experience in crisis management. A campus minister or counselor will have skills in comforting the distraught. Buildings and grounds managers will know how to deal with major facilities issues. The collective expertise of the team is sure to be impressive. Because many issues involve both the campus and the surrounding town, campus representatives should also be actively engaged in state or local disaster planning and training, and local officials should be included in campus training. Positive relationships with external constituencies such as police, hospital staff, and mayors can be vital in times of crisis. Two specific training activities are tabletop exercises and simulations.

Tabletop Exercises

Tabletop (or desktop) exercises are discussion-based activities that can be used in crisis management training to "assess the effectiveness of plans and . . . work through the mechanics of simultaneously handling the operational and communication challenges and demands of crisis situations" (Seymour & Moore, 2000, p. 203). They are low-cost activities and provide opportunities to develop and enhance capabilities of people and institutions to respond to crises. For example, Harvard University tested its crisis response system with a tabletop exercise in which a student died of a mysterious illness with flu-like symptoms and three others were hospitalized with similar symptoms (Gewertz, 2002). The case involved many departments across the university, and new developments in the case were revealed throughout the activity.

Exhibit 8.1 presents an example of a tabletop exercise.

With tabletop exercises, small groups of participants discuss how they would respond to hypothetical crisis situations. Facilitators ensure "that participants recognize and address all the critical issues surrounding a crisis, and . . . [help] them identify policies and tools to approach and manage those situations" (Loewendick, 1993, p. 16). Tabletop exercises can be especially helpful early in the crisis management planning process. They can be used to "develop and enhance employee skills, formulate policy, and build team cohesion and consensus" (p. 16). They occur in low-stress environments and can help reduce the terror some feel in responding to crises. Tabletop exercises based on an institution's particular risks and vulnerabilities are best.

Seymour and Moore (2000) stressed several key points in using tabletop exercises. First, the goals of the exercise must be clearly articulated so crisis management response team members will have

Exhibit 8.1. Sample Tabletop Exercise: Fire on Campus

4:00 A.M.   The vice president for student affairs receives a phone call from public safety reporting a fire in Noyer Complex. No further information is available at this time. Noyer is located across the street from the football stadium where graduation ceremonies are scheduled to begin at 10 A.M.

4:05 A.M.   Fire is determined to be on the first floor of Howick Hall in the complex.

4:10 A.M.   Initial reports are of two dead, fifteen to twenty injured.

4:15 A.M.   Explosion reported. Fire engulfs the entire first floor.

4:20 A.M.   Death toll now at three. At least one of the dead students used a wheelchair. More than thirty students and emergency responders are reported injured. Fire marshal reports that fire involves entire first and parts of second floor. Fire units from several surrounding cities asked to respond.

5:30 A.M.   Fire marshal reports fire is nearly under control. Death toll now at four. First network news affiliate arrives on campus.

7:30 A.M.   Fire contained. However, water has disrupted power throughout Noyer Complex. Campus police sergeant enters building with police dog and finds suspicious area in first floor room, suggesting arson. Remains of what is suspected to be a fifth student are discovered in the same room. Witnesses report hearing a loud argument between a resident of the room and another student earlier in the evening. Some describe the scene as a "lovers' quarrel." All network affiliates go live from campus. *Daily News* reporter begins asking questions about the rumor of arson in retaliation for a relationship gone bad.

8:00 A.M.   Several students from Howick Hall report to campus medical clinic complaining of minor injuries and smoke inhalation. One student collapses and goes into cardiac arrest.

Source: Adapted from Robert S. Pritchard, U.S. Navy captain (retired), assistant professor of journalism and training coordinator of the crisis management team, Ball State University.

the experience and training necessary to be successful in their roles. Second, scenarios should come from the list of threats that the campus is most likely to face. They should be facilitated by those with strong experience in responding to crises and excellent training skills. Next, if major problems arise, it may be necessary to interrupt the flow of the exercise to take corrective action or discuss important issues. Finally, tabletop exercises may highlight additional needs for training and briefing of team members. This process can lay a foundation for simulations; these are described in the next section.

Loewendick (1993) described four steps in developing a tabletop exercise. Designing the exercise is the first step: What objectives should be addressed? What risks and vulnerabilities are faced? What aspects of response capabilities need to be examined? The second step is to develop the exercise. Specific scenarios are created based on the following questions: What events could realistically occur and cause significant short- and long-term consequences? How can exercise objectives be met? What internal and external personnel should be involved in responding? What would be observable in the event (for example, a student death, hurricane damage)? What information will be available about the event and when in the course events will it be available? Scenarios should be challenging and realistic, and participants need to consider their response roles both individually and as a group. What prompting questions or materials are needed for participants to respond? Conducting the tabletop exercise is the third step. Exercises typically last two to eight hours. Scenarios can be presented in verbal or written form, or through video clips. As in an actual crisis, information may be limited or come in at staggered intervals. Participants can be pressured with demands for decisions or actions, even though information may be incomplete. Participants discuss what actions they would take if there are resources available to support that response. Recommended actions may change as more information becomes available. Evaluating the group's work is the final step in the tabletop exercise. The person responsible for the activity should work with the group to evaluate their "ability to address pertinent issues, reach decisions, and meet objectives" (Loewendick, 1993, p. 16). Performance should be assessed based on achievement of the stated objectives of the exercise and on the skills and processes that were used effectively. It is also important to make recommendations for continued improvement of plans, procedures, and skills.

Simulations

Simulations are designed to give participants an experience comparable to one they would face in practice; they mimic actual crises to be managed (Eitington, 2002). Crisis simulations are a common tool for training crisis management response team members. They can be used to help assess team members' readiness to handle crises and determine needed improvements to the crisis management process (Coombs, 1999). Simulations may involve campus policies, procedures, and protocols; managing on- and off-campus crises; responding to student deaths; managing natural disasters; working with parents, faculty, staff; and dealing with the media. Simulations can also strengthen cooperative relationships. If a local municipality carries out a disaster simulation—on handling a biological attack, for instance—campus officials should be involved in it. Conversely, local officials including police, fire, and government officials could participate in campus simulations of events that would involve off-campus constituents.

According to Mitroff, Pearson, and Harrington (1996):

> A good simulation tests every aspect of the [crisis management] process. . . . [T]he simulation should not be so transparent that the decisions and actions to be taken at every step are obvious or reduced to a single choice. Rather, a good simulation contains generous amounts of uncertainty. This forces the members of the [crisis management team] to state their assumptions as clearly as they can, reach agreement where they can,

tolerate disagreement where they cannot, and identify at each step what they (1) know, (2) do not know, (3) must do immediately, (4) must postpone, and (5) must monitor and keep track of over time. [pp. 89–91]

Simulations are complex activities requiring a great deal of planning and coordination.

Silberman (1998) promoted the use of simulations because they encourage participants to confront their attitudes and values and help test their behavioral style and performance. Eitington (2002) listed several benefits to simulations. First, participants are involved in real-life situations that facilitate readiness to handle actual situations. Second, learning is active, not passive. Third, participants use experiential or discovery learning, which is the best approach to adult learning. Fourth, mistakes can be made in a risk-free and no-cost situation. Fifth, participants can learn to deal with high-stress situations in a low-stress environment. Sixth, time spans can be compressed. Seventh, simulations provide for immediate feedback so behavior can be rewarded, corrected, or improved immediately. Finally, the training role is facilitative, not didactic. Eitington also pointed out some potential drawbacks of using simulations. They will not replicate all situations or complexities that may arise. Participants may overgeneralize their experience and develop a false sense of confidence. Simulations are also very time-consuming.

If simulations are to be successful, facilitators need to have a high tolerance for ambiguity to handle unpredictable or emotional outcomes. Finally, simulations must be carefully designed to ensure that intended learning outcomes are achieved.

Sample Training Activities

Throughout this book, several training activities are suggested or implied. The crisis management cycle explained in Chapter Two depends heavily on training. The five phases of the cycle—planning, prevention, response, recovery, and learning—all involve ongoing training. For instance, effective training plays a significant role in preventing and mitigating crises. Planning requires training key personnel for their roles in the crisis management cycle. That training is put into practice during the response and recovery phases. The learning that results from those processes can initiate new training to address weaknesses or vulnerabilities that emerged during response and recovery.

The issues addressed in Part Two of this book can also provide an agenda for training. In forming a crisis management team (Chapter Three) it must be determined which members of the team should be involved in responding to various incidents and what those members would do given different scenarios. They need to be trained for those roles. Chapter Four deals with developing a crisis management plan, including creating crisis protocols for common events in the crisis matrix presented in Chapter Two. Practicing those protocols and ensuring that staff have the knowledge, skills, and attitudes to enact them should be part of training. This helps participants internalize their roles and test the systems to identify problems and issues that may have been overlooked in the planning process (Coombs, 1999). Crisis communication (Chapter Five), working with emergency personnel and outside agencies (Chapter Six), psychological first aid in the aftermath of a crisis (Chapter Seven), and crisis debriefing (Appendix) are all important topics to cover during training as well. Finally, staff should also learn about contemporary threats such as riots, terrorism, and technological attacks (Chapter Twelve).

All team members should conduct a skills assessment to determine what skills are needed to respond effectively to the types of crises in which they are most likely to be involved. Coombs (1999) argued that simulations typically emphasize group-level responses to crises, so attention needs to be paid to ensure that individual members have the knowledge, skills, and attitudes necessary to effectively carry out their specific crisis duties. Exhibit 8.2 illustrates an assessment tool that can be used to identify the myriad tasks that will need to be accomplished in various crisis protocols and the knowledge, skills, and attitudes necessary to complete them. This task assessment can help set a training agenda for team members.

Using the Crisis Matrix

The crisis matrix presented in Chapter Two can provide a useful framework for planning crisis management training. An event may be a critical incident, campus emergency, or disaster that is an environmental, facility, or human concern and it may be intentionally or unintentionally activated. A fire set in and contained to a residence hall lounge would be an intentional facilities critical incident. A shooting in a classroom would be an intentional human campus emergency. A hurricane is an unintentional environmental disaster that is likely to have significant impact on humans and facilities. For training purposes, it is helpful to follow Exhibit 8.3,

Exhibit 8.2. Sample Task Assessment

Task	Knowledge	Skills	Attitudes
Participate in interview with reporter	Effective communication strategies (listening and speaking) Danger of long pauses, "no comment" responses, and arguing with reporters	Public speaking Staying calm under pressure Clear communication Quick thinking	Assertive Confident

Source: Adapted from Coombs, 1999.

Exhibit 8.3. Crisis Matrix Worksheet

Level of Crisis[1]	Type of Crisis[2]	Intentionality of Crisis[3]	Example
Critical incident	Environmental	Intentional	
Critical incident	Environmental	Unintentional	
Critical incident	Facility	Intentional	
Critical incident	Facility	Unintentional	
Critical incident	Human	Intentional	
Critical incident	Human	Unintentional	
Campus emergency	Environmental	Intentional	
Campus emergency	Environmental	Unintentional	
Campus emergency	Facility	Intentional	
Campus emergency	Facility	Unintentional	
Campus emergency	Human	Intentional	
Campus emergency	Human	Unintentional	
Disaster	Environmental	Intentional	
Disaster	Environmental	Unintentional	
Disaster	Facility	Intentional	
Disaster	Facility	Unintentional	
Disaster	Human	Intentional	
Disaster	Human	Unintentional	

1. *Disaster:* Nature and impact extends beyond the institution, disrupting institution operations and functions and surrounding community. *Campus emergency:* Disrupts the orderly operations of the institution or its educational mission; may prompt temporary closure of institution. *Critical incident:* Initial impact limited to a specific segment or subgroup.

2. *Environmental:* Originated in the environment or nature (for example, flood, hurricane). *Facility:* Originated with a facility or structure (for example, building fire, bomb threat, water main break). *Human:* Originated with or initiated by human beings (crime, mental health issue).

3. *Unintentional:* Initiated accidentally or unintentionally (heart attack, blizzard). *Intentional:* Initiated deliberately or intentionally (assault, arson).

having participants work in groups to generate an example that could happen on campus from each of the "boxes" in the matrix. Next, groups should identify those examples that are most likely to occur or where significant risk of them occurring exists. Some schools may face little risk of floods or blizzards but significant risk of tornadoes or hurricanes. Every campus must be prepared to deal with alcohol abuse and student deaths. (See Scott et al., 1992, on preparing staff to respond to student death.)

Training should emphasize preparation for the types of incidents for which significant risks are present. In a survey of American universities' preparedness for crisis, Mitroff, Diamond, and Alpaslan (2006) found that campuses were "generally prepared only for those crises they had already experienced" (p. 65). Provosts were given fourteen types of crises identified as those that campuses are most likely to face. Then they were asked which they were prepared for and which they had experienced. Fires, lawsuits, and crimes were the situations most prepared for and most experienced. Based on the difference between preparation and experience, campuses seemed to be underprepared for environmental disasters, athletic scandals, and data tampering, but overprepared for serious outbreaks of illness, revenue shortfalls, damage to institutional reputation, ethical problems, data loss, employee sabotage, and terrorism. Mitroff et al. (2006) suggested that training a broad-based campus management team in at least one of the risks in each of the fourteen categories strengthens the campus crisis portfolio.

Using Case Studies

Case studies can be based on an incident on one's own campus or another. Prepared case studies are available in books (for example, Stage & Dannells, 2000) and on the Internet. A sample case study involving a serious fire the morning of graduation was shown in Exhibit 8.1. A number of steps need to be taken when working with case studies. First, the key facts of the case should be identified, distinguishing facts from rumor or innuendo. Second, all stakeholders (individuals and groups) should be listed, along with their likely stakes in the case and potential conflicts among them. Next, short-term decisions that need to be made and who should be involved in those decisions should be identified. Then, long-term decisions that need to be made and who should be involved in those decisions should be determined. Finally, an immediate plan for handling the situation should be developed. What needs to be done and who needs to do it? In this process, it is important to know what policies and procedures are relevant to the case. To analyze a crisis (or in this instance, a case study) systematically, Mitroff and Pearson (1993, pp. 5–6) recommended that four principal factors be considered: "*What* is the crisis? *When* did it begin? *Why* has it occurred? (What are its *multiple* causes?) *Who* is affected?" They also suggested examining which stakeholders affect crisis management and which are affected by crisis management. In training settings, these questions aid in conducting a thorough analysis of cases to better prepare team members to prevent and respond to actual incidents.

Debriefing Incidents

When an incident occurs on one's own campus or another, the crisis management team and other student affairs staff should debrief those events. This can facilitate an assessment to determine which systems worked well and which did not. It can highlight persistent risks and vulnerabilities to be addressed and may indicate the need for additional training. An independent special commission appointed to investigate the Bonfire collapse at Texas A&M that killed eleven students and a graduate and injured twenty-seven others examined three major controls or barriers designed to prevent problems and encourage safe and reliable procedures. Individual human performance barriers include adequate skills, knowledge, and good judgment. Effective programmatic barriers include adequate levels of procedural guidance, and methods to identify and resolve problems. Strong organizational and management barriers include effective risk identification and management, and adequate management and supervisory actions. Although the commission determined that those control barriers were not directly responsible for the collapse, some related failures ("subbarriers") were relevant. Two related to organizational and management barriers: an active risk management plan was lacking and cultural bias impeded risk identification. Therefore, for example, excessive injuries from constructing the Bonfire resulted in safety training programs, and alcohol violations resulted in alcohol awareness programs. However, individual problems were not addressed collectively and did not initiate a broad, overall reexamination of the Bonfire (Special Commission, 2000). So, although most campuses do not have the Bonfire tradition, they likely have some long-standing, culturally embedded, recurring programs in which major controls or barriers (individual human performance, programmatic, and organization and management) are lacking.

Training should include identification and discussion of current vulnerabilities on campus. This way, administrators and members of the crisis management response team can develop a greater sensitivity to risk factors, examine cultural factors that promote vulnerability to danger, and learn how to avert such tragedies while also fine-tuning the response plans for a large-scale crisis. Similarly, training can involve using an incident from another campus and developing a tabletop exercise to work through the crisis management plan that is in place.

Chapters Nine through Eleven focus on environmental, facility, and human crises. Written by administrators who were involved in managing them, they describe the incidents, responses to them, and lessons learned. Each includes a list of discussion questions that can be used in training. Debriefing these valuable chapters will allow others to learn from the experiences of those who have managed very complex campus crises.

Conclusion

Crisis training is an ongoing, cyclical process that requires extensive planning, practice, and evaluation. A carefully developed, thoughtful training program that is evaluated and updated regularly to ensure that staff members are prepared to respond effectively to critical incidents, campus emergencies, and disasters is vital.

References

Abent, R. (1999). Managing in a time of crisis. *NASPA NetResults*. Retrieved March 14, 2005, from http://www.naspa.org/Results/pubrelat/managing.html.

Borodzicz, E., & van Haperen, K. (2002). Individual and group learning in crisis simulations. *Journal of Contingencies and Crisis Management, 10*, 139–147.

Coombs, W. T. (1999). *Ongoing crisis communication: Planning, managing, and responding* (Vol. 2). Thousand Oaks, CA: Sage.

Duncan, M. A., & Miser, K. M. (2000). Dealing with campus crisis. In M. J. Barr, M. K. Desler, & Associates, *The handbook of student affairs administration* (2nd ed., pp. 453–473). San Francisco: Jossey-Bass.

Eitington, J. E. (2002). *The winning trainer: Winning ways to involve people in learning*. Boston: Butterworth-Heinemann.

Gewertz, K. (2002, October 24). Schools practice "table-top" crisis response. *Harvard University Gazette*. Retrieved March 2, 2006, from http://www.news.harvard.edu/gazette/2002/10.24/01-emergency.html.

Loewendick, B. A. (1993). Laying your crisis on the table. *Training & Development, 47*(11), 15–17.

Mitroff, I. I., Diamond, M. A., & Alpaslan, C. M. (2006). How prepared are America's colleges and universities for major crises? *Change, 38*(1), 61–67.

Mitroff, I. I., & Pearson, C. M. (1993). *Crisis management: A diagnostic guide for improving your organization's crisis-preparedness*. San Francisco: Jossey-Bass.

Mitroff, I. I., Pearson, C. M., & Harrington, L. K. (1996). *The essential guide to managing corporate crises: A step-by-step handbook for surviving major catastrophes*. New York: Oxford University Press.

Pfeiffer, J. W., & Ballew, A. C. (1988). *Design skills in human resource development*. San Diego: University Associates.

Scott, J. E., Fukuyama, M. A., Dunkel, N. W., & Griffin, W. D. (1992). The trauma response team: Preparing staff to respond to student death. *NASPA Journal, 29,* 230–237.

Seymour, M., & Moore, S. (2000). *Effective crisis management: Worldwide principles and practice.* London: Cassell.

Silberman, M. (1998). *Active training: A handbook of techniques, designs, case examples, and tips.* San Francisco: Jossey-Bass/Pfeiffer.

Special Commission on the 1999 Texas A&M Bonfire. (2000, May 2). *Final report.* Retrieved September 29, 2006, from http://www.tamu.edu/ bonfire-commission/reports/Final.pdf.

Stage, F. K., & Dannells, M. (Eds.). (2000). *Linking theory to practice: Case studies for working with college students* (2nd ed.). Philadelphia: Accelerated Development.

Part III

Lessons from Crisis Management

Norbert W. Dunkel

Learning from experience is a learning approach that has been developed to advance educational processes in campus crisis management. Chapter Two provides the crisis matrix as a way to conceptualize the types of situations that colleges and universities experience. Campus administrators never imagined their communities would have to face, and eventually recover from, such horrific events. These same campus administrators were able to draw from the experiences of their colleagues to assist them through these terrible times.

In contacting institutions that have experienced tremendous loss, it was difficult to limit their number. Chapter One provides a historical context of incidents occurring in the United States, and we recognize the enormity of crises over the years. The cases selected for Part Three represent ten intentional and unintentional incidents that have occurred in the past fifteen years.

The authors from all the campuses responded to a general writer's outline that provides a summary of the incident, the agencies and individuals involved, the types of communication issues, the public relations considerations, the long-term implications for the campus, state, or nation, whether protocols were revised due to the incident, and how the incident has affected the lives and jobs of the faculty, staff, and students on campus. For some authors, this was an easy task, because they have written and presented on their incident for many years. Other authors needed to make several drafts due to their level of personal emotional attachment.

In discussing these incidents with the authors, it was evident that the various campuses were at different levels of preparedness. Even at campuses with comprehensive, well-coordinated crisis protocols, the enormity of the incident was overwhelming. One could agree that the campuses that possessed crisis management plans where the various campus entities (that is, police services, physical plant, health and safety, and so on) came together to advance plans, discuss, and even hold mock drills were the campuses that knew their resources and were best in responding. Whether the incident occurred directly on campus, such as the Texas A&M Bonfire tragedy, or adjacent to the campus, such as the off-campus apartment balcony collapse in Blacksburg, Virginia, or at a distance from campus, such as the Oklahoma State University plane crash, all greatly affected the campus community.

The authors of the following chapters agreed to share their experiences with readers in order to advance the approach of learning from experience. Readers may discover common themes, new approaches, different techniques, or new processes to consider on their campus through these collective experiences. That is the value of learning from experience.

9

Environmental Crises

Pat Whitely, Jacinta Felice, and Kevin Bailey

The crisis matrix presented in Chapter Two identifies three types of crises that are common to institutions of higher education: environmental, facility, and human. An environmental crisis is any event or situation that originates in the environment or in nature. Typical weather-related crises such as hurricanes, earthquakes, and floods fall into this category.

This chapter reviews three environmental crises affecting campuses: Hurricane Andrew, which struck the University of Miami (described by Pat Whitely); a tornado that struck the University of Maryland, College Park (described by Jacinta Felice); and Hurricane Katrina, which struck Tulane University (described by Kevin Bailey). Following each incident is a collection of questions designed to provoke reflection and discussion. Readers can use these questions to advance their own campus preparedness for crisis situations.

The University of Miami: Hurricane Andrew

The Incident

On the afternoon of Friday, August 22, 1992, the University of Miami, like many universities ready to open for the fall semester, had just concluded its resident assistant training. As we finished, our thoughts turned to welcoming eighteen hundred new students and twenty-five hundred upper-class students to our residential colleges. Less than four hundred miles to the east, however, a Category Four hurricane loomed. Because Miami-Dade County had not sustained a direct hit from a hurricane in thirty-two years, many believed this one would turn north up the eastern seaboard toward the Carolinas. Unfortunately for us, however, that prediction was very inaccurate and our worst fear became reality.

On Saturday, August 23, the University of Miami began full-scale preparations for a direct hit by Hurricane Andrew, which would become the worst disaster to strike the United States up to that time. Our staff teams met constantly, food was prepared, and we began meeting with students only twenty-four hours before the storm was to make landfall.

On Sunday evening, August 24, Hurricane Andrew devastated southern Miami-Dade County. The storm lasted approximately seven hours, and created damage not previously experienced. The university had four thousand students and parents living on campus. The university sustained $13.7 million in damages—including fifty-two roofs, thirteen hundred trees, and eight hundred windows. Fortunately, students and parents were safe and no injuries were reported, even though winds of 145 miles per hour were recorded on campus, and students and their parents had to move into the hallways. At the height of the storm, staff walked the hallways trying to calm new students, who, though excited to be "Hurricanes," did not believe this was the way they would be welcomed into the UM community. Afterward, the campus was barely recognizable.

Agencies and Individuals Involved

The minute the storm ended, the university went into action. The senior leadership team, on which a number of student affairs staff served, met twice a day. President Edward T. Foote chaired the meetings each morning and expected an assessment and major issues report from all in attendance. These meetings also helped coordinate all aspects of support needed and helped curtail rumors.

The most important determination initially involved whether classes could resume in three days. Considering the condition of the campus and community, the answer was an emphatic *no*. Thus, a major decision was made to close the campus for two full weeks until September 10, 1992, and students were encouraged to go home. In order to expedite this process, the university reimbursed students for automobile mileage or paid for round-trip airline tickets home. Travel reimbursement was offered because we believed that the campus could return to "normal" more quickly if it were empty. The university negotiated special airfares with three carriers, which made this offer even more attractive.

Communication Issues

Our communication plan was certainly not sophisticated, but it was effective. After the senior leadership team conferred each morning, meetings were held at noon with the resident assistants (RAs), the residence coordinators (RCs), and the faculty of the residential colleges who were the real heroes during Hurricane Andrew. Each staff member was given a comprehensive list of issues and decisions that were to be reviewed with students at 2:00 P.M. Students had to be briefed about food schedules, safety, sanitation, water, and campus closures. Since we never lost phone service, we established immediately a toll-free number, staffed twenty-four hours per day, seven days per week, so students and parents could receive hourly updates. Our computer connections were not 100 percent reliable, even after the power came on, so the RAs and the hot line were the main avenues of communication. The staff, faculty, and RAs in the residential colleges were clearly among the main reasons we were able to handle successfully the challenge of over four thousand students and faculty living on campus for three days. The RAs were asked to identify students who might need counseling or additional support. The university then provided the counseling staff accordingly.

It was important for the senior leadership team to be highly visible to students. The president and student affairs staff walked the two cafeterias each evening and answered students' questions. This ritual also provided an opportunity for the residence hall staff to spend significant time with the president and provost, briefing them about pertinent issues and requesting various resources. It was essential to communicate to the staff and students that the well-being of our students was our highest priority, despite all the damage to the campus and community.

We established a phone bank immediately to reach out and contact all university staff and faculty, trying to ascertain the extent of resources and support they would need. This task proved to be extremely difficult and time-consuming because almost four hundred staff members had lost their homes.

The campus administrative offices closed for one week to allow us to take care of the students, encouraging them to leave for two weeks, and to allow some of the major damage to be cleared. When we reopened, student affairs and communication staff were stationed at all university entrances to provide updates about university resources available, including food, water, and clothing. This small symbolic gesture went a long way toward beginning the healing process for those who had lost so much.

As a result of Hurricane Andrew and with the help of crisis management consultants, we developed a state-of-the-art communication system. Technology has grown by leaps and bounds since 1992, and the improvements we have made since Hurricane Andrew have been dramatic. Highlights of the current system include these:

- A hurricane/crisis Web page is updated hourly for students, faculty, staff, and parents. We also have a server in Canada that we can utilize if the university server becomes unavailable.

- A state-of-the-art Emergency Operations Center is activated twenty-four hours a day as soon as a hurricane watch is announced. Staff from university communications and student affairs undergo training and answer the special emergency hot line number that is published widely in all communications to parents and students.

- A complete set of walkie-talkies has been issued to the emergency operations team to be used in the event of an emergency. Cell phones cannot be relied on during a crisis of this nature and communication is essential to successful management.

- We have completely reorganized our crisis management teams. There are now two distinct groups: a large group of approximately one hundred with representatives from every area of the university, and a much smaller group consisting of ten senior leaders who meet with the president and discuss the key decisions points. It is interesting to note that all of our communication changes were activated during an extremely challenging hurricane season in Florida in fall 2004. Also, these strategies were absolutely essential during the tragic events of September 11.

Public Relations Issues

Moving from communications to public relations, the University of Miami experienced several challenges. One of the most important public relations issues was to ensure that the university had a unified message, while at the same time remaining sensitive to the fact that the medical school and clinical practices also had a consistent message to the community about their ability to maintain a level of care. Luckily, the damage to the medical school was not significant compared to the Coral Gables campus.

The communication staff had to ensure that the decision to close for a two-week period was understood and perceived nationwide as a positive step. We did not want our freshman enrollment to drop for the fall or inquiries and applications to be affected in subsequent years, which easily could have happened. We also needed to communicate to all students, staff, and faculty that, even though classes would be delayed two weeks, the entire semester, including finals, would be completed in time for the holidays because we would use the two-week finals period as actual class time.

Other public relations strategies included organizing our students and medical school resources to volunteer in the South Dade community that had been absolutely devastated by Andrew's wrath. The university and President "Tad" Foote believed strongly that our role in volunteer efforts would be helpful and comforting to those who had been affected so deeply.

We needed to continue coordinating with our Employee Assistance Program and psychological services and to lend support to faculty and staff living in that area. It would take years for this area to return to normal. Our faculty and staff needed support to return to work, and at the same time, know that the university recognized their need for flexibility and compassion during these extraordinary times.

Although our RAs and RCs were not able to travel home for the two-week break, the associate director of residence halls met with the staff to determine a schedule that would allow each of them to get some much needed rest. The RAs and RCs had been through a vigorous training program, only to have to prepare and live through a major disaster, while at the same time caring for many new students and their families. They had served admirably and handled more issues in one week than most staff members handle in any given year.

Protocol Revision

Before 1992, the university had not known what it meant to live through and survive a real hurricane. Hurricane Andrew was a true wake-up call for our community. We were lucky that we did not sustain a direct hit, but winds of 145 miles per hour were too close for comfort, especially with vulnerable young students living on the campus.

Several protocols were revised as a result of Hurricane Andrew. They include these:

- The development of a comprehensive university-wide hurricane plan for each department or area, which not only includes a step-by-step preparation process, but an updated list of names, addresses, and contact numbers of university employees. A major frustration after Hurricane Andrew was the inability of directors and department chairs to contact staff because they did not have the correct information.

- The Department of Residence Halls and the Department of Purchasing worked together and identified and solidified standing purchasing orders for all the essentials—water truck, "porta potties," and the like, and we completely revised protocols regarding the availability of food from our food service vendor. We decided that at least a solid five-day supply of food needed to be available, recognizing that the university would feed all essential workers and staff, as well as commuter students who moved on campus.

- The university designed a state-of-the-art Emergency Operations Center with the latest computer technology. Housed at the Department of Public Safety, this is where trained staff operate our rumor control hot line, which can be activated at a moment's notice and is published widely among students and family members. During the more recent 2004 hurricane season, the rumor control hot line was activated twice and answered over two thousand calls.

- The university has partnered extensively with the Federal Emergency Management Association (FEMA). Through this partnership, we have received recognition for being a "Disaster Readiness University," a classification that has meant federal funding for our initiatives, including the installation of hurricane shutters and hurricane glass throughout campus.

- All the residence hall housing protocols were revised. No longer are students allowed to stay in our apartment area or in a fraternity house. Arrangements have been made to house students in various areas in the residential colleges, primarily lounges and common areas where shutters and hurricane glass have been installed. In addition, arrangements have been made to house students who are commuters but, as noted earlier, may not want to stay in their own homes. Although this policy is flexible, we do encourage students to initially seek out the local shelters available.

- We have completely revised all of our policies and resources regarding disaster recovery efforts. The Department of Facility and Planning has clearing equipment available, and preassigned trained damage assessment teams are organized to be on campus prior to the storm in order to move quickly after the storm ends. So power can be restored quickly, it has been essential to make prior arrangements with Florida Power and Light to house and feed crews on campus.

- Protocols have been revised to provide off-site complete payroll and business operations support. One of the most amazing outcomes of Hurricane Andrew was our ability to handle payroll literally six days afterward for all university employees, despite the roadblocks that were encountered when cash and checks were not readily available to obtain the most needed services.

Author Notes on the Incident

Hurricane Andrew clearly defined the University of Miami family for several years. The university community will never feel complacent about a pending hurricane threat. Our policies, procedures, and operations, as well as our relationship with FEMA, have all been enhanced because of Hurricane Andrew.

When Hurricane Andrew struck, we were not afraid to improvise, while always remembering that our students and guests came first. For many on that fateful day, surviving and thriving after Hurricane Andrew defined the strength and perseverance of the University of Miami community.

Questions for Discussion and Reflection

1. What was the most important meeting scheduled prior to Hurricane Andrew reaching land? Why?

2. What three communication strategies used during this incident could other institutions duplicate in a large-scale incident?

3. What factors do you believe went into the decision to close the campus for two weeks following Hurricane Andrew?

4. What was the role of the campus president before, during, and after Hurricane Andrew?

5. What should be included in an annual review of hurricane protocol?

6. Should a campus consider closing prior to a hurricane and sending all students home, including residence hall students? What considerations are made for students unable to travel home?

7. When a hurricane strikes, both personal property and the institution are damaged. What alternatives exist to identify employees willing to come to work to assist the institution when their own property has been damaged?

8. How can a campus develop a rumor control hot line that can be activated within one day's notice? Who should be involved in the decision to activate this hot line?

9. What are the advantages and disadvantages of possessing an off-site Web server?

The University of Maryland-College Park: Tornado

The Incident

On September 24, 2001, two tornados struck the metropolitan Washington, D.C., area. At approximately 5 P.M. that day, one of those storms, a Category Three tornado, struck the University of Maryland-College Park campus. Given the time of day, the campus was in transition when the tornado struck, with many faculty, staff, and students headed home for the day and others arriving for evening classes and activities. On-campus residents were going off to dinner, to events in the Student Union, and elsewhere on campus. The tornado was the third stressful event of the month for the campus. Earlier in September, a student died in a fraternity house, and two weeks prior to the tornado, the campus community was affected deeply by the September 11 terrorist attacks on the World Trade Center. The tornado itself took the lives of two University of Maryland students, sisters leaving campus on their way home for the day, when their car was carried off by the tornado's winds.

Upon seeing the weather turn ominous, many looked to escape the impending rain by seeking shelter in campus buildings. The tornado struck an area of campus known as North Campus. This quadrant of the campus is home to the Campus Recreation Center, two dining facilities, a performing arts center, and eleven residence halls housing approximately five thousand students. An apartment complex known as University Courtyard, housing seven hundred students, is located adjacent to the north quadrant. This complex, one of the university's two public-private housing partnerships, is managed by a private company on property leased from the university.

Agencies and Individuals Involved

After the tornado hit, as word of it spread, campus officials proceeded to the affected area of the campus. UMD Department of Public Safety Police Officers, Prince George County's Fire Department, and state police quickly responded and set up a command post adjacent to one of the residence halls. No serious injuries were reported. A review of building and grounds conducted by campus officials revealed uprooted trees, broken windows, roof damage, and many overturned cars. Almost immediately, staff members from facilities management, environmental safety, and residential facilities began to thoroughly inspect buildings for occupancy and use. When the tornado struck, residence hall staff directed students to move to the lower floors and prohibited them from going outside. Shortly thereafter, students in these halls were safely relocated to other campus buildings. Public safety and emergency personnel also ordered the evacuation of students from the University Courtyard apartments.

Staff from the offices of the vice president for student affairs, residence life, residential facilities, and campus recreation services set up a campus command post in the campus recreation center. From here, staff gathered and disseminated information to various student affairs staff who were deployed throughout campus. Staff at this campus command post confirmed where groups of students had been temporarily relocated and identified a staff member to be the point person for communication at each of those locations. Staff used a combination of radios, campus land line phones, and cell phones as prime means of communication. Later that evening, Maryland Governor Parris Glendening arrived on campus to view the damage and meet with senior university officials. He visited the campus again the next day. Classes that evening and the next day were cancelled. University facilities and grounds staff worked through the night to remove trees and debris from roads and sidewalks, to board up broken windows, and to further assess damage.

Several residence halls sustained minor damage such as broken windows and some roof damage. Several other university buildings were damaged, including a dining facility near several residence halls, as well as trailers that temporarily were housing the Maryland Fire and Rescue Institute. Facilities management and residential facilities staffs determined that students could return to their residence halls approximately six hours after the tornado had hit the campus. The University Courtyard apartment complex sustained significantly more damage to its garden-style apartments, so students residing there were not permitted to return. Many University Courtyard students spent the night with friends or at the Student Union, which remained open overnight for them and any others who could not get home. Public safety officers, along with the Maryland State Police, patrolled the University Courtyard apartment complex to ensure the security of the property until residents could return.

The next morning, the vice president for student affairs convened the campus's incident response team. The team had been created by the vice president for student affairs in February 2001 to respond to campus incidents. The team had met earlier in the month to respond to the other campus incidents. The team's purpose is to provide a cohesive approach to the management of campus incidents by ensuring that the appropriate university staff are able to consult, share information, and manage incidents collaboratively. Standing members of the team include the university legal office staff, the campus's chief of police, the vice president for administrative affairs, the president's chief of staff, the provost's office staff, university relations staff, and other department staff as needed (such as residence life, counseling center, health center, Office of Information Technology, athletics, fraternity and sorority life, and the Student Union). The president may also join the team when he deems it appropriate, and he did so on the morning after the tornado.

Also on that morning, the incident response team reviewed what had been done in the hours immediately after the tornado and provided an up-to-date assessment of the state of the campus. The team decided to designate one person, the director of residence life, to act as the university's liaison with University Courtyard's property manager, the Ambling Corporation, as well as to the students who resided there. One of the first steps for this liaison was to determine the needs of these students, including finding temporary housing options. Staff from student affairs and University Courtyard invited all University Courtyard residents to a meeting to give them an opportunity to ask questions, to learn when they might be able to return to their apartments, and to help provide housing options to anyone who needed assistance. Although many students stayed with family or friends, some needed temporary lodging. When asked, countless residence hall students quickly volunteered to host displaced University Courtyard students. Residence life and residential facilities staffs made cots available for students to borrow. University chaplains also secured toiletry packs from the Red Cross for these displaced students.

The incident response team also discussed the impact of the two student deaths on campus. Students across campus were affected deeply by these deaths, by the manner in which the two women had died, and by the fact that this tragedy followed so soon after an already emotionally arduous first month of the academic year. Staff from the university chaplain's office, the counseling center, and the health center's mental health unit were ready to respond to the needs of the campus community. Plans for a memorial service were soon under way.

The storm and the tornados caused a significant amount of damage to a number of communities in the College Park area. University officials from facilities management, residential facilities, and environmental safety helped the University Courtyard staff with property assessment, structural assessment, and the removal of many damaged cars. The university also assisted University Courtyard management in identifying contractors to make necessary repairs to the apartments. Residents were escorted to their apartments for a short amount of time to collect books and other possessions. In addition to having belongings in their apartments damaged by the wind and rain, many students found their cars damaged by the high winds, carried and dropped on top of other cars, or wrapped around trees. Approximately four hundred cars across campus sustained damage. Leaking gasoline created a hazardous situation in the parking lots that needed to be cleaned up before students could be given access to their cars. In the meantime, student affairs staff were assigned to parking lots with cameras so students could take pictures for insurance purposes.

Public Relations Issues

The university's Web site served as the main source of information for University of Maryland students in the days and weeks following the tornado. The Web site provided a means for concerned family and friends to stay informed. Because of the university's proximity to the nation's capital, it is not unusual for local news to become national news. University officials are accustomed to campus incidents receiving national press attention from time to time, and this incident was covered in papers such as the *Washington Post* and the *Baltimore Sun*. The university's public relations staff was informed as decisions were made and implemented in order to be able to respond to questions from the media.

Implications

The tornado that hit the College Park area was the first in seventy-five years and caused approximately $15 million in damages. In the past few years, there has been an increase in tornados in the metropolitan Washington, D.C., area. After the 2001 tornado, the campus researched and purchased an early warning siren system. The campus also contracted with a weather data service to provide the campus with up-to-the-minute weather information. The early warning siren is used in conjunction with information received from weather data to alert the campus of severe weather (tornadoes, hurricanes, and so on) and to inform those who hear the siren to take shelter inside a building immediately and seek further information.

The University of Maryland now has approximately twenty-five hundred students living in apartments managed by private companies. While students sign a lease with these companies, the campus is responsible for identifying resources to assist these students in the event their housing is affected by a tornado, fire, power outage, or other significant event. Since 2001, residence life officials have worked together with the management companies of both public-private partnerships to review and collaborate on plans to respond to emergencies in these venues. It is vital for universities that have similar public-private partnerships to determine, in advance, if the property is complying with their property insurance requirements and to fully understand the scope of the coverage of the property, displacement costs, and what the insurance policy covers in the event of a major disaster.

Protocol Revision

Following the tornado and the terrorist attacks, the university has reviewed and updated its plans for campus emergencies. The Department of Public Safety has extensively trained its officers to deal with a wide variety of situations and has supplies on hand to deal with situations involving hazardous materials. Communication with other police agencies in the area is more integrated than in the past, and a mobile command center is ready to quickly respond to an incident of any type. The campus still relies on the university's Web site as a primary source of information for those on and off campus. Other communication means include the campus cable television channel, a dedicated information phone line, and two radio stations. Staff from many offices, such as facilities management and environmental safety, have open purchasing and vendor agreements in place to assist the university quickly should the need arise. Most recently, the Department of Public Safety has conducted a number of tabletop training exercises for university officials focusing on different types of campus emergencies. These exercises allow officials to discuss plans and to share information and resources. During any emergency, as well as over the days that follow, collaboration and communication are essential between departments and across the campus. Debriefing and reviewing what happened and how the campus responded are also essential in ensuring that future incidents are well managed.

Author Notes on the Incident

The tornado of 2001 and the terrorist acts of September 11 taught our campus valuable lessons—lessons of compassion, outreach, collaboration, reflection, and careful planning. Communication in and across the departments has increased, as has communication with the campus community in general. The campus's plan of "shelter in place" mirrors the plan communicated to residents living throughout the Washington, D.C., metropolitan area. The campus's Department of Public Safety and many other departments now regularly review their written emergency plans, revise them as needed, and ensure that the plans are comprehensive yet flexible enough to be adapted to any type of incident. Training of new staff in all departments, implementation of the incident response team, and communication to incoming students about safety and security expectations and emergency preparedness resources are now routine for our campus. The events of fall 2001 taught our campus that careful advance planning, along with coordination among talented, dedicated, and caring staff, students, and other volunteers, are the keys to successfully managing the most trying times for a campus community.

Questions for Discussion and Reflection

1. What was the campus president's role in this incident?

2. What impacts, if any, did the events of September 11, 2001, and the death of the fraternity member earlier in the month have on this incident?

3. Did the fact that the apartment complex was managed by a private company impede the response to this incident?

4. How would the institutional response have differed, if at all, had the apartment complex that was most significantly affected not been managed by a private company?

5. Are there members of the university community currently not on the incident response team who should be on the team?

6. What was taken into consideration in deciding to cancel classes for two days?

7. What was the most important communication issue immediately following this incident? One day later?

8. What was the best means of communication to distribute information following this incident?

9. Which university staff members should receive training regarding crisis procedures?

10. What support should the institution provide to staff members who played a role in handling this incident?

11. Was the level of communication among parents and students adequate? If not, what changes should be made?

12. What effect did this incident have on the institution's budget? Are there ways of lessening this impact should a similar incident occur?

13. Are there other campus, community, state, or federal resources that could have been tapped in the wake of this incident?

Tulane University: Hurricane Katrina

The Incident

Saturday, August 27, 2005, began as any typical freshman move-in day at Tulane University. Lines of cars waited to make their way to various residence halls. The mood was generally upbeat, for move-in day signaled the start of these students' first year of college at Tulane.

In the administration building, however, the mood was far more somber. Senior-level administrators were contemplating what course of action to take in response to Hurricane Katrina's sudden and unexpected shift toward New Orleans. With move-in day well under way, the decision was made to close the university that evening and to reopen on Thursday, September 1, 2005—a day later than classes were originally scheduled to begin.

The university's standing evacuation plan called for faculty, staff, and students to have a personal evacuation plan. Students who are unable to leave the city would be evacuated to Jackson State University in Jackson, Mississippi, where the president is the former general counsel for Tulane University. Because of the timing of the hurricane, many international students did not have their personal plans in order and needed to evacuate through the university as well. The sign-up process began at 4:00 P.M., and approximately six hundred students in charter buses, fifteen passenger vans, and personal vehicles departed at 8:00 P.M. bound for Jackson with Tulane police and Tulane EMS as escorts.

Hurricane Katrina made landfall on Monday, August 29. The initial assessment after the storm was that the campus could be ready in a few days, once the debris had been removed. However, on Tuesday, August 30, the levees broke and northern sections of the uptown campus were flooded by at least three feet of water. Many first-floor offices and equipment, residence hall rooms, and student belongings, athletic fields, and vehicles were submerged underwater for two weeks.

Agencies and Individuals Involved

The evacuation and closure of Tulane University was a coordinated effort through the Office of Emergency Preparedness. Department of Housing and residence life staff swept through all residence halls to make sure that all students were gone. Tulane police conducted a similar sweep of academic and nonresidence hall buildings. University communications provided information on the Web site about the evacuation and reopening of the university as well as important numbers to call for more information. Deans, directors, and department heads disseminated information to their respective employees.

The recovery and renewal of Tulane University could not have been accomplished without the generosity and collaboration of various corporate partners. Coca-Cola provided space in Houston for the establishment of a call center to which phone calls and e-mails were directed. Yahoo, Sun Systems, and Internet2 provided various technological support, from hosting servers to providing a non-Tulane e-mail account to which questions could be directed. In addition, the Association of American Universities (AAU) worked to craft an unprecedented arrangement in higher education where host institutions did not charge tuition to evacuated students. In cases where this was not possible because of state regulations, such tuition was remitted back to the home institution. The National Collegiate Athletic Association (NCAA) supported the temporary relocation of all athletic teams between five college campuses across the country and allowed the teams to compete from their new "home" fields.

Communication Issues

A Category Four storm with the storm surge brought by Hurricane Katrina derails even the most acutely written plans. The City of New Orleans ordered a mandatory evacuation on Sunday, August 28. Based on previous experiences, the overwhelming consensus of the public was that residents would be allowed to return in a day or two at most. No one anticipated the levee breaches. No one anticipated the failure of all communication systems, which left Tulane University in the dark and out of touch with constituents for several days. No one dreamed that an entire semester would be lost.

Power lines and cell phone towers fell. Communication via cell phone in the Gulf Coast area was initially impossible. As staff made their way to evacuation locations, land lines in hotels and the dwellings of friends and family residing in unaffected areas became the main communication vehicles. Staff and faculty purchased alternate cell phones with non-Gulf Coast area codes in order to obtain information. Some staff, with assistance from an experienced preteen, learned how to use text messaging for the first time because it was more reliable than placing a call. The e-mail server was inoperable, which rendered Tulane e-mail accounts useless. Once again, staff and faculty resorted to alternate providers—Yahoo, AOL, gmail, and other third-party vendors—for e-mail communication.

The emergency Web site for the university became the official source of all information about Tulane. President Cowen was diligent about providing daily and timely communication on the status of the campus, the lost fall semester, and the need to locate and communicate with faculty, staff, and students. In the days and weeks to follow, a call center was established in Houston to provide didactic communication sources via telephone and e-mail.

Public Relations Issues

Tulane University and other Gulf Coast universities became high-profile news after Hurricane Katrina. President Cowen appeared in major newspapers across the country including the *New York Times* and *Wall Street Journal*, as well as the *Chronicle of Higher Education*. He was interviewed by Matt Lauer on the *Today Show* and lauded for the quick and decisive action to negotiate arrangements for Tulane University and other Gulf Coast students to visit at other colleges and universities in the fall.

The plight of international students also gained attention, as the Department of Homeland Security required an accounting of all those enrolled at the university by September 30. The university did not know where some of these students were or how to contact them.

A select few senior-level administrators were designated to speak to the media in order to maintain a consistent voice. Staff contacted by a media source were instructed to inform their area vice president, who would choose who would speak on the university's behalf.

Implications

The strengths and weaknesses of an organization are amplified in a time of crisis. The administration followed the emergency plan, but it offered only limited solutions. We learned some lessons that will be incorporated into future planning. Computer servers should be centralized in one location; this eases the backup of the devices and provides timely retrieval. Similarly, staff and faculty need to back up all research data, notes, and other important documents on CDs, jump drives, or other portable media. Staff should review notification procedures or "phone trees" to share important information with the community and make sure faculty are aware of the notification. Some divisions at Tulane were far better at this than others. The security needs of international students during a crisis must be considered, including notification, returning to homelands without jeopardizing their status in the United States, and Department of Homeland Security registration. Many international students had just arrived at Tulane and did not know to bring their passports, I-20, or other important documents that would have allowed them to return home or transfer easily. Finally, in the technology and information age the answer to one question remains paramount: *If all communication and information media fail, how will the institution function?*

An environmental crisis like Hurricane Katrina forced the university to think differently about itself in order to survive and remain financially viable. In the short term, many aspects of the university's evacuation plan and individual unit plans have been revised, including measures to deal with total communications failure. To this day, there is a local workforce shortage that affects the delivery of services, including maintenance, grounds keeping, custodial, dining, and mail. Additional financial measures have been implemented to regulate expenses as the university's financial health improves. The university is developing the infrastructure to support aspects of a renewal plan for the future that call for the merger of the men's and women's liberal arts coordinate college system, centralizing academic advising, and eliminating several academic programs and associated faculty and staff positions.

In the long term, Tulane University will be a more focused institution. Tulane will home in on academic programs in which it has demonstrated or emerging areas of expertise. A new partnership with three other New Orleans universities will be devoted to the transformation of urban communities and improving human life in the city and the Gulf Coast region. The newly created Center for Public Service will centralize and expand the connections between academic study and public service while serving non-Tulane students who wish to study and provide service in the area. All of these initiatives will secure the survival and recovery of the university in case of another unprecedented environmental disaster.

Author Notes on the Incident

Tulane University is indebted to the 590 colleges and universities across the country that educated our students, the eight higher education associations that collaborated with the Gulf Coast universities to devise the tuition policy, the NCAA for making arrangements for athletes, our corporate partners who provided services to Tulane in its recovery and renewal phases, and the countless colleagues who called or e-mailed to provide support, guidance, and encouragement.

As of this writing, hurricane season is only three months away. One cannot help but be a little nervous about what this season will bring, despite claims that a storm like Hurricane Katrina should only occur once in a lifetime. Hurricane plans are being updated with the new knowledge learned as a result of the storm. Undoubtedly, there will be extra precautions when (not if) an evacuation is called and decisions that err more on the side of paranoia than practicality. Perhaps this is to be expected until Hurricane Katrina becomes more of a distant memory than the constant reminder that she remains.

Questions for Reflection and Discussion

1. What was the campus president's role in this incident?

2. What do you do when your campus president is not available during an incident of this magnitude?

3. What types of arrangements can institutions form with other institutions when planning for environmental crises such as hurricanes, earthquakes, floods, volcanoes, and so on?

4. When the institution's workforce is not present to provide the basic essentials for campus operation, who can be called on to assist?

5. What communications issues can you learn about on your campus based on this incident?

6. What two actions taken by institutional staff showed students that the institution cared about them?

7. What ceremony (if any) should be considered by the institution one year following this incident?

8. The failure of the levees resulted in the flooding of the northern part of campus. Which entity is responsible for reimbursing the institution and the students for the replacement of institutional and personal items?

9. What is the role of student leaders in this type of incident? How would you involve student leaders if a crisis of this magnitude occurred on your campus?

10

Facility Crises

Tom Brown, Craig Allen, Jim Conneely, and Claire Good

The crisis matrix presented in Chapter Two identifies three types of crises that are common to institutions of higher education: environmental, facility, and human. A facility crisis is any event or situation that originates in a facility or structure.

This chapter reviews three facility crises affecting campuses: the apartment balcony collapse that occurred in Blacksburg, Virginia (described by Tom Brown); the Seton Hall residence hall fire (described by Craig Allen); and Eastern Kentucky University's power outage (described by Jim Conneely and Claire Good). Following each incident is a collection of questions designed to provoke reflection and discussion. Readers can use these questions to advance their own campus preparedness for crisis situations.

Virginia Tech: Apartment Balcony Collapse in Blacksburg, Virginia

The Incident

All the planning in the world cannot prepare student affairs professionals for some of the crises we face, but collaborative relationships and a standing crisis response team can abate some of the challenges we confront in a dramatic incident. An April 1996 off-campus student party ended abruptly with the collapse of a third-floor apartment balcony. The balcony collapsed under the weight of fifteen to twenty students and a keg of beer in a trash barrel full of ice, and took the second-floor balcony, which held another twenty students, with it on its way down. Students spilled onto the lawn below and hit the concrete at the base of the building, as well as inside and onto the resulting rubble of wood.

Approximately forty students were on the two balconies when they went down. The injuries ranged from none to serious physical injuries requiring hospital admission. Three students had extensive injuries including a broken back, lacerated kidney, and fractured vertebrae. Sixteen of the students were treated and released from the local emergency room.

Agencies and Individuals Involved

The response by Virginia Tech's Division of Student Affairs was both intense and extensive. Staff members from the Dean of Students Office worked with the local Blacksburg Police Department to establish presence both at the scene of the accident and at the hospital. Emergency personnel covered the first line of response. Staff members were assigned on-site to assist by fielding questions, trying to calm bystanders, and acting as buffers between students and members of the media.

Student affairs staff members also assisted emergency room personnel, because many students descended on the waiting area to check on friends and confirm whether acquaintances might be hospitalized. Establishing order, calming fears, and rumor control were the primary tasks of student affairs staff members. Emergency room staff members appreciated the Virginia Tech support in managing the numbers of students at the hospital.

Communication Issues

Students involved in the accident, both on the scene and in the emergency room, were concerned about delayed class assignments and missing class in the short term. Student affairs staff generated lists of students to assist in verifying who was involved in the incident. Typically, the Dean of Students Office is the point of contact for students requesting any form of academic relief due to missed classes. Verification of student absence was sent to colleges and departments in the university by the end of the day following the incident. Family notification was also a concern; friends of those involved were encouraged to contact the families if they had connections to the injured students and their families. Family contact was also made by hospital officials pending signed patient release and primarily related to student and family insurance concerns.

Uninjured students on the scene were quickly concerned about where responsibility would lie. Was this the renter's problem or the responsibility of the building owner? Some students fled the scene out of fear of being found present at a party and involved in underage drinking. However, most of the partyers who were inside the apartment, and therefore not injured, acted responsibly and helpfully to their fellow partygoers.

Public Relations Issues

Reporters and other members of the media were on the scene immediately. The hype and concern caused by the presence of the media were expected, and of course, not helpful at the time. The immediate needs of both injured and uninjured students were more important than the breaking news of the balcony collapse. Students were quickly counseled by student affairs staff about the pros and cons of talking with the media.

Implications

Fallout was extensive, both in the apartment complex and on campus. Word of the accident spread quickly, and many students were worried about who might be among the injured. As with any campus crisis, rumors ran rampant and many curious students and townspeople came to the scene. Staff members worked closely with the student reporters for the campus newspaper in order to ensure that the story be told accurately, hoping to get a handle on rumor control.

The Student Affairs Division possesses a "Care Team" that meets weekly throughout the year. Care Team members, representing the Dean of Students Office (now renamed Student Life Office), residence life, health, and counseling, held a special meeting to assess the situation. Provisions were made to offer counseling and other needed support to students who were involved in the crisis.

Town officials were responsive. The town manager did not dodge questions about town codes or owner responsibility. He was consistent in his message to the university and to the media that the welfare of the injured students came first and foremost. Apartment owners had complied with local ordinances requiring inspections during and after construction. Subsequent inspections were only made at the request of an owner or in response to a complaint. A town inspection showed the apartment balconies were constructed according to state standards. In addition, the apartment handbook, given to all residents, specifically gave balconies an occupancy limit of ten people. Shortly after the incident, local police adopted a policy of knocking on doors with a word of caution when the number of people on a balcony appeared to exceed limits.

Protocol Revision

The cause of the balcony failure was ruled to be overload and not a flaw in construction. The management company for the apartment complex inspected all other balconies as a preemptive measure, finding no faulty construction, rotting, or other concerns. Although balcony limits were stated in the lease of the student who had given the party, and in the policy handbook for the apartment complex, management added signs to each apartment balcony warning of the ten-person limit.

Families of injured students continued to contact the university for some time after the incident. Their questions primarily related to legal issues. Those callers were referred to our Student Legal Services Office for advice. No lawsuits came to fruition to the knowledge of the university. All of the students involved made full recoveries and continued their academic pursuits at Virginia Tech.

Student affairs protocol did not change after this incident. The on-call communication between the university, law enforcement, and hospital administration worked effectively. Our protocol was reinforced and we believe our response was both timely and thorough. This incident confirmed that our on-call system works and our procedure to call for backup is invaluable. Multiple staff members were needed to respond effectively to needs at two locations and with multiple students involved.

Author Notes on the Incident

Staff advice is to emphasize having a system in place to respond to off-campus crises. The development of and ongoing rapport with local community responders are crucial. The relationship and partnership with hospital staff can be invaluable when students and families need the support of the university along with the care of a hospital. Appreciating legal constraints while working toward mutual relationships on behalf of students pays off. In addition, talking with apartment managers and tenant associations to encourage posting of weight limit signs on apartment balconies is an important preventative measure.

Questions for Reflection and Discussion

1. What is the role of the campus president in this kind of incident?

2. What was the most important communication issue during this incident? After the incident?

3. What information was provided to family members of the students?

4. How can rumors be minimized in a similar incident?

5. Did the campus have any legal liability as a result of this incident?

6. Should the campus student government play a role in this type of incident? If so, what is its role?

7. What should the role be for the Office of University Relations, media relations, or the information officer?

8. What should the provost's role be?

9. What were the decision-making protocols followed in this incident? How often should such protocols be reviewed?

10. What was the visibility of the senior administrators? How important is their visibility during a campus crisis?

11. What should the role of campus victim services be? If such a service does not exist, what steps should an institution take (if any) to establish such an office?

12. Which other members of the campus community could be called on to assist in such times (for example, faculty, campus leaders, students, and so on)?

13. What is the immediate role of the counseling center in this incident? Is there a continuing need for the counseling center's involvement?

14. What information should be provided and how frequently should campus operators and campus Web page managers provide it? How else can technology be used to one's advantage in a campus crisis?

15. What is your evaluation of the Care Team? Is there a need to review the protocol or membership for such a team?

16. What were the long- and short-term communication needs?

Seton Hall: Residence Hall Fire

The Incident

On January 19, 2000, three freshman students died in a tragic fire in Boland Hall, the first-year residence hall at Seton Hall University in South Orange, New Jersey. More than fifty other students were treated for injuries related to the fire that broke out at approximately 4:30 A.M. in a third-floor lounge. Built in the 1950s, Boland Hall did not have a sprinkler system, and codes did not require there be one.

Boland Hall was the residence for about 650 freshman students. There were eight or nine fire alarms during finals week at the end of the fall semester, and many of the involved students were heard to say they did not believe this alarm was "real."

On that cold January morning, the quiet fifty-eight-acre campus located about fifteen miles outside of New York City became a surreal setting for dozens of emergency vehicles, firefighters, and rescue personnel, as media helicopters hovered overhead. University administrators, faculty, and staff came to campus in the predawn hours to begin what would be the first of many long days to come.

Agencies and Individuals Involved

The Essex County Office of Emergency Management was on campus almost immediately after the fire was extinguished. They assisted the university in dealing with local and state authorities. A crisis team, consisting of the police, the prosecutor's office, the fire department, and university and town officials, was formed to manage the crisis. The scene of the fire was designated a crime scene, so police and county investigators, along with the fire department, had "control" of the building for many days. This meant that university officials were not allowed inside. Throughout the day of the fire, different state and local agencies were present on campus. State police were on the scene, the governor arrived on campus by helicopter, the Red Cross came in to assist students displaced by the fire, county health officials and numerous mental health organizations sent volunteers to campus, and there was an outpouring of support from the community.

The volunteers were organized and the crisis management plan was implemented after the first briefing meeting held around 7 A.M., if not earlier. The delineation of duties was the next most immediate aspect of dealing with the aftermath of the fire. Seton Hall's president was clear that our students' needs must come first, and everyone took that charge to heart. Seton Hall is a Catholic university, and its priest community was a vital part of the university's response. Priests were assigned and dispatched to every area hospital to talk to students and families within hours of the fire. Other members of the Seton Hall community from faculty to varsity coaches were on campus in the University Center, in the residence halls, and outside to provide a shoulder for students to lean on.

Every division of the university was involved in the management of this crisis in one way or another. Student affairs at Seton Hall consists of health and counseling services, community development (campus life/student activities), housing and residence life, public safety and security, the Career Center, and ID card services. The vice president for student affairs met with all of her directors early in the morning, tasking each with caring for our students in many ways. Managing the people managing the crisis was the vice president's focus, and to do this she relied on her knowledge of the capabilities of her staff. Knowing that housing and residence life would be dealing with immediate shelter needs, and planning for longer-term needs, staff in the Career Center served as case managers for the students who lived on the floor where the fire had occurred. Several of these staff members had housing backgrounds, and thus were able to handle the sensitive issues raised by students and their families. Community development coordinated essentials—blankets, clothing, food, and the like that were donated to the university. The health and counseling services staff held debriefing sessions for student affairs staff throughout the first day and in the days after the fire, and set up a twenty-four-hour volunteer center to coordinate the more than seventy-five counseling volunteers from other universities, state agencies, and local hospitals who were available to the students. Student affairs colleagues at local colleges and universities came to support the Seton Hall community almost immediately. They answered phones, made copies, helped find accommodations for students, and offered emotional support. It was important to have volunteer coordinators so that people did not get in the way, and we were lucky to have colleagues close by who knew the university well and took the lead coordinating volunteer efforts.

Communication Issues

Communication among university officials and the various agencies on campus began immediately, and a formal communications center, or "command center" location, was established in the central administration building, Presidents' Hall. It was here that university officials met regularly with the outside agencies. Briefings on the status of the crisis were held to share information and discuss the next steps for managing the crisis. Access to communications equipment and technology was critical to the management of the crisis so that persons who stayed in the command center could receive and send information to university officials in their offices, or to outside agencies assisting from off-site locations. Multiple phone lines and data ports were needed, all in a location that was secure and relatively central to campus.

Communication was the most critical component of managing the crisis. The director of public relations was on campus from the very beginning in her baseball cap and casual attire. She attended all the briefings and then worked with university leadership and her staff to manage the immediate media rush to campus. The dean for community development held regular town meeting–style updates for students and also collaborated with information technology and public relations to regularly update the university Web page with information that students, parents, and the university community needed to know. The dean's office also gave students displaced from the residence hall who did not have a phone access to telephones in the University Center to make outgoing calls to family and friends. The Department of Housing and Residence Life posted information for students about temporary housing, how to get assistance, available resources, and more in all the residence halls because many displaced students went to other buildings to seek comfort. By the end of the first day, and for days following the fire, phone banks were set up and volunteers from across the Division of Student Affairs called students who had lived in Boland Hall and their families to keep them up to date and answer questions about their belongings and when they would be permitted to return to the residence hall.

Students and parents had many questions, but it was important to resist the temptation to speculate about what might have happened, when students might get into the halls, or how damaged property would be handled. Much of the information the university needed in order to answer these questions depended on local and state authorities, and the facts were not always readily available. Information changed as the investigation unfolded and the scope of the crisis became evident. Fortunately, the many methods used by the university to communicate with its publics helped ease anxieties.

Public Relations Issues

Seton Hall University was fortunate to have strong leadership in its public relations department. Given the university's proximity to New York City and the time the story broke—with the morning commute—and the scope of the tragedy, the fire quickly became national news. From the very beginning, behind closed doors on campus, and for the public at the first press conference early in the morning, the message was clear: a terrible tragedy had occurred. Our first priority as a university was to care for our students. As we gained information to answer other questions we shared it with the public, but we were a community of faith, and a community that would take time to heal. Directors in the Division of Student Affairs worked closely with public relations before the fire, and our good working relationship was evident as the crisis unfolded. Student affairs provided information to public relations when needed, but the primary role of student affairs was to care for our students and allow public relations to handle the media.

Implications

The Seton Hall fire was an incident that grabbed the attention of colleges and universities across the nation. The director of housing and residence life received hundreds of calls and e-mail messages, and for years after the fire those same colleagues would speak of how they reviewed their fire safety policies and procedures. Although the cause of the fire was ruled arson, much was written and discussed in the media about the role a fire suppression system or sprinkler system might have had in the Boland Hall fire. The impact in New Jersey came within six months. Then-Governor Christine Todd Whitman came to Seton Hall in July 2000 and signed legislation requiring sprinkler systems in all New Jersey college and university housing. This legislation was thought to be the beginning of a wave of similar federal and state laws to be passed, but to date it remains the only one of its kind in the country. Fortunately, there have been no multiple fatality fires in traditional college residence halls since the Seton Hall fire, but it is estimated that to this day as many as half of all residential facilities in the United States do not have sprinkler systems.

Seton Hall's president made a bold announcement soon after the fire: all Seton Hall residence halls would have a fire suppression sprinkler system installed by the time school started in fall 2000. For housing and residence life, this meant working with contractors to have access to rooms while buildings were occupied during the academic year, rescheduling summer conference programs, and working with contractors to accommodate their needs in the residence halls for summer school housing and summer orientation programs. Other facility needs were addressed, such as upgrades to the fire alarm system and renovations to the floor damaged by the fire. Policies on acceptable appliances and furniture in residence halls, evacuation protocols, student and professional staff training, and fire safety education for all students were enhanced, and the university continues to evaluate and improve all aspects of fire safety on campus.

The Seton Hall community is reminded of the tragedy every day: once every quarter-hour, a bell tolls for Frank Caltibolata, John Guinta, and Aaron Karol, the three freshmen who died in the fire. Outside Boland Hall is a memorial garden with the word *Remember* engraved in stone. Freshmen who now live in Boland Hall (that is, in 2005, when this was written) were in seventh grade when the fire occurred, and in the Department of Housing and Residence Life, just three of the current seventeen full-time professional staff were on campus at the time of the fire. The role of student affairs, especially housing and residence life, can best be summed up as constant vigilance. Every day in everything that is done, fire safety is a consideration. The university maintains a close relationship with the South Orange Fire Department, and together, they educate staff and students about fire safety. And as a community, they remember.

Author Notes on the Incident

In the five years since the Boland Hall fire, I have spent a considerable amount of time on work related to the fire. There was a lot of follow-up with students and families as the healing process unfolded, and this tragedy will always be a part of those who were at Seton Hall in January 2000.

Any tragedy causes us to reflect, learn, and improve on all aspects of our work. I am confident that my colleagues in student affairs and housing and residence life have also spent much time reflecting on what happened at Seton Hall University. My hope is that my colleagues across the country will make improvements to their facilities, policies, and training and to student education and student orientation so that a tragedy of this magnitude will never happen again.

I end with a few words of advice:

- *Put the needs of the students first.* Basic needs for shelter, food, and emotional support are critical. Develop plans to address those needs prior to a crisis.

- *Communication is key.* Almost as important as those basic needs is the need to know what is happening, what will happen, and where to get help. Develop communication plans, and expect to spend time getting accurate information to all members of the community who can help you manage a crisis and to the students and their families. It is important to know and work with your university public relations or media relations personnel. At Seton Hall, several directors in student affairs had media relations training, and this training, combined with a strong relationship, was invaluable in the management of the crisis.

- *Take your time.* There is a tendency to work fast in a crisis, and although a quick response is important, it is equally important not to rush. Taking some extra time to gather information or formulate a plan is time well spent.

- *Recognize your limitations.* You have no control over local and state authorities, and the sooner you understand that you need to work with them the better you will be able to manage a crisis. This does not mean you cannot make suggestions, or request specific information or action, but it is best not to spend too much time doing so. Rather, focus on items directly under your sphere of control.

- *Manage those managing the crisis.* It is important to know the depth of skills and abilities of your student affairs staff. It is important that units come together to support and assist one another. Having and using connections to outside agencies is also useful in organizing those who may come to campus to manage a crisis. Cultivate connections and good relationships with agencies prior to a time of crisis.

Questions for Reflection and Discussion

1. What should the role of the campus president be in this kind of incident?

2. Many students were heard to say that they did not believe the fire alarm was real. How can colleges and universities increase student awareness to ensure immediate evacuation of a building when a fire alarm sounds?

3. What alternative housing options are there for students displaced in a residence hall fire? What campus entity determines who pays for the students' loss of books and other personal items?

4. What is the campus's role, if any, when state or federal legislation is proposed as a result of a campus incident?

5. In a residence hall fire resulting in student deaths, identify the various persons affected by the incident. What decisions should be made for each group of affected persons?

6. Develop a communication plan for this incident. Note the campus entities that should have awareness of the plan and direct involvement in execution of the plan.

7. Develop a short-term (one-week) plan for managing the various staff and community volunteers involved in such an incident. In what ways would a long-term plan be different?

8. What are the short- and long-term facility assessment points to consider?

9. What type of support should the students who are directly affected expect from the campus?

10. Which community agencies can be helpful and what services can they provide to affected students?

11. What is the institution's role in initiating and supporting a campus remembrance ritual after a student fatality?

Eastern Kentucky University: Power Outage

The Incident

In January 2004, Eastern Kentucky University (EKU) experienced a significant power outage that affected a large portion of family housing, academic buildings, athletic facilities, residence halls, and service facilities. This narrative is intended to provide accurate, complete information about the problems that occurred with the electrical systems on campus and the decisions made regarding relocation and other services for affected students.

- On Sunday, January 25, at 10:15 A.M., an electrical cable failed, causing power to be lost to all those buildings serviced by a specific circuit known as Circuit 6 in EKU's electrical system. Sixty-one families and forty-four single graduate students in on-campus apartments, called the Brockton Apartments, lost all power. All had to be relocated.

- On Monday, January 26, work outage diagnostics continued on Circuit 6.

- On Tuesday, at 1:30 A.M., power to Circuit 6 was restored, including the Brockton Apartments. Then, at 7:55 A.M., there was a cable failure in Circuit 5, with collateral damage found on Circuit 1. There was critical damage to cable insulation at electrical manholes 60 and 61 behind the student services building. Family housing was once again without power from 7:55 A.M. through 5:15 P.M.

- To allow for repairs, a power outage was scheduled for Circuits 1 and 5 on Wednesday, January 28. The outage began at approximately 10:00 A.M. and lasted for approximately twenty-four hours, until the repairs were completed. More damage was found between electrical manholes 59 and 60. This outage affected a larger number of students—294 residence hall rooms and 156 student apartments were without power and all of these students had to be relocated.

- Repairs continued to Circuits 1 and 5 on Thursday. On Friday, Circuit 5 power was restored at 10:30 A.M. All EKU facilities regained power. Power to the model lab was restored at noon.

- On Sunday, February 1, there was a cable failure on Circuit 6 and a conductor failure between EMH 14 and 15. Families living in the apartments were once again without power from 12:40 to 6:30 P.M.

- Repairs continued to Circuit 6 on Monday, as did the replacement of conductors and transformers for Black Building (the garage).

- The terminations and pulling of new conductors to Black Building continued on Tuesday. Circuit 6 was scheduled down at 10:00 A.M. for connection back at EMH 14. Family housing residents were told to expect a power outage for the entire day. Power was out from 10:00 A.M. until 3:00 P.M.

- Repairs and connections to Black Building continued on Wednesday, February 4, with power restored at 2:00 P.M.

As one can glean from this time line, the repairs to the electrical system were complex and the logistics of providing housing to students similarly so. Outages occurred unexpectedly or were necessitated by the need to make repairs in a safe environment. EKU personnel worked diligently to restore power to campus and minimize any inconvenience to its students. Information was communicated to students in as many ways as possible, and updated frequently.

Providing food was another challenge associated with the power outage. Approximately four hundred apartment units with kitchens were affected, and these students were unable to prepare meals or even keep items in their refrigerators. Because so many families were affected, staff faced additional challenges.

Students were offered meals in the Fresh Food Company on the second floor of the student center at no cost. The Division of Student Affairs paid for 184 meals during the first days of the outage. The decision was made to continue to offer these meals to the apartment residents. This decision was made because of the continued loss of power and because these individuals had been relocated from apartments with full kitchens. All residence hall students affected by relocation were welcome to eat in the Fresh Food Company or other dining facilities, either using their meal plans or at their own cost. Apartment residents without meal plans signed in for 329 meals. The cost of meals for the period between January 25 and January 29 totaled close to $2,700.

Details about the emergency food voucher program through the Chaplain's Office was provided to residence hall desks, facilities services, housing, and student affairs receptionists. The chaplain is on the student affairs staff and is able to provide food vouchers in case of emergencies. Also provided was information about the availability of an emergency student loan of up to $100.

After the January 25 outage, arrangements were made to temporarily relocate sixty-one families and forty-four single graduate students from the apartments. There were enough clean, empty residence hall rooms to fit all the single students, and rooms in three local hotels were reserved for the families affected. The university shuttle was made available to students to assist in the relocation. Students checked into twenty-nine of the sixty-one hotel rooms reserved, but no single students checked into available residence hall spaces. The larger number of residents affected by the January 28 outage led to a need to house seventy-seven male graduate students, fifty-four female graduate students, and thirty-four families in hotels. Approximately 468 other residence hall students were relocated to other residence halls. The approximate cost of hotels for the period between January 25 and January 28 was $10,371.

After losing all power, student health services was forced to cancel all appointments. However, a physician remained on campus for consultation by telephone. Information about this physician was posted in the residence halls, on the Web, and on the dedicated phone line. In addition, all medicines and supplies that needed to be refrigerated were moved to locations that had power on campus.

In response to questions about reimbursement for damage and lost food items, the following information was provided via the Web site and dedicated phone line: *Students may compile a list of any food items that spoiled during the outage and submit the list to Facilities Services. Student Affairs and Facilities Services are working on procedures for possible reimbursement.* The contract for residence hall students and the contract for Brockton Apartments both expressly set forth that the university would not be responsible for loss of personal property, and each resident was encouraged to purchase renter's insurance to cover any such losses. For students who desired to seek recovery of any such loss nevertheless, it was determined that the Kentucky Board of Claims was the appropriate avenue through which to pursue such claims. Printed information describing the claims procedure was made available both to apartment residents and students who lived in the traditional residence halls. Board of Claims forms also were made available at facilities services, university housing, and the Division of Student Affairs.

Communication Issues

As can be imagined, communication is key in dealing successfully with any crisis on a college campus. This is especially true when the crisis has an impact on the campus communication network, such as during a power outage. This outage necessitated not just using new methods of electronic communication but also reverting to some more traditional methods.

A dedicated telephone line was established to provide up-to-date information on the status of the outage and other details about relocation. Letters were hand-delivered to each affected apartment with specific information about the temporary assignments to residence halls and hotels. The letters reiterated the invitation to dine in the Fresh Food Company at no cost, and reminded students that the university shuttle was available until 2:00 A.M., and again in the morning, at the specific time requested by each student. This same information was posted on the university and the student affairs Web sites.

On a regular basis (several times during the day and evening), the dedicated phone line and Web site were updated. The phone messages and Web page could be updated by approved staff from their homes in order to expedite the transferal of information as well as make it easier for staff to communicate with the campus. In addition, when new information about hotels, food, or relocation was needed, hand delivery of letters remained a primary and more personal source of communication.

These methods for communicating to the campus population remained in force until all the necessary repairs to the electrical system were completed and students were able to move back to their homes for good. These methods then continued to be operational for about forty-eight hours after all of the repairs were completed.

Public Relations Issues

Public relations issues included getting timely and accurate information out to the students, but also keeping the community informed. We relied on the hotels to be sensitive to the university's needs—to hold rooms and rates for displaced students during this situation. There was a need to reassure our students and their families that all was being done to correct the situation as quickly as possible.

The university tried to help the students understand what we were required to do legally, but also what we felt compelled to do morally to help them get through this crisis. The university needed to make sure that the students' safety and security topped the list of priorities as students moved from on-campus to off-campus locations.

Another public relations issue was keeping the president and other members of the leadership team informed so they could respond quickly and accurately to inquiries from media, parents, board members, and community leaders. The media played a crucial role in helping us meet the needs of the students by printing accurate information on the situation and serving as a verifier that EKU was taking the situation seriously and going the extra mile to accommodate students.

Implications

With the help of a debriefing session, we learned some lessons that will be used for planning purposes in the future.

We should have erred on the side of caution—that is, made plans beyond the original estimated time and date for restoration of power. Students did not like the "not knowing" where they would be until the last minute. We should have made decisions based on the safest scenario, rather than on when we thought the power would be restored. We also should have found a way to educate students about the services we were providing compared with those they could expect if they were living in the community. Dealing with facilities is very unpredictable, and we tried to make it predictable.

We also realized that we needed to make sure all information on family housing residents was up to date and provided to our housing department on a regular basis. Facility services does not have an electronic data file, so the first night we had to call a secretary to come into the office to read us the names and family status of all their residents!

We realized as well that we were too accommodating in trying to respond to students who lost food due to spoilage. We should have told them up front to make alternate plans if possible, and that, if they did not, we could not be responsible for any food spoilage.

In the buildings where services were interrupted, such as the student health center, instead of keeping a physician there to give advice by phone, we should have transferred the phone line and had him set up in a building that was not affected by the power outage. We did not realize at the time that the doctor was working in a dark, very cold building!

We should have included information in our notices to residents that explained what to do if they had medications that needed to be refrigerated.

As we move forward, we will surely learn other lessons. The benefit of a debriefing session is not to place blame but to evaluate and plan improvements for the future.

Author Notes on the Incident

In reflecting back on the situation, it has become obvious that no matter how much you prepare and how much experience you may have in dealing with a crisis, no two are the same. There will always be wrinkles that affect all the preparation, and you just need to be flexible. An institution needs to know what resources are available at all times and what communication mechanisms will be most effective for a specific crisis. No matter how much you think you are ready, the unexpected will arise and you will need to put it all into perspective in order to do what is best for the students as well as the institution.

One last thought: often, a situation becomes a true crisis only if you allow it to become a true crisis. Preparation, flexibility, and resourcefulness can minimize the impact of a crisis on the campus community.

Questions for Reflection and Discussion

1. What was the campus president's role in this incident?

2. What was the most effective means of communicating with the students during this incident?

3. Which two actions taken by institutional staff helped students believe that the institution cared about them?

4. How would this incident have been different if it had occurred in an institution located in a northern U.S. state in January?

5. How would this incident have been different if it had occurred in an institution located in a more southern state during late August or early September?

6. How would your institution handle the replacement of student food items?

7. Would your institution provide alternative locations for storage of a student's personal medications? Would that location be on campus or off campus?

8. What process would your institution use to determine where to relocate students if there was no space available on campus? Who would make the final decision on relocating students?

9. What departments at your institution and which individuals in those departments would be involved in making the decisions about the outage, the extent of the electrical distribution system that needed to be turned off, and the duration of the outages? Would your housing operation be involved in making and understanding those decisions?

10. Would your institution initiate a debriefing following this incident? Who would initiate this debriefing?

11. Would it be necessary for your institution's staff to follow up with the residents to determine if there were any continuing

issues, such as refrigerators, air conditioners, lighting, and other electrical components that are not working properly? Who would be responsible for this follow-up?

12. Numerous building systems are controlled by electricity, such as steam, chilled water, heating hot water, domestic hot water, and all the pumps and controls associated with these systems. Who would be responsible for checking these components for proper operation after each outage? (After a power outage, steam controls may be lost and the steam may need to be shut down when the power is turned back on.)

13. If a facility is several stories high, domestic water booster pumps may be involved. If so, the toilet flush valves may need to be checked. After a drop in pressure, they may not reset properly and will start running continuously. What campus operation would be responsible for checking these items?

11

Human Crises

Brent G. Paterson, Lee E. Bird, Suzanne M. Burks, Cindy K. Washington, Tom Ellett, and Anthony Daykin

The crisis matrix presented in Chapter Two identifies three types of crises that are common to institutions of higher education: environmental, facility, and human. A human crisis is any event or situation that originates with or is initiated by humans, whether through error or conscious act.

This chapter reviews four incidents of human crises affecting campuses: the Texas A&M Bonfire tragedy (described by Brent G. Paterson); the Oklahoma State University plane crash (described by Lee E. Bird, Suzanne M. Murks, and Cindy K. Washington); the 2001 terrorist attacks on the World Trade Center (described by Tom Ellett); and the shooting at the University of Arizona College of Nursing (described by Anthony Daykin). Following each incident is a collection of questions designed to provoke reflection and discussion. Readers can use these questions to advance their own campus preparedness for crisis situations.

Texas A&M University: Bonfire Tragedy

The Incident

November 18, 1999, is a day that every Texas Aggie remembers and will never forget. In one week, a year of planning and over two months of work by thousands of students would culminate in the burning of a three-layered forty-two-foot stack of wood logs known as *Bonfire*.

Bonfire was a time-honored tradition initiated in 1909 to show Texas A&M University's burning desire to beat the University of Texas in its annual Thanksgiving weekend football game. No one ever imagined that this symbol of Aggie pride would result in the death of eleven bright and energetic students and one former student, and serious injuries to twenty-seven others.

At 2:47 A.M. there were close to seventy students at work on Bonfire. Within seconds, the massive column of logs toppled. Some students were injured by falling logs, some were trapped in the pile of logs, and some were killed instantly by falling logs or the wire that helped hold the stacks together. A university police officer on duty at the site immediately contacted his dispatcher. Within minutes, emergency response personnel arrived at the chaotic scene, which was now in total darkness. The collapse had damaged spotlights erected on the site. Miraculously, some students were thrown from the stack and suffered only minor injuries.

Agencies and Individuals Involved

The Division of Student Affairs Critical Incident Response Team received an immediate call from the university police dispatcher. A member of the team responded to the site and notified other members of the team. Following established protocol, additional university officials were contacted by a team member.

In Brazos County, where Texas A&M University is located, the fire chief of College Station (the city in which the university is located) was the designated leader for disaster response. It was his role to coordinate the response from local fire departments, police departments, Emergency Medical Services (EMS), the local chapter of the American Red Cross, and any other agencies that might be needed. As events evolved, state and federal agencies such as the state police, Occupational Safety and Health Administration (OSHA), and Task Force One (Federal Disaster Response Team trained and stationed at Texas A&M University) joined the recovery effort. In total, over two hundred emergency workers responded to the incident that day. There were also thousands of volunteers, ranging from members of the Aggie football team, who helped move logs until heavy equipment arrived, to local clergy, who helped counsel those affected, to local restaurants, which donated food for workers over the next twenty-four hours until the last body was retrieved from the pile of logs. Individuals feeling a need to help in some way continued to volunteer their time and service in the following days and weeks. Responding to the offers to help became a full-time job for several weeks.

Communication Issues

The coordination among the various agencies and the university was tremendous. It certainly helped that protocols existed, were reviewed annually, and practiced. Fortunately, the Division of Student Affairs had developed a crisis response plan and established the Critical Incident Response Team (CIRT) four years earlier. The CIRT on-call staff included the dean of student life and the three associate directors of student life. During its four years in existence, CIRT had responded to numerous car accidents, apartment and residence hall fires, suicides, and even plane crashes. During this time, the team developed excellent working relationships not only with campus departments including residence life, university relations, environmental health and safety, and the university police, but also with local fire departments, police departments, and hospitals. These relationships and experience paid huge dividends in responding to this tragedy. The various agencies and university entities quickly assumed their respective roles.

One of the first tasks in this particular crisis was to verify who was working on Bonfire that night, account for those who might have left the scene after the collapse, determine who was being treated for injuries, and identify those still trapped. A member of CIRT contacted the commander of the Corps of Cadets and the student body president. These student leaders contacted other student leaders and residence hall staff to account for every student who might have been working on Bonfire that night. With an enrollment of forty-three thousand students, this was no small task. Within a few hours, the commander of the Corps of Cadets and the student body president produced a list of those who had been working on Bonfire. That list would provide an accurate accounting of students injured, students who escaped injury, and students still trapped.

Within minutes local media outlets arrived on the scene of the tragedy and began transmitting news reports. By daybreak, satellite news trucks had arrived from television stations in Houston, Dallas, Austin, and San Antonio. Following our protocol, one of the first calls was made to the director of university relations. On hearing the numerous emergency vehicles rush past her house with sirens blaring, she recognized that the situation was much larger than she had first imagined. She would spend that day and the days and weeks that followed serving as the university spokesperson and arranging interviews with the university president and other university officials.

The university quickly established two command posts. University police in cooperation with other local emergency response agencies established a command post on the site of the Bonfire collapse. Student affairs established a command post in the office suite of the vice president for student affairs. Cell phones were used to transmit information between CIRT members on-site, in the VPSA command center, at local hospitals, and in offices. Staff in the VPSA office called parents of students seriously injured or trapped to notify them of the incident. A comfortable room in the student center was identified as the location for parents to gather while awaiting word of their son's or daughter's fate. The associate vice president for student affairs made several trips to that room to inform parents that their loved one had been injured or found dead. Maintaining an accurate and timely transmission of information became more difficult as the day progressed. With thousands of students, staff, community members, media, and emergency personnel using cell phones in a very limited territory, the cell telephone networks were overloaded and shut down temporarily. "Runners" were called upon to relay messages between the various offices and agencies managing the crisis.

A phone bank was quickly established using space in the Association of Former Students building, and an 800 number was published through the media. Staff were called and asked to report to this area. They were briefed on the incident and instructed on how to respond to calls from anxious parents and others. Regular updates were sent to the phone bank. Various staff were called on to relieve those who started earlier in the day.

Meanwhile, the president and vice presidents met to determine the university's official response to the incident and consider implications for the days, weeks, and months ahead. From the beginning, the president stressed his concern and sympathy for the students and their families. He also stressed a need for the university to do what was right and not be concerned about potential lawsuits or other legal action. Within days of the accident, the president appointed an independent commission to investigate and report on the causes of the Bonfire collapse. He charged the commission "to satisfy itself that the truth about what caused the accident is known as far as it can be discovered and to report its findings and conclusions with recommendations for corrective actions, if warranted." In May 2000, the Special Commission on the 1999 Texas A&M Bonfire released its final report, which determined that the physical failure and causal factors of the Bonfire collapse were driven by an organizational failure. "This failure, which had its roots in decisions and actions by both students and University officials over many years, created an environment in which a complex and dangerous structure was allowed to be built without adequate physical or engineering controls." At the time of this writing, lawsuits filed by some of the families of those injured and killed are still pending against Texas A&M University, the president, and other university officials affiliated with Bonfire.

Protocol Revision

One of the positive outcomes of the commission's report was a Division of Student Affairs effort to review risk management procedures for division programs and student organization activities. A task force was formed and submitted recommendations for implementing a comprehensive risk management program in the division. The risk management program found its basis in the 1999 work *The Rights and Responsibilities of the Modern University*, by R. D. Bickel and P. F. Lake. (See Chapter Seven References for complete information.) The goal of the program was to "advise organizations of the potential and perceived risks involved in their activities as well as supervising organization activities and taking corrective actions and proactive steps to minimize accidental injury and/or loss." A risk management program was established in the Department of Student Activities a year after the tragedy. It significantly changed the planning and execution of programs and activities.

The Critical Incident Response Team learned that established procedures worked well. However, we could not have imagined the magnitude of such an event and the impact it would have on so many people. Fortunately, there were staff in the Department of Student Life and other departments of the division that had worked with CIRT over the years and were ready and willing to assist. We also learned that you need to pace yourself and others. Everyone felt a need to be immediately involved in the response. Everyone needed rest, but no one wanted to "leave their posts."

From the day that CIRT was formed, the members were well aware that the day would inevitably come when a team member would personally know a victim in one of the team's incident responses. That day came with the Bonfire collapse; the CIRT on-call person had been visiting with students at the Bonfire site hours before the collapse and returned to discover that some of those students were now buried under the fallen stack of logs. The incident had a lasting impact on that individual and she would not be able to return to CIRT duty in the future. Prior to the incident, CIRT had established a critical incident stress debriefing process utilizing staff in the Employee Assistance Program. These services were put to use immediately after the incident and in the following weeks. Later several staff in the division would complete training to become critical incident stress debriefing facilitators.

Implications

The last student was removed from the pile of logs about twenty-four hours after the collapse. Staff from across the Division of Student Affairs had been enlisted to aid in responding to the incident. Some staff were sent to the hospitals to be with injured students, their families, and friends. Others met with groups of students in residence halls, the student center, or anywhere students had congregated. Still others answered the never-ending phone calls to department offices. The work for CIRT had only just begun. There would be weeks spent visiting injured students and their families in the hospital. Numerous students and staff had been affected by the incident and needed attention and follow-up contacts. Normality would not return during that academic year.

The university made some difficult decisions at the time of the incident and in the following weeks, months, and years. Classes were held the morning of the incident. It was decided that students needed a place to go instead of visiting the incident site. Faculty were asked to assist in identifying students most troubled by the incident who might benefit from counseling services. The students organized a memorial service even while rescue efforts were still under way. A service was held at 7:00 P.M. the evening after the tragedy with more than twelve thousand students, faculty, and staff in attendance. The university provided public transportation for students wanting to attend the funerals of students who died in the accident. The university even leased a commercial airplane to fly students and university officials to a funeral in California. Scholarships were established in the names of the deceased. Through the Association of Former Students, a fund was established to help defer medical costs incurred by the injured that would not be covered by insurance. The annual football game with the University of Texas was held on November 26, as scheduled, and seen as a time to begin the healing. On November 18, 2004, the Bonfire Memorial was dedicated on the site of the collapse five years earlier. These are only a few examples of how the Aggie community came together in a time of tragedy.

Author Notes on the Incident

At the time of the Bonfire collapse, I was out of town. I returned to campus on the next available flight. As I flew into College Station and saw the media trucks at the Bonfire site and the media helicopters lining the tarmac at the airport, reality hit. This incident would affect all of our lives in ways we had considered when we established the Critical Incident Response Team but hoped would never occur. I am most proud of the efforts of CIRT members and all of those who responded to this crisis.

Questions for Reflection and Discussion

1. What was the role of the campus president in this incident?

2. As state and federal agencies became involved (such as the American Red Cross, OSHA, and so on), who was in charge of the incident?

3. What was the most important communication issue immediately following the Bonfire collapse?

4. As media outlets continued to arrive on campus, who was responsible for coordinating media efforts? What type of meetings would have been most beneficial for that person to schedule?

5. What considerations should go into the planning of an event of a size and a scope similar to the Bonfire?

6. Which campus and community offices, leaders, or agencies should be involved in the planning?

7. The anniversary date of a major incident has become an important date on many campuses. What considerations should be given prior to the one-year anniversary date of a major incident?

8. What response should the families affected by a campus tragedy expect from the institution? Which offices should be responsible for coordinating this response?

9. What types of support services should be provided for the crisis responders?

10. What training, if any, should faculty members be given in order to be able to identify students potentially in need of counseling services?

Oklahoma State University: Plane Crash

The Incident

On January 27, 2001, a plane carrying ten men affiliated with the Oklahoma State University basketball team crashed shortly after takeoff in a field near Strasburg, Colorado. Those killed included two student athletes, a student manager, a sports information coordinator, an athletic trainer, a basketball staff member, two media personnel, and two pilots. The crash devastated the OSU campus and community.

Agencies and Individuals Involved

At approximately 9:00 P.M. Saturday night when a TV news break reported that only two of three planes had arrived in Stillwater, members of the executive team including the president, athletic director, vice president for business and finance, and public information officer had already converged in the basketball office. Support staff including counseling services staff, the vice president for student affairs, residential life, and campus life staff were checking in and being assigned to residence halls where several of the men lived. The vice president for student affairs and director of counseling arrived at the basketball office to help comfort players and others associated with the basketball program who gathered to grieve and await details of the crash.

Head coach Eddie Sutton began the painful task of calling each family in hopes that family members would learn of the crash from him and not the media. In most cases, this was successful. The media arrived in force. Attempts to protect the grieving players from the glare of cameras required the help of the campus police and staff.

Between 2:00 A.M. and 4:00 A.M. on Sunday morning, the executive team plus the athletic department staff and the director of counseling (who made up the core group) met at an off-campus location to plan next steps. Concerned that the OSU campus was over one thousand miles from the crash site, three individuals were selected to travel later that same day to Colorado to serve as the eyes and ears of the campus and family members. An OSU police officer, university comptroller, and an attorney who worked in the athletic department formed the on-site team. They worked with local rescue and recovery agencies and the NTSB to keep the core group informed. Another critical decision was made to assign a counselor and athletic department staff member to work directly with each family. These individuals were available to each family to answer questions and address needs on a "24/7" basis.

Last, a campus-community memorial service was scheduled to be held Wednesday, January 31, 2001. Initial planning for the memorial service began during that early-morning meeting. Each person around the conference table was given specific tasks, such as choosing the venue, choosing music, making arrangements for family transportation, developing the program, recruiting parking volunteers, handling food, and handling security of dignitaries, among the hundreds of tasks to be performed. The family support representatives would help determine family wishes for the service. Hundreds of volunteers were recruited to help. By 10:00 A.M. Sunday, the director of counseling and the vice president for student affairs were making home visits to the families of the deceased.

The Wednesday memorial was attended by thirteen thousand people. The service represented the culture of the campus and was covered widely in the media. Each family was given a teddy bear to hold and was accompanied by a counselor who had been working with them since Sunday. As family members and the basketball team made their way to the arena floor, the audience rose and remained standing in absolute silence. In the background, *One More Day* by Diamond Rio played on the sound system. Two additional memorials (one in Colorado and another in Gallagher-Iba Arena) would be constructed and dedicated over the next year.

Communication Issues

Communication during the crisis was excellent. Cell phones and call lists made lives easier. The Colorado on-site team checked in regularly and supplied accurate information. Each person assigned a family or task was given the responsibility and authority to act. The greatest communication failure was the inability to connect with every family before news of the crash aired publicly.

Public Relations Issues

All staff were instructed to avoid discussing speculation about the causes of the crash. Campus spokespersons were designated to make statements for the university. Staff was challenged to find an appropriate balance between helping tell the story and protecting grieving family and friends. Media focus may have been heightened because one of the deceased was a prominent Oklahoma media personality as well as "the voice of OSU basketball." Members of the executive team, counselors, and athletic representatives attended family funerals over the next two weeks. The governor and lieutenant governor spoke at the memorial, which required additional security measures.

Implications

During the initial campus-community memorial service, the university president, Dr. James Halligan, made promises to build memorials on the Colorado crash site and at Gallagher-Iba Arena and to educate the children of the deceased at OSU free of charge. This was not scripted, but all promises were kept. Coping with litigation uncertainty and the cost of doing the right thing never superseded the desire to help and care for family and friends. The OSU administration granted exceptions to campus policy in allowing nonstudents full access to counseling services, because the counselors and family members developed close ties. Another campus challenge was the fear of air travel, which affected several athletic teams over the next few months.

Protocol Revision

A task force consisting of the athletic department staff, risk management, the vice president for business and finance, parents of the victims, coaches, student athletes, university purchasing, and flight industry representatives developed a new, comprehensive athletic travel policy for consideration at a national level. In addition, the university began work on a comprehensive emergency plan after the crash, which was designed to comply with a state mandate following 9/11.

Incident Effects

In the days following the crash, the entire campus was depressed. The counseling center made available brochures about grief and loss. Counselors not assigned to families extended themselves to help friends and classmates of the men who were killed. There was very little sleep for the executive team members, athletic department, counselors, and others who had a dual focus: helping family members with any need and preparing for the memorial service. Students prepared black and orange ribbons (our school colors) to be worn at the service. Volunteers were put to work cataloging cards and flowers. During the next few weeks community members cried more, hugged more, and reveled in the minor miracles that happened in their lives daily. Everyone said thank you to each other much more often—and meant it.

Author Notes on the Incident

It is most important to put the needs of survivors above cost accounting. Recognize that you will never be able to change the source of grief and sorrow; all you can hope to do is ease the suffering. Support must be a long-term commitment. It is essential to make immediate and regular contact with grieving family and friends. Build strong campus relationships. Develop call lists before you need them. Stay flexible as needs evolve and change. Encourage staff to foster a make-it-happen attitude. Plan and prepare for the unexpected. Debrief after the incident to ease the stress and grief of staff who were directly involved. Thank people for their extraordinary kindness and professionalism. Be prepared for an outpouring of feelings: cards, flowers, and volunteers wanting to help.

Staff and family members were overwhelmed with the generosity of so many people during the aftermath of the crash. This was especially true of the citizens of Strasburg, Colorado, when the memorial was dedicated there. They took OSU community members under their wing and helped immediately with the healing process.

Questions for Reflection and Discussion

1. What was the role of the campus president in this incident? The athletic director? The various vice presidents? The public information officer? Other support staff?

2. When a plane crashes with students or staff onboard, on university-related business, who, if anyone, should represent the university on-site at the crash scene?

3. The OSU administration sent a police officer, comptroller, and attorney to the crash site. What skills might staff in these positions be able to provide in this type of crisis? Which other administrators might be sent to the site, and why?

4. What were the two most important communication issues involved in this incident, which occurred one thousand miles from campus?

5. Who were the persons affected by this incident? What considerations were made for each group of affected persons?

6. What counseling services were considered after this incident? What counseling services were considered through the first year anniversary of the incident? Beyond?

7. Staff were instructed to avoid speculating on the causes of the crash. Discuss this strategy, both during the time period prior to determination of the causes of a crisis and after the causes are determined.

8. The OSU president's promises during the memorial service to build two memorials and educate the children of the deceased at OSU free of charge was "unscripted." Discuss the potential short- and long-term ramifications of such actions.

9. Discuss the short- and long-term challenges of this statement: "Coping with litigation uncertainty and the cost of doing the right thing never superseded the desire to help and care for family or friends."

10. Discuss the advice offered in the Author Notes on the Incident in this section of the chapter. What other advice would you add?

New York University: Terrorism Strikes the Towers

The Incident

Tuesday, September 11, 2001, began like any beautiful early autumn day in New York, but will be remembered as the most tragic day in contemporary American history. The details of this day have been permanently etched in people's minds and need not be retold. For those staff members on college and university campuses in the New York City region, that day forever changed our definition of a campus crisis.

Working as a new employee in the student affairs division at the largest private university in lower Manhattan provided a significant learning experience. Although the hub of the campus is approximately two miles from the World Trade Center (WTC) location, the institution has residential properties housing approximately sixteen hundred students and faculty members and rented classroom space located within a quarter of a mile from the site of the WTC.

Agencies and Individuals Involved

Prior to the 9/11 attacks, New York University had established a number of crisis command centers that were wired for multiple telephone lines, Internet connections, and computer access in case of an emergency. Within an hour after the first plane hit the towers, the university stakeholders congregated at one command center. This delegation included staff from campus safety, academic affairs, student affairs, public affairs, information technology, budget administration, environmental services, the counseling center, the health center, and auxiliary services.

Communication Issues

Communication was a significant challenge in the local region. Cell phones went off-line as a result of the volume of calls in the system and the damaged towers and infrastructure problems. Mobile radios proved helpful when most telephones were not operational. Whereas other forms of communication proved inconsistent, Web technology functioned throughout the crisis and served as the most effective mechanism for posting information to campus and external constituents such as parents, alumni, and students attending study abroad programs. The university communicated daily updates to the community through the institution's Web site, mass e-mails, and regularly scheduled town hall meetings.

The director of campus safety took a lead role during the crisis because he had a direct connection to the information being provided by the city's police headquarters and other governmental agencies. This allowed the university command center team to make informed responses that suited the needs of the institution. The most immediate concerns included ensuring the safety of all institutional members (faculty, students, and staff). To address this, the institution created numerous assembly areas that provided space for people to rest, receive the latest news, obtain food, get counseling services, and make free telephone calls (the institution's phone system was one of the few systems that remained active and intact throughout the crisis). Although the majority of students stayed in the city, students who lived in the tri-state region left campus to return home.

The greatest challenge was the discovery that over sixteen hundred students were displaced from their residence halls, and that many other students, faculty, and staff members resided in locations that were deemed danger zones. The institution worked diligently to accommodate short-term housing needs by creating a makeshift care shelter at the recreation center. Students were also placed in temporary spaces made available through fall semester no-show and housing cancellation lists. Furthermore, over twelve hundred beds were secured at local hotels for the displaced students. Those students who were unable to return to their residence halls in the downtown region were supplied with free replacement books, school supplies, and loaner laptop computers. The institution also provided cash allotments of $200 to purchase necessary items and offered a university meal plan in an attempt to assist displaced students.

Another challenge facing the university was the necessity for staff and faculty to support students in need while simultaneously handling their own personal concerns related to the tragedy. Many had family members, relatives, and friends who had perished or who were injured as a result of the collapse. In some instances, staff members were relieved of duties to be with their families.

Public Relations Issues

The administration made a concerted effort to follow the mayor's lead in returning the city to a sense of "normalcy" as quickly as possible. The university opened for classes three days after the attack, and within four weeks almost all students had returned to their former residences. The institution's response was well received by parents, faculty, and staff.

After the immediate crisis, the institution's challenge was to communicate to incoming freshmen, transfer, and graduate students that the region was safe from further terrorism. Admissions staff handled endless phone calls with concerns from parents and prospective students, hoping that the applicant pool would not decrease based on the events. Despite the attacks of 9/11, there was no change in the quality or quantity of applications for the following year's admissions process, and there appeared to be little or no impact on the retention of faculty and staff, many of whom see New York City as their home.

University staff mitigated concerns about the air quality from the debris generated by the collapse of the WTC. Unfortunately, one year later a report from the federal government reversed earlier findings and stated that the air quality was in fact a long-term potential danger for people exposed to the air.

Protocol Revision

While there were many written protocols in place prior to these events, the experience of the 9/11 attacks was not something we could have planned for in a protocol manual. Meetings with key stakeholders at designated command centers equipped with appropriate technology at regular intervals each day assisted in making informed decisions.

Implications

Terrorism, like the crisis of 9/11, was not something staff had been trained to handle. So much was unknown about what precautions might be necessary that few institutions planned effective responses. From this experience, the following serve as suggestions for other campuses. Ideally, institutions should have multiple methods of communication in place to share information, such as the Internet, phone banks, two-way radios, crank radios (battery-free radios), campus plasma screens, and prominent message boards. Certain supplies are necessary during a crisis of this magnitude, including first aid kits at all satellite locations across the campus to assist with minor cuts and abrasions; cots for students and staff to sleep on should the crisis not allow people to leave the campus; and an ample supply of water, flashlights, batteries, and granola bars. Staff should be made aware of command center locations, which should be established at various places throughout campus in case one location is inaccessible. Finally, it is important to remember not to "burn out" staff and rotate them during a crisis; fresh minds make better decisions.

Author Notes on the Incident

Based on the terrorist attacks and continued threats against New York City, the institution has engaged in a comprehensive review of all crisis protocols. We have hired an outside consultant to prepare for other potential incidents that might occur in our urban environment. Crises come in all shapes and sizes and we in student affairs need to be ready and prepared, because expecting the unexpected is now a reality in our society.

Questions for Reflection and Discussion

1. What should the campus president's role be in this kind of incident?

2. What were the two most effective means of communication after this incident of such tremendous magnitude?

3. What can other institutions learn from this incident regarding means of communication?

4. What was the institution's greatest communication issue after this incident?

5. What considerations should be made in deciding whether to close all or part of an institution following this kind of incident?

6. What two "lessons learned" from this incident could be transferable to almost any other institution?

7. Educational communities are often known for working to bring together groups with differences (ethnic, religious, philosophical, and so on) while still highlighting their individual diversity. Although the initial efforts surrounding such an event will be immediate crisis/survival management, within a few days various groups may want to hold a rally or protest. What are some considerations and concerns when it comes to such an event? What sort of planning or logistical issues may need to be considered? Under what conditions should such an event be allowed to proceed or be prohibited from proceeding?

8. This author discussed the need to rotate staff to keep them "fresh." What are other staff concerns in a crisis of this duration and how could they be addressed?

9. Crisis planning often involves prior rehearsal with various stakeholders. However, in a large or unexpected crisis, stakeholders may be unavailable or unable to reach a command center for an indeterminate amount of time. Some may even perish in the crisis. How does lack of "rehearsed leaders" affect a crisis such as 9/11? What factors go into deciding how long to wait for designated leaders to arrive at a command center? In the absence of a clear chain of command, how should leaders be determined in a crisis?

10. The 9/11 incident took place in a large city. This gave the university some advantages in dealing with the situation. What are some disadvantages that smaller cities and institutions might face and how might they work to minimize those disadvantages?

University of Arizona College of Nursing: Shooting

The Incident

On the morning of October 28, 2002, Robert Stewart Flores Jr., a nursing student at the University of Arizona, entered the College of Nursing armed with five handguns and more than two hundred rounds of ammunition, shot and killed three of his professors, and then killed himself. Emergency calls came into the University of Arizona Police Department (UAPD) and the Tucson Police Department (TPD) while the shootings were taking place. Both departments dispatched officers immediately.

It became significant to the response that both departments had additional officers on duty because of an early-morning call to handle a disturbance at the McKale Center ticket office. Thousands of students had gathered during the early morning hours for distribution of student basketball tickets and many were trying to be first in line. UAPD officers responded and made an initial assessment that more officers would be needed to disperse the crowd. Officers from UAPD were called to duty from home and TPD officers from throughout the city responded. In addition, TPD called out a mobile field force. The police chiefs of both departments also responded to the disturbance. The crowd was successfully dispersed and all officers involved attended debriefings held by their respective departments.

It was during these debriefings, at 8:37 A.M., that the first frantic call about the shootings was received. Many calls followed to both departments' 911 centers. Information was received that at least two victims were shot and down and that the suspect was moving through the building. All officers at both debriefings responded to the call. A partial description of the suspect was provided while the officers were en route.

UAPD officers arrived on scene within two minutes of the first call and immediately began an extraordinary deployment, during which officers moved rapidly through the building toward the threat. Ten TPD officers arrived on scene at 8:40 A.M. and immediately followed UAPD officers into the building using an extraordinary deployment.

Both departments had trained using the same techniques. However, they had not trained together, which created concerns about the lack of knowledge of consistent training in pairing up officers from both departments. While this deployment was taking place hundreds of people consisting of students, faculty, and staff were fleeing the building. Officers had to scan the crowds for the suspect as they moved into the building toward the fourth floor where the shooting had been reported.

Both chiefs responded to the College of Nursing and established a unified command center between UAPD and TPD at 8:43 A.M. TPD responded with an additional thirty-three officers from the mobile field force for deployment. The UAPD mobile command post was dispatched and set up in a parking lot proximate to the College of Nursing. After the suspect was identified, it was discovered that his vehicle was parked in the same lot as the command post. A positive response by an explosive-detector canine on the suspect vehicle necessitated relocation of the command post.

At 8:52 A.M. a UAPD officer located two victims and the suspect, all dead in a classroom on the fourth floor of the college. At this point it became apparent that this event was going to require far more resources than existed in UAPD. Both chiefs discussed the situation and TPD agreed to take primary control of the incident. At 8:53 A.M. officers reported that there was no active shooting on any floor. However, at 9:31 A.M. officers were told there was a man with a gun in the College of Pharmacy, directly adjacent to the College of Nursing.

Officers were now conducting concurrent searches of the College of Nursing and the College of Pharmacy, which consist of 67,018 square feet in five floors and 74,166 square feet in five floors, respectively. Locked doors, lack of keys, the evacuations, and safe escorts of people found hiding in the buildings created challenges for the SWAT teams conducting the searches. In addition, there was concern that a backpack carried by the suspect, and still in the classroom, might contain explosives, and all necessary precautions were taken. Knowing that it would be critical to the investigation, officers were also trying to contain and account for all the evacuees from both buildings. At 10:23 A.M. a third victim was found dead in her office on the second floor of the College of Nursing. It was later learned that she had been the first person killed.

When the buildings were secured, TPD detectives assisted by UAPD detectives conducted the homicide investigation. In total, over two hundred police officers from various agencies in the area assisted UAPD in the response and investigation of this tragic event. The Tucson Police Department alone provided over one hundred officers and investigators. Also assisting were the Pima County Sheriff's Department SWAT and EOD officers, Arizona Department of Public Safety, Bureau of Alcohol Tobacco and Firearms, Federal Bureau of Investigation, and U.S. Air Force EOD personnel from Davis Monthan Air Force Base in Tucson. The Tucson Fire Department, American Red Cross, and the Pima County Emergency Services also provided invaluable assistance to the responding law enforcement agencies.

Communication Issues

Communications between so many agencies on different radio frequencies created difficulties. However, the establishment of the unified command center helped mitigate the problem. Communication within the university community was difficult at best. Rumors spread quickly as people who had been in the buildings made cell phone calls to friends and family, who in turn called police and university offices. A central point of contact for university information was not established early and an attempt to post information on the UA Web page was unsuccessful when the server went down as a result of extensive "hits" on the site.

The University Medical Center (UMC), a privatized hospital, and the Colleges of Medicine, Pharmacy, and Nursing all share the university's north campus. Communication with UMC administration and their security force was not adequate beyond very basic information. In the absence of information, UMC initiated their lockdown procedure for the hospital.

Public Relations Issues

At the same time that the command post was established, a media staging area was established by the public information officers (PIOs) of UAPD and TPD in a safe, controlled area that still afforded the media a view of the colleges. University News Services joined the law enforcement PIOs at the media staging area and were thus privy to information that was being distributed. The PIOs regularly distributed information cleared by the command post and scheduled regular press conferences by both police chiefs for the more than one hundred media representatives, who gathered within hours. This quickly became a leading national story.

The location and the regular releases and conferences at the media staging area encouraged the media to stay close to the area and virtually eliminated conflicts between tactical units and the media at the scene. As soon as it was determined that there was only one suspect and the scene was secured, the university president joined a press conference with the police chiefs to tell the community that this was an isolated incident that was now under control. His appearance and message provided information to the community that helped calm concerns and played a large role in starting to return the rest of the university to normal operations.

Public safety personnel who responded were familiar with and had practice in incident command. However, the academic and administrative segments of the university were not familiar with this concept at the time of this event. This led to some confusion as to how public safety and university administration would coordinate their efforts to deal with the event and the eventual return to normal operations of the university. The inability, due to staffing needs at the scene, of the UAPD to place someone with the Campus Emergency Response Team (CERT) necessitated that communications between the police chief and the president of the university and CERT take place by phone. While this was effective, having the chief or a senior commander at the same location with CERT would have reduced confusion and facilitated better communication.

Virtually every department of the university responded based on their established protocols and were effective in marshalling resources to assist with issues at the scene and the related issues affecting the rest of the campus. A reception area for evacuees, witnesses, and others affected by these events was quickly established at the alumni building. Resources were made available to assist people who were traumatized by the events and with the emergency evacuation of two colleges and the extended closure of the College of Nursing. A critical incident stress debriefing was conducted for all UAPD personnel involved in the event.

Protocol Revision

Since this event, there has been a commitment by the university administration to educate the rest of the university about the Incident Command System (ICS). The ICS provides an overall structure so that multiple agencies can simultaneously communicate, receive commands, and understand their responsibilities. It began with a presentation to the president and his cabinet and has included presentations to department heads, colleges, building managers, CERT, and other members of the campus community. The university also established and equipped an Emergency Operations Center (EOC) for use in any event in which ICS is employed and that requires the activation of CERT. More extensive formal education about ICS has been conducted for the primary members of CERT.

The UAPD maintained a constant presence at the College of Nursing while it was closed and provided escorted entry to the building by those who fled so quickly that they left behind items such as house and car keys, wallets, and other personal items. Escorted visits also allowed retrieval of items and information necessary for the continuation of the business of the College of Nursing at an alternative site. The college reopened November 4, 2002, with a special ceremony following a memorial service for the three victims.

For months, members of the UAPD, Counseling and Psychological Services (CAPS), Human Resources' Life & Work Connections, and the Dean of Students Office conducted workshops for concerned campus groups and provided extensive assistance to groups and individuals affected by this tragic event. Counselors continued to see people from nursing through 2004. Tolerance for disruptive or threatening behavior on campus was virtually nonexistent, and calls for assistance to offices reached all-time highs. The university consolidated its policies on disruption and threats into two concise policies that were widely distributed and discussed.

Author Notes on the Incident

The success of the entire response was possible because of the relationships, collaborations, and partnerships established between local and federal law enforcement agencies before the need arose. These same conditions existed in the university between key departments. The importance of collaboration cannot be overemphasized in the success of any major event and must be established before the emergency. Only the very largest police departments will have sufficient resources to handle an event such as this and even they will need assistance from other agencies.

Extraordinary deployment works. Students in the classroom after the shooting of two of the two professors later said they could hear officers in the building before the suspect shot himself and believe that the suspect heard them too. This may well have played a part in his decision to shoot himself before seeking out any more victims.

Even if agencies train in the same way, it cannot replace training together to build trust and confidence that they can operate together in a critical situation. UAPD and TPD have since conducted joint training with integrated teams of officers. Other local, county, state, and federal agencies are included in emergency drills conducted on campus.

Communication internally and externally is critically important. The adoption of the ICS and the establishment of an EOC by the university create formalized channels for internal communication by those dealing with the emergency. In times of emergency people first need to know what to expect, what to do about the immediate emergency, and then what to do afterward. Regularly scheduled releases of information and press conferences kept the media informed and through them, the public.

The university identified a need to have one coordinating point for emergency planning and preparedness. This position has been created within the UAPD. This commander will help departments develop their individual emergency plans to support the campus emergency response plan, develop emergency exercises, provide and facilitate training, maintain and update existing plans, and be the university point of contact for all outside emergency response agencies.

People who choose nursing as a career are remarkable people. The night following the shootings, several nursing students walked up to the media command with plates of cookies for the police and fire personnel. Even while they were dealing with their own tragedy they were concerned for the well-being of the public safety personnel.

All the best planning, training, and practices cannot guarantee that an act such as this will be prevented if committed by someone who is not concerned about the personal consequences.

This was a tragic event that immediately galvanized the university and Tucson communities. The overall response and handling of the situation was determined to be good and illustrated that the university was prepared. However, areas for improvement were identified. Although it is hoped such a tragedy will not occur again, the university's commitment and work since October 28, 2002, have created an even greater capacity to respond to any type of emergency situation.

Questions for Reflection and Discussion

1. What was the campus president's role in this incident?

2. What was the most important communication issue during this incident? Following the incident? Why? What types of communications plans and contact lists should be established in case of a crisis like this one?

3. What "lessons learned" from this incident are transferable to almost any other institution?

4. As numerous media arrived on campus, who was responsible for coordinating media services? Was there any difficulty in coordinating media services because of the numerous agencies involved? What were the successes—that is, what went well?

5. What counseling services were made available following the incident? One week later? In the long term? What are some means or resources for determining groups or individuals who might require services but may not reach out for publicized offerings?

6. How important are relationships with outside agencies in planning and training for crises on campus? What type of meetings should be established with these agencies?

7. Although the media can play a large role in assisting with communications to all interested parties, what responsibility does the institution have to provide information to those

affected and involved? By what means can they provide information? What are the tools for rumor control?

8. What tools were needed by the response team—both what they had and did not have at their disposal? How does the answer inform emergency planning (tools equals resources)?

9. This incident highlights the need for and value of a command center. What considerations inform the planning for and success of a functional command center?

10. What role did existing plans and protocols play in the successes and challenges faced in dealing with this incident? How might this type of event provide an opportunity for review and revision of those documents and the campus knowledge of them?

Part IV

Maintaining a Crisis Management Focus

12

Contemporary Issues in Campus Crisis Management

Beth Hellwig-Olson, Merna Jacobsen, and Azfar Mian

Whereas the other chapters in this book examine a range of contemporary crisis management topics, this chapter focuses on four specific types of crises. These four, while not the only ones faced by the modern university campus, warrant further consideration because they represent the changing types of crises present in today's educational landscape. Furthermore, there has been an escalation in either frequency or level of violence of these types of events in recent years. Indeed, in some cases legislative action has been taken at the federal or state level to address such circumstances. Each of these crisis types falls into the intentional-acts-perpetrated-by-humans category described in the crisis matrix discussed in Chapter Two, and for university officials, they provide unique management issues.

The four types of crises explored in this chapter are: (1) disruptive fan behavior and celebratory violence; (2) technological crises as they relate to business continuity and internal security; (3) missing student cases; and (4) acts of terrorism. We will identify the issues unique to each of these crisis types and provide a range of strategies for dealing with them.

Disruptive Fan Behavior and Celebratory Violence

"America doesn't ask a lot of its citizens. We don't have a draft, we have comparatively low taxes, we don't have compulsory voting. But we do have certain rules that you have to follow as a citizen, certain expectations of behavior—and one's passion for a sports team doesn't waive these expectations" (Geraghty, 2005, p. 3).

There is a long history of sport spectator violence, which has been documented since the Roman era. Audiences watching the Roman chariot races engaged in violent behavior that was "unparalleled by even the worst violence today and continued into the fifth and sixth centuries in the Byzantine Empire" (Canter, 1989, p. 104).

Violence among the fans and participants in European football, known in the United States as soccer, can be traced back to fourteenth-century England, when brutal fighting became so violent that Edward III banned the game in 1365. Almost three hundred years later, Oliver Cromwell also banned this sport to maintain order throughout the country (Canter, 1989). History may provide some insights into the behavior we see in contemporary America.

Yet although violence has been associated with athletic events throughout history, the technological sophistication of photography and television makes it a contemporary issue. The whole world can view major sporting events almost instantaneously, where brawls between players, managers, coaches, and fans are often glorified.

The Media

Fans attending professional sporting events in the United States are notorious for poor behavior, jeering at opposing teams, throwing objects onto the field, and being unruly. In recent times, television cameras have captured fans taunting players and players responding by entering the stands to engage in physical fights, with fists flying and chairs and bottles being thrown.

The more intimidating the fans are to the opposition, the more they feel a part of their team's effort to beat opponents. Geraghty (2005) suggests that fans frequently rationalize their behavior (in part owing to a sense of entitlement over paying high prices for tickets) and seem to feel a need to be part of the game, not just spectators.

A potentially deadly combination of alcohol abuse and fans whose behavior goes over the line of acceptable conduct during and after athletic events such as football, basketball, baseball, and hockey is occurring. What began years ago as fans experiencing the joy of witnessing their team's victory and cheering in the stands has evolved to include outrageous behavior on the part of some college students. In an alarming trend, this kind of fan behavior has been seen at a growing number of colleges and universities throughout the United States.

Universities can work with local media representatives on an agreement not to air violent and disruptive behavior on television or show it in print media. They can also partner with professional sporting associations to focus on positive fan behaviors by employing popular sports figures to promote appropriate behavior and to model good sportsmanship.

Alcohol

Students frequently attend activities prior to games, such as tailgate parties, and may drink alcohol there and already be intoxicated when they arrive at the main event. Basketball and football stadiums often seat students together in large sections, which may include over a thousand individuals fueled by intense competition and a desire to help their team. Exacerbating the situation, in many cases the university itself, needing to raise revenues to address expenses incurred, often sells alcohol during sporting events.

All of these factors contribute to a crisis situation. Large crowds, alcohol consumption, and high emotions combine to spark behavior that can turn violent and cause damage to fans, property, athletes, and law enforcement personnel.

A variety of ideas can be solicited from different constituencies on campus and adopted to deal with the issue of alcohol abuse at university events. A thorough discussion of university policies on disruptive fans should occur annually to identify and evaluate promising suggestions.

One policy that has proven successful as a deterrent to inappropriate behavior is to take the privilege of attending a number of future sporting events away from intoxicated students and other disruptive fans. Most students will do what it takes if they understand that they can lose the privilege. This policy and others need to be put in writing and included in the university student handbook.

Event managers should also hire and train staff to prevent intoxicated individuals from entering large events and identify alcohol concealed in purses, blankets, and elsewhere if alcohol abuse has proven to be a problem. A uniformed security force or crowd management team can also be helpful at some events and needs to be highly visible to spectators as they arrive at the event venue. It is important for the staff to be courteous and friendly, but to assert their authority when needed. Undercover agents stationed throughout the venue can also help identify underage drinkers.

Universities can also work collaboratively with the liquor control board in their area to monitor underage drinking and identify strategies to deter abusive alcohol-related behavior. It is important to critically examine alcohol sales and set consumption limits during events. These ideas need to be evaluated by each university with its own special circumstances in mind before being put into place.

Poor Sportsmanship

A number of college fans plan ahead and design customized T-shirts to wear to the game that insult opponents. Athletes may be targeted with crude chanting planned to embarrass and distract them throughout the game (Snider, 2004). Even mascots and pep bands may participate in unbecoming behavior.

Fans have been known to "salute rival players who have been caught at some malefaction, hurl women's underwear, aspirin, pizza boxes," and other items onto the court or field, according to Deford (as cited in Geraghty, 2005). Countless athletes are verbally assaulted throughout their careers. It is not unusual to witness a dead animal, representing the mascot of the opposing team, being thrown onto the ice at hockey games.

More in-depth research is needed to understand the causes of aggressive fan behavior in the United States. Studies conducted on hooliganism and soccer in Britain (Coakley & Donnelly, 2004) and lessons in crowd management may be learned from those in Europe who have dealt with this issue for many years.

Many preventative strategies are currently being used at universities throughout the United States that can prove helpful in dealing with poor sportsmanship on other campuses. The NCAA makes several excellent recommendations. An important first step is to convene a meeting of invested individuals, including the athletic department, campus security, student life, and students, as well as community police departments, referees, athletes, and neighbors, to discuss ideas for preventing and responding to both disruptive fan behavior and celebratory violence (covered in the next section).

It is also critical to meet with individuals from student governing groups, such as the residence hall association, council of athletes, Greek councils, and associated student organizations, to draft a student code of conduct outlining expectations of fans during and after athletic events, thus gaining buy-in to the policies. The university president or vice president for student life should be asked to write to students before they arrive in the fall, establishing clear expectations for appropriate fan behavior and consequences for inappropriate behavior.

Another important group that can help set a positive tone at sporting events is the pep band. It is essential to engage the pep band director and student leaders to discuss how the choice of songs played during games can add to antagonism. Inappropriate songs designed to incite the crowd to chant profanity at the opposing fans and team should be eliminated from the band's repertoire.

A number of schools play high-quality commercials before sporting events and during the game to promote sportsmanship by team members, coaching staff, and fans. Popular athletes, coaches, faculty members, and student leaders are often highlighted in these commercials. The NCAA has created a short video clip that can be used as this kind of commercial. Regulations for developing a university's own commercials may be in place depending on the athletic conference in which the school is a member. As an example, some conferences may not allow coaches to appear in commercials. These regulations should be researched with the NCAA before commercials are developed.

It is also critical to develop a positive working relationship with the cheerleading squad and student spirit club in order to tone down inappropriate cheers and to guide them in what cheers may and may not be used during the games. Having this kind of relationship may prove to be the key factor when some fans get out of control. Some schools with religious affiliations ask the crowd to join in a prayer prior to the athletic event, and this helps set a respectful tone from the beginning.

Although many schools create student-only sections, others ask that student leaders, faculty, staff, and administrators be visible by having them sit among the crowd. This helps defuse and control the behavior of the group. Again, a good working relationship between the spirit club leadership and university administrators is key. Self-policing by responsible students can also be instrumental in maintaining a positive student section. Section leaders at many schools have also been helpful; they address unruly behavior among their peers and can help minimize the use of security or crowd management officials in confronting students. This model can be particularly effective and is seen as a positive use of student empowerment.

A practice that has gained popularity at some schools is to provide "cool" T-shirts to exchange with students who arrive wearing offensive shirts. It is important to enforce a no-tolerance policy for clothing and signs that present demeaning messages. Offensive signs should be removed immediately, as soon as they are observed. A practice at some schools is to create an agreement that all ticketholders must sign prior to the season; this agreement outlines behavioral expectations of fans. Some schools also publish these expectations on their athletic department Web sites.

Celebratory Violence

When fans are disruptive during the game it is usually a strong signal that there will be behavioral problems afterward. Crowds in the past have occasionally rushed the field after a football game and torn down goalposts, or run onto the basketball court to celebrate a team victory. This behavior still takes place, potentially injuring bystanders, athletes, and law enforcement officers as a result of the sheer numbers of individuals pushing forward. The practice of "piling on" can have devastating results if several people land on one individual; severe injuries can be sustained.

Property damage on campus and in the community is also occurring with increased frequency (McCarthy, Martin, McPhail, & Cress, 2002) as violence erupts between fans of opposing teams. The ultimate tragedy—two student deaths—occurred in 2004 after the Boston Red Sox beat the New York Yankees in the last game of the World Series and following a Super Bowl victory for the New England Patriots.

Celebratory violence has erupted throughout the United States over the last decade in a wide array of states, such as West Virginia, Colorado, Minnesota, Indiana, South Carolina, Connecticut, Illinois, Hawaii, Maryland, Ohio, Massachusetts, and Washington, to name a few (NCAA, 2003). There have been literally millions of dollars in property damage as a result of riots, primarily from fires being set and cars being overturned, and the cost of paying firefighters and overtime for police officers.

Carr (2005, p. 10) clarifies: "The distinction between celebratory and other forms of violence is that celebratory violence is recreational and expressive." This does not mean that celebratory violence has any less an impact on those who are caught in the chaos.

Even if a school is not a Division I athletic powerhouse, events that transpire miles away in another county still may have a profound effect on a community—as was seen in Greeley, Colorado, after the Denver Broncos won their first and second National Football League Super Bowl victories in 1997 and 1998. Greeley was home to the Broncos' summer training camp. In their excitement over the long-awaited wins, students, along with thousands of other fans in college towns throughout Colorado, ran outside to celebrate. Students lit numerous bonfires in the streets, fueled with couches, chairs—anything they could find that would burn. Some climbed up light poles. Alcohol was consumed throughout the day and many individuals continued to drink after the game. Students tried to leap over the fires, yelled and screamed, and some started fights. University and community officials in some cases had not foreseen the behavior that erupted after the first incident. Police departments in these communities scrambled the first year to control the outbreaks with the assistance of other police departments from surrounding areas, and together with university officials, anticipated a similar response after the second Super Bowl victory. Many arrests were made throughout Colorado both years, and there were severe sanctions at the universities for those students found responsible for breaking university policies and local laws.

A number of strategies can be implemented to provide some relief from destructive celebratory violence. It makes sense to start with a new student orientation to provide the opportunity for coaching staff and athletes to speak to incoming students and set a civil tone for behavior at athletic events.

Those who plan events need to include in the game management plan enough staff or volunteers to deter students from running onto the court or field after the event. Announcements can be made before the event begins to make it clear fans are not allowed onto the playing field or court. Consequences for such behavior should also be clearly stated and enforced.

Policies can place students on interim suspension if found to be involved in rioting or other inappropriate behavior. Videos can be instrumental in identifying violations when large crowds are involved in the destruction of property and violent activity.

A proactive approach to deter celebratory violence is to work with various clubs and organizations on campus to provide late-night programming events as well as more athletic events and festivals during daytime hours, rather than in the evening.

Finally, it is important to explore the latest technology advances in finding goalposts that can easily collapse and be put away after football games. Such technology has the capability of saving lives or preventing serious injury.

Legislation and Reports on Celebratory Violence

After the brawls in Colorado, the General Assembly passed a bill on June 3, 2002, specifically to deal with college students enrolled in state-supported institutions who could be proven to have participated in riots. The bill outlines mandatory suspension from school for a designated period of time. This legislation came about after frustration over the number of incidents of violent fan behavior throughout the state's institutions of higher education. The full text of the bill can be read at http://www.state.co.us/gov_dir/leg_dir/olls/sl2002a/sl.290.htm.

A major crisis occurred when the University of Michigan faced Ohio State University in a 2002 football game in Columbus, Ohio. What followed the game stunned the university and the city, where "the scale and level of destruction" far exceeded past disturbances involving student unrest, which had occurred as far back as the 1950s (Andrews & Buettner, 2003, p. 6).

According to an article in GQ *Magazine* ("GQ Names the Top Ten Worst College Sports Fans," 2005, n.p.), the riot included "more than one hundred fires, including a nine-car victory pyre and cost the city of Columbus over $135,000 in police overtime." Students and nonstudents alike were involved in the destruction. The mayor of Columbus and the president of Ohio State University were compelled to form a task force to investigate the causes of the violent behavior and propose methods to deal with problems that might arise in coming years. The Ohio State University Task Force on Preventing Celebratory Riots wrote a final comprehensive report that defined terms, identified strategies for dealing with future riots, and included results of a national survey the team had initiated and theories on the cause of the disruptive behavior (Andrews & Buettner, 2003). The members of the task force interviewed students and conducted a number of focus groups to gather information to help understand what had occurred.

The task force members broke into smaller subcommittees to research the issues and found little data on the subject of celebration riots. According to the report, there is a "perceived increase in disrespectful, inappropriate, and uncivil behavior among students and other young adults." The report goes on to speculate that four areas might be linked to celebration riots: "alcohol consumption that includes high-risk and binge drinking; the role of the community, culture and the media; the nature of young adult risk taking; and effective celebration management" (Andrews & Buettner, 2003, p. 7).

Similar events have erupted throughout the United States, creating havoc for town officials, neighbors, university officials, and other students who watch with disapproval. Newman (2004) describes comparable behavior in a different region of the country after the University of Connecticut's men's national basketball championship game.

A number of elements that are common in celebratory violence across the United States were identified by the Ohio task force (Andrews & Buettner, 2003):

> A large group typically gathers for an official activity that might include a variety of celebrations such as festivals, holiday events, or sports. Mass alcohol use is observed.

Police are called in to bring about order and are generally met with a lack of respect. Sporadic disruptions begin to escalate and eventually violence and destructive behavior occurs. Sizeable numbers of individuals, the majority [of whom] are white and young, turn out. Interestingly, many participants in the violence are not students but join the college crowds in the chaotic behavior. [p. 2]

General Strategies to Deter Fan Violence

It is imperative that universities develop strategies to offer students alternatives and to modify negative behavior.

Categorize with the Crisis Matrix

The crisis matrix introduced in Chapter Two of this volume can help college administrators analyze celebratory violence and disruptive fan behavior and break the crisis down into meaningful elements:

- The level of the crisis is *critical incident*.

- The type of crisis is *one created by humans*.

- The crisis is *intentional*, because it is created by the instigators. However, there are also individuals who get caught in the middle of the violence, not realizing what others might do to engage in destructive behavior.

Plan Ahead

Some steps to take are as follows:

1. *Provide organized activities and events throughout the day of the main event that are designed to engage students in positive behavior.* Student union and residence hall viewing parties with food and other activities can offer students the chance to enjoy camaraderie and a sense of community.

2. *Plan late-night events that are exciting, safe, and fun.*

3. *Communicate with law enforcement officials to create a unified approach to celebratory violence.*

4. *Plan to have a strong police presence to serve as a visible deterrent for illegal activities.* The presence of uniformed officers can prove invaluable during large events.

5. *Photograph large gatherings that might have the potential to erupt in violence.* This practice may discourage students from engaging in inappropriate behavior, and documentation can assist in the case of judicial proceedings.

Do the Research

A Sportsmanship and Fan Behavior Summit was held in 2003, where representatives from higher education and intercollegiate athletics convened to "examine issues related to fan violence, raise awareness, and initiate national communication" as well as identify best practices that could be compiled into a report that would be easily accessed on the NCAA national office Web site and available to download (NCAA, 2003). The NCAA has developed resources to help college administrators deal with disruptive fan behavior and celebratory violence, including a video clip that can be shown prior to athletic events, as described earlier.

It is imperative that the student affairs professional confronted with disruptive fan behavior and celebration violence learn about the nature of this phenomenon, be prepared for it, and take preventive measures to curb it. Hong (2002, p. 12) suggests that a public health approach to campus violence prevention encourages administrators, faculty, and staff to collaborate "with the local community [and] modify those campus and community policies, practices, infrastructure and culture which promote violence and tolerance for it." University health administrators are calling for an organized response to reduce violence resulting in injury and death to college students.

Develop a Concrete Plan of Action

More proactive steps that university administrators can take to confront fan aggression are as follows:

1. *Create a "bystander policy" that encourages students to report behavior that infringes on the rights and safety of community members.* Offer anonymity to the student sharing information "when possible" (Epstein, 2002, p. 118).

2. *Engage students in their neighborhoods, creating a sense of pride in their surroundings.* Plan a series of opening week events where neighbors and students can meet and interact with one another.

3. *Encourage student government representatives to participate in the surrounding neighborhood councils, thus offering opportunities to hear from neighbors about student behavior.*

4. *Work with state representatives to create legislation designed to discourage individuals from participating in riots.*

5. *Use police surveillance tapes to analyze and identify students who engage in illegal and inappropriate acts.*

6. *Be careful in placing opposing team supporters in the event facility.* Analyze for possible aggression among fans.

7. *Work with student leaders to identify effective strategies to combat celebratory violence.* This was the case at the University of Maryland, where a student task force was created to recommend voluntary compliance (Snider, 2004).

Many additional suggestions can be found in the full Ohio State University Task Force report (Andrews & Buettner, 2003; see http://hec.osu.edu/taskforce/FinalReport.pdf) and in the *Report on the Sportsmanship and Fan Behavior Summit* (NCAA, 2003).

Summary

We Americans have great enthusiasm, a love of sports, and a competitive spirit, all of which are reflected in the attitudes of many college-age individuals. Collegiate traditions can be very positive and help build a true sense of belonging. However, when those traditions become injurious to others either physically or psychologically, college administrators together with athletic department colleagues, law enforcement, and city officials need to plan ahead and design realistic responses.

Disruptive fan behavior and celebratory violence must be addressed proactively and dealt with through a united effort that crosses territorial lines. Resources are available to help colleges and universities plan. Colleges and universities must have the will to create a concrete plan of action.

Technology, Business Continuity, and Internal Security

The first section of this chapter explored a type of crisis type that has deep historical roots. This section delves into a relatively recent development: potential threats associated with technology, which are emerging as quickly as the new technologies themselves. Technological crises affect both internal security and business continuity.

Data security and disaster recovery are becoming increasingly important in our global economy. Higher education institutions are recognizing how much they rely on their technology services, such as data storage, communication processes, and network systems. These days, there is much less emphasis on the traditional paper processes. Instructors and institutions are embracing Web-based course management for grade record keeping, assigning homework, posting resources, and encouraging out-of-class communication. Research data and findings are stored on the campus network, which is accessible from anywhere.

Business Continuity Plans

Universities have had to reevaluate the techniques they use to maintain business continuity during crises. Unanticipated events such as blackouts, thunderstorms, hurricanes, fires, earthquakes, system hacking, and even terrorist attacks can lead to significant losses. University executives are thus being held accountable for developing business continuity plans to deploy in such moments of crisis.

What is business continuity? According to a 2004 Sun Microsystems communication, it is "simply the uninterrupted provision of operations and services to customers, united with continuous accountability for key decisions. It requires more than just data preservation and restoration of data systems." A business continuity plan explains how to resume business operations across the institution in case of a crisis. Plan preparers must be detailed, thorough, and able to foresee potential risks. The plan should cover all technical and nontechnical areas of the university business operations, including a communication plan, data storage, data recovery, system applications, network access, institutional processes, and human resources. Once the plan is in place, it should be readily accessible and tested annually.

Franz (2003) points out some of the difficulties of crisis recovery planning in university settings: universities have decentralized computing services, the number of technological systems continues to increase, universities have limited resources with which to respond to less likely events, there is limited publication on industry standards as they relate to educational institutions, and finally, crisis preparedness is low on universities' planning list compared to competing needs.

The primary reason for developing a business continuity plan is to answer the following question: Is the university technologically prepared to outlive a crisis or will it become a target?

Before a crisis occurs, the institution needs to develop a secure and robust infrastructure. After the event, the institution needs to recover immediately. The focus needs to be on restoration or replacement, depending on the situation. A business continuity plan will help the university accomplish these objectives because it includes a trustworthy backup and restoration system.

Regardless of the size of the university, the costs and impact of downtime can be significant. Absence of services for an extended period of time has consequences. There can be long-term damage in the form of a delay in the delivery of services, lowered customer satisfaction, and perhaps most significant, a negative impact on the university's reputation and image. A substantial business continuity plan is always a worthwhile investment.

Creating the Plan

The first step in creating a business continuity plan is to thoroughly assess the services the university system offers and the needs they cater to. Staff should evaluate the impact that an unexpected event can have on these services. The assessment must consider all types of possible crises. Staff should be sure to include some noncatastrophic occurrences, such as the loss of important data or release of confidential information.

Organizations must prepare for some possibilities regardless of their geographic location. If an institution is in an area that is prone to such drastic weather conditions as floods, hurricanes, earthquakes, blizzards, and so on, then these are important threats to prepare for. But nonenvironmental factors, though not predictable, should be considered as well. There may be power outages, corruption of data, software failures due to viruses and worms, equipment failure, or attacks by hackers, as already noted.

Planners should assess the duration of downtime, costs, and potential forms of liability. Some downtime is unavoidable and should be anticipated. The most important responsibility of stakeholders and decision makers is to make arrangements to minimize the downtime, thus minimizing the costs to the institution. Assessments should evaluate the length of time that systems may be nonfunctional, the financial consequences, and legal ramifications. This information is critical in designing a business continuity plan that promises successful system restoration within a clearly defined response time.

Maintaining the Plan

To maintain a successful plan it is important to regularly monitor changes and update relevant inventories to ensure accurate system records, functions, backups, and plans. Having this updated information readily available will help reduce recovery time. It may be a good idea to use external support services for data storage, such as alternate local and off-site backup venues. Having a third-party storage facility located outside the affected region offers an additional guarantee of data safety. In a large-scale disaster, for instance, backup storage in the same geographical area, city, or physical structure could mean immediate loss of all pertinent information in one clean sweep. Planning for the worst-case scenario ensures coverage for all types of recovery concerns.

IT continuity. The plan needs to take two kinds of continuity into account. First is IT continuity, second is business continuity. Both are critical elements of the business operation and they require different approaches to resolve. The most important applications should be brought online as soon as possible; the remaining information can become available later. Staff should arrange for vital physical functions to be restored promptly. The plan should identify which information is valued and relevant.

In an emergency the response must be quick in order to minimize downtime and associated costs. University systems must be running within hours of plan activation. Yet restoring normalcy on campus may take several days depending on the university's preparedness and the magnitude of the crisis. Insurance coverage pays for loss of physical resources and damage. Good planning helps normal university business resume in the shortest time.

It is critical to have regular backups so that the data restored after the disaster is the latest version and available for all systems. Testing backup recovery in a tabletop exercise is the only way to know for sure that the data recovery will work as intended. Universities can benefit if central IT manages and plans for the whole institution rather than for individual departments. All systems, procedures, and personnel are tested when a university is trying to overcome a disaster. Annual testing, such as tabletop exercises, should be conducted to check that the solutions are practical and realistic during a real crisis.

As noted previously, it is also a good idea to arrange for an off-site data storage facility, a stable network, and regular data backup procedures. This will help speed the data restoration process.

Essential university staff should be aware of their roles. Staff who will be expected to respond in the event of a crisis must be familiar with the plan so they can respond promptly when the need arises. The plan does not need to be available to all staff, but first responders should have access to it.

Business continuity. There are really no alternatives to actual hands-on testing of a business continuity plan. Tabletop exercises should be realistic and performed on an annual basis. The goal of the exercises should be to evaluate how staff performs and find loopholes in the plan. Changing the scenarios during the exercises can help staff learn to adapt their approach as the crisis continues. Changes should be relevant to realistic changes in circumstances during a particular kind of crisis. As the testing proceeds, tasks should be shuffled among responding staff to ensure that several people are familiar with the responsibilities of that particular role, because there is no assurance that all the right people will be available at the time of the event.

Internal Security

Data security is another important consideration; the goal is to prevent unauthorized individuals from gaining access to or destroying data. Universities need to consider a data storage strategy that combines all data centers into a single virtual data center, which will help in restoring data immediately.

When it comes to internal security, universities should consider three factors: threats, vulnerabilities, and controls. *Threats* are events that can have a negative impact on a university, such as fires, environmental disasters, security breaches, and computer viruses. *Vulnerabilities* are the areas where a threat can appear. For example, if there is no firewall, a network is vulnerable to attack, such as from a virus or a hack. *Controls* are the measures taken to protect vulnerabilities from the threats they face. These measures foresee, discourage, and avoid or address potential threats.

Universities still find themselves affected by virtual security breaches despite all the investments that they are making in data and network security. The primary reason seems to be the minimal attention paid to establishing a secure network. Most of the focus has been on perimeter defenses, such as firewalls, authentication services, intrusion detection, and antivirus scanners. The mission, however, needs to be to protect the computing hardware resources on the internal university network.

Most of the weaknesses in internal network security are what may be called *application layer weaknesses*. These vulnerabilities avoid the perimeter controls and also the controls in the internal network. A few years ago, there were fewer network connections into universities. Drastic reduction in prices for hardware and computer technologies has contributed many more actual and potential paths into the university's network. Examples of these are virtual private networks technology, wireless local area networks, and handheld devices. Worms and viruses can enter the network from either a mobile user coming into the university after being away with an infected machine, simply through opening e-mail, or by visiting an external Web site. All provide an avenue into the university's network. To ward off these threats additional perimeters that are closer to the individual assets being protected are needed. Also, access control should be enforced for all inbound and outbound network access.

Bouchard (2005) asserts that a mixture of many different controls are needed to secure internal networks. He divides these controls into three categories: fundamental, intermediate, and emerging.

- *Fundamental controls*. These include physical security, user awareness, and antivirus scanners.

- *Intermediate controls*. A step up from fundamental controls, these include using routers, switches, and virtual local area networks and firewall hardware resources that require different levels of security; giving users access to what they need rather than giving access to everything; if financially feasible, monitoring suspicious activity through intrusion detection systems.

- *Emerging controls*. These include paying close attention to user rights and privileges as their positions and status in the university changes; having firewall capabilities at individual computers; establishing user names and passwords requiring digital certificates; domain structuring to identify and establish a physical separation between resources and within each collection of resources.

Summary

Business continuity must be addressed on an ongoing basis. Investing in a business continuity plan makes good sense. Universities cannot afford to be caught unprepared because they can face disruption of infrastructure, processes, IT systems, and the ability to continue operations. Surviving a crisis depends on the creation of a solid business continuity plan and the ability to carry it out. Because application layer attacks and virus attacks are increasing, perimeter defenses need to be supported by internal security measures. Universities can benefit from using products that are successful at dealing with the unique challenges of internal security.

Missing Students

The previous section of this chapter demonstrated how technological crises can affect an entire campus. This section explores a type of crisis that, although it revolves around a single individual, also has far-reaching implications: a missing student. When a student goes missing, a number of critical leadership decisions may be required; also, the campus will get involved with external agencies and stakeholders playing significant roles in the crisis. Here is an example.

> On March 2, 1998, we received a telephone call that changed our lives forever. We were informed that our daughter, Suzanne, was missing from the State University of New York at Albany. Our reaction was one of disbelief and shock, leaving us confused and unable to think clearly. We know our daughter well and we were positive that she had not run away. Reluctantly, we faced the realization that we would not wake from this "bad dream." Life would not return to normal. We began to accept the unthinkable, that harm had come to her. [Lyall & Lyall, n.d., n.p.]

Douglas and Mary Lyall's heartbreaking journey to discover what happened to their daughter, missing college student Suzanne Lyall, would prompt more than an investigation into her disappearance. The Lyalls would discover the complexities of handling missing college student cases, illuminate the shortcomings of both higher education and law enforcement agencies in responding to such crises, and initiate legislative action that has changed the way missing college student cases are addressed.

Suzanne Lyall's story is not the only one to be told. In 2004, the *National On-Campus Report* identified several cases that prompted

states and institutions to create and implement plans for responding to such crises:

- Ohio State University student Chris Gerspache was
  reported missing by his parents in 2002 after he did not
  return home for winter break.

- Indiana University student Jill Behran was last seen in
  May 2000. She was reported missing after she did not
  show up for work at the campus recreation center.

- Ohio University student Keith Noble was reported
  missing in April 1998. He was last seen attending
  a party.

- North Carolina State University student Kristen
  Modaferri spent summer 1997 at the University of
  California-Berkeley taking summer classes. She left cam-
  pus to go to a job at a coffee shop and was not seen again.

- In May 1996, Kristin Smart went missing after walking
  home from a party at California Polytechnic State University. Local police were not called into the case until
  she had been missing a month. ["Improving Our
  Response," 2004, p. 4]

According to the National Crime Center, nearly one hundred
thousand people are missing in America at any given time. Of these,
nearly thirty-five hundred are between the ages of twenty-two and
twenty-nine ("Improving Our Response," 2004). Some are enrolled
college students. While many cases are resolved quickly, response
to missing student cases has been inadequate. As the Lyalls discovered, reports of missing students have not historically been viewed
as serious. And even with the cooperation and support of campus
police, response efforts are hindered by inherent system barriers.
Jurisdiction issues between campus and local police and ineffective

working agreements between these entities can cause costly delays in response time. Poorly defined protocol and inexperienced law enforcement agencies further complicate the issue. Poorly defined processes for handling the media hinder efforts. Uncoordinated efforts between university departments prevent parents and others from getting the advice, counsel, and referral support they need (Lyall & Lyall, n.d., n.p.).

Taking Action

In response to the Suzanne Lyall case, New York enacted the New York State Campus Safety Act of 1999. The act focuses on eliminating the historical waiting period to launch an investigation into the disappearance of a college student, as well as accelerating access to missing person information. "The law requires all public, private, community colleges, and universities in New York State to have formal plans that provide for the investigation of missing students. It also expands the responsibilities of the New York State Division of Criminal Justice Services' Missing and Exploited Children Clearinghouse to provide assistance with the dissemination of information regarding missing college students" (Lyall & Lyall, n.d., n.p.). In 2002, then-Governor George Pataki announced the distribution of a guide entitled *Missing College Student Cases: An Investigative Guide* (2002). The guide, which was designed to assist New York institutions of higher education in meeting the requirements of the New York Campus Safety Act, offers an action response plan for institutions of higher education to follow when a student is reported missing. It was the first guide of its kind in the nation to focus on missing college students. It stresses close collaboration between university officials, law enforcement agencies, and the child's family. "The plan includes techniques for gathering information and making assessments about a missing student; critical information to relay to law enforcement; how to disseminate information quickly to the community; how to work with the media; as well as how to liaison with a victim's family. The guide also stresses the importance of immediate coordination of efforts and information sharing between all law enforcement agencies in the vicinity of a disappearance" (*Missing College Student Cases*, 2002, n.p.).

The Lyall case was also the driving force behind federal action. In 2003, President Bush signed Suzanne's Law, which is now part of the Amber Alert system. It requires law enforcement to notify the National Crime Information Center immediately when someone between the ages of eighteen and twenty-one is reported missing rather than waiting twenty-four hours, as is the historic practice in cases when the missing person is eighteen or older ("Improving Our Response," 2004, p. 4).

The work of the Lyall family, coupled with legislative action in New York and at the federal level, has brought focus to a contemporary area of crisis management that has historically been plagued with ambiguity. In light of these recent developments, universities are reviewing their practices regarding missing students.

Defining the Institution's Role, Scope, and Responsibilities

A missing student crisis presents an interesting initial question: Who owns the crisis? (L. Elsinga, personal communication, March 3, 2004). Defining the crisis as a college, rather than a law enforcement, issue is a long-standing criticism of the response to these cases ("An Adequate Response," 2004). Framing the situation as a campus crisis has resulted in delayed response, uncoordinated efforts, and failure to understand the serious nature of the situation, critics say. Recent legislation more clearly defines the roles and responsibilities of on-campus and external law enforcement agencies that assume the lead in handling the investigation. However, this does not mean that the institution has no role. The first, and perhaps most important decision institutional leadership makes, is a symbolic one. By choosing to "own" the crisis, the university conveys goodwill and openness, both essential to communicating that it is doing the right thing. In a more practical sense, assuming a role in the crisis allows the institution to have a bearing on information about the school, the student involved, and the strategies used to address the situation. One factor affecting this decision is the residential status of the missing student. However, even when the missing student resided off campus, the institution has a clear role to play (L. Elsinga, personal communication, March 3, 2004).

The institution can define its role, scope, and responsibilities by doing the following:

1. *Identify the nature and needs of the myriad groups who will come to campus as a result of the crisis.* Media, law enforcement, immediate and extended family members, close friends of the missing student, and community volunteers are among those who will need tending to. The resources these groups require include personnel, facilities, and information. Each group should be assigned university personnel who have the knowledge, expertise, and authority to interact appropriately with them. For example, family and friends of the missing student may benefit from access to counselors. The media may begin a probe into campus security. Campus and community members may want to hold vigils or other events. Thoughtful planning for interactions with entities the institution does not regularly interact with will establish positive working partnerships and prevent combative relationships.

2. *Define and communicate to staff and external entities the roles and responsibilities of all involved.* Not interfering with law enforcement is essential to successful management of the crisis. Clearly identifying what role the institution will play is critical.

Dealing with Institutional Privacy Policies

Although institutions of higher education continuously balance students' constitutional rights to privacy with safety issues, a missing person case will challenge institutional practices as no other situation can. Law enforcement agencies, the student's family, and the media may seek access to information about the student's life not normally granted by the institution. They may want access to the student's residence hall room, disciplinary files, personal computer, and academic, attendance, counseling, and health records. Requests from investigative agencies about friends and acquaintances of the missing student will present yet another dilemma for the institution. If these individuals are also enrolled students, their rights to privacy are also at stake. Violations involving the student's family as well as those associated with him or her are possible when there is probing into the student's life. Scrutiny and speculation about the student, as well as his or her experience while in school, may become a focus for both law enforcement and the media. A common fallout of a missing student case is questioning by the media and others about campus safety and security, including the campus's reporting of crime statistics. The university can take several key steps:

1. *Educate key university officials and staff on laws and policies governing protection of privacy.* Foremost among these are the Family Education Rights and Privacy Act (FERPA) and the Health Information Portability and Accountability Act (HIPAA). Staff should have a working knowledge of these legislative acts, their implications during a campus crisis, possible exceptions in a missing student case, and the consequences for violating the laws. It is not only the senior-level administrators who should be knowledgeable of FERPA and HIPAA but also entry and midlevel professionals who have substantive direct contact with students: residence life and housing staff (resident advisers, hall directors, and area coordinators), student organization advisers, and coordinators of student services programs.

2. *Coordinate with campus public relations officers.* A high-profile missing student case is likely to bring an onslaught of local and national media attention. Well-defined communication plans and policies can replace rumors with accurate information and communicate the desired message of the institution.

3. *Include issues related to privacy laws in campus crisis response planning and drills.* Common understanding across campus about specific issues related to privacy laws (for example, identification of parties who have an "educational interest" and right to know, student information that can be shared, who in the institution is permitted to speak to outside parties) can prevent blunders. Discussions about the institution's obligation to the missing students' circle of friends and acquaintances should be part of the rehearsal process. Internal memoranda that address various scenarios (if the missing student lives in a residence hall or off campus, is a member of a Greek organization, and so on) can help delineate staff roles.

Managing Volunteers

If foul play or imminent danger is suspected in a missing person case, the early stage of the crisis most often involves comprehensive search efforts, perhaps with hundreds of volunteers. While law enforcement agencies direct volunteer efforts, the institution can play important secondary roles, offering hospitality functions (food, housing), coordinating schedules, providing facilities for meetings and gatherings, disseminating information, and managing difficult or inappropriate volunteer behavior or volunteers (such as psychics claiming to have information about the missing person and demanding access to the family). One of the compounding factors associated with the management of volunteers is concern for their safety, because they may be traversing treacherous terrain or working in adverse weather conditions. When university staff and students are among the volunteers, yet another layer of concern is added (L. Elsinga, personal communication, March 3, 2004). Here are some steps to take:

1. *Allow experts to oversee volunteer operations.*

2. *Match volunteers to tasks for which they are best suited.* Volunteers with specialized skill or knowledge should be identified

and placed in appropriate roles. They may be counselors, facility coordinators, or information technology personnel. Consideration should be given to volunteers with physical or other limitations.

3. *Monitor staff activity to prevent burnout and undo stress.* It is not uncommon for staff to dedicate long, emotionally draining hours when a student goes missing. Appropriate briefings and debriefings, recognition of efforts, and clearly defined work hours and roles can help alleviate the potential for burnout.

Coordinating with External Agencies

Cooperation with external agencies is essential to avoid confusion and allow for quick response. The desire is to have clearly defined partnerships that allow all involved to meet their needs. Two strategies are important in addressing this issue:

1. *Be knowledgeable of the understandings and protocol that exist between local, state, and federal law enforcement agencies.* Formal memoranda that delineate such information are typically in place between these agencies.

2. *Plan for the effect of having external agencies on campus.* Local and national media and law enforcement agencies can change the nature of campus life for students and staff. If designated meeting areas, a regular schedule of meetings, and guidelines for appropriate interactions are established, it can provide some degree of normalcy in what otherwise can become a chaotic milieu without boundaries (L. Elsinga, personal communication, March 3, 2004).

Managing a Potentially Lengthy Waiting Period

Unlike a crisis that comes on quickly and moves quickly to resolution, in missing student cases the period of time before resolution may be prolonged. This presents several unique issues for university administrators. Speculation and rumor about what could have happened keeps the crisis alive in an uneasy state. It can be difficult to determine when and how to move on while still dedicating resources and maintaining relationships. Memorials for a missing student may occur long after the student's peer group has graduated. The ultimate resolution of the case may renew emotions and media attention. The nature of the case—abduction, murder, self-determination, or the rare occurrence of a staged disappearance—can have a bearing on the decisions made by institutional leadership. Here are some strategies:

1. *Prepare for ongoing public coverage and investigations into the safety of the other college students.* If the missing student lived on campus this scrutiny will be intensified. It is important to demonstrate due diligence in the review and improvement of campus safety precautions in the aftermath of a missing student case.

2. *Prepare for anniversary events.* Weekly and monthly anniversaries are monitored in a missing student case. Significant anniversary dates may involve press conferences and emotionally trying times for staff, students, and family members. Sustained support systems such as counseling services, media releases, and family communications can ease the distress of anniversary dates.

Summary

Recent developments at the state and federal level have illuminated the shortcomings in how missing student cases have historically been handled. Colleges and universities can join the national conversation by continuing to contribute to the dialogue on how best to respect the autonomy and privacy of students while looking out for their best interests.

Acts of Terrorism

This section addresses the most recent type of crisis to manifest itself in the educational environment: terrorist acts. As we will see, just as in our broader society, when we contemplate and prepare for potential terrorism on the college campus, vulnerabilities we had never thought of before are illuminated.

The attacks of September 11, 2001, on the World Trade Center in New York City and the Pentagon in Washington, D.C., forever changed the face of crisis management in higher education. In an attempt to protect the physical and psychological safety of the college environment, university officials have since sought answers to questions that have the potential to change the very nature of the college experience: *Is our campus a potential target for terrorism? How much and what kind of security should be present on campus before the historically treasured open nature of the environment is compromised? How do we deal with the loss of control of institutional borders that result from significant reliance on external agencies needed in a terrorist attack?*

In his guide *Protecting Schools and Universities from Terrorism: A Guide for Administrators and Teachers*, Adams (2003) warns of horrifying possibilities. "Although there have been few specific terrorist threats against schools and universities in the United States, captured videos of training by al Qaeda operatives in Afghanistan reveal their intention to conduct such warfare in the near future" (p. 2).

The threat of terrorism presents university administrators with significant challenges when it comes to personnel, facilities, legal issues, and student relationships.

Expanding the Role and Knowledge Base of the Campus Crisis Response Team

A critical element in preparing a campus for the possibility of terrorism is ongoing training for the crisis response team (CRT). Team members need to become knowledgeable about the different kinds of threats to the campus (bombs, biological attacks, suspicious packages, technological sabotage, chemical terrorism, nuclear and radiological attacks, and other types of terrorist acts). Training should also explore implications of each threat and how best to respond to the crisis. The Department of Justice and the Office of Domestic Preparedness are good sources for information. They have cosponsored opportunities for colleges and universities to attend specialized training with regard to terrorism.

It is important to analyze what makes particular campuses more inviting to domestic and international terrorist attacks. The FBI suggests that certain universities might be susceptible to terrorism for numerous reasons, including the following ("Helping Campus Heal," 2001):

- They are state or federally funded.

- They have a religious affiliation.

- They house research and lab experiments.

- They house political pundits, economic theorists, or religious scholars.

- They symbolize the power, prestige, economics, and influence of the United States.

The location of a college campus and its proximity to high-level security risk facilities such as military bases, nuclear power plants, chemical plants, hydroelectric dams, and others should also be considered. Zdziarski (2003) points out that large concerts, athletic competitions (such as the NCAA Final Four basketball tournament), and other major events may also have potential as targets.

The CRT can plan for the possibility of a terrorist act in several ways:

1. *Conduct a crisis audit of the institution.* Littleton (1983) describes the crisis audit as a method to critique threats the

institution is exposed to through the use of a systematic assessment process. Crisis audits are discussed more thoroughly in Chapter Four.

2. *Identify subgroups to thoroughly assess if elements on the main campus or satellite campuses in the United States or abroad make it an attractive target.* Areas to be addressed include those mentioned earlier: facilities; cybertechnology, research and experimentation; political, religious, or structural symbolism; proximity to key targets in the surrounding community; study abroad programs; major campus events; and high-profile faculty, staff, students, or administrators.

3. *Address unique issues related to bioterrorism.* The campus's health center will be instrumental in developing a plan of action to respond to bioterrorism and should be included in information dissemination to the public. If the staff is not well trained in this area, the institution should contact a state emergency management agency capable of conducting the necessary training.

Utilizing Outside Resources

As has been noted throughout this volume, being prepared means building and expanding relationships with external agencies before a crisis occurs. Planning for possible terrorist acts is no different. Emergency planning has to be a community effort. It is impossible to anticipate which key individuals might be unavailable or out of town when a crisis occurs, and the university cannot rely on a few people to know what steps to take. Network building and knowledge sharing are essential. Establishing a community coordinating committee to work with the university is an important and critical step. Other coordination efforts include the following:

1. *University officials need to make critical contacts with law enforcement, fire departments, hospitals, phone companies, transportation*

departments, fire, gas, and power companies, hotels, food service organizations, churches, and schools, as well as other colleges and universities in the area, to develop action plans and share resources. If positive working relationships are already established, they can save precious time when a terrorist act is committed.

2. *Identify housing options off campus in case the campus loses the ability to accommodate students and staff.* An off-site housing area can provide valuable space for rest and comfort for staff working in the aftermath of a crisis. Gyms, cafeterias, churches, and schools are some examples of spaces that could accommodate displaced individuals.

3. *Become fully informed about the services state and federal emergency agencies can provide and make contact with appropriate offices.* The state FEMA affiliate can help train citizen response teams and provide an emergency management course complete with crisis simulations conducted on campus. FEMA's Web site (www.FEMA.gov) contains important information on this subject. Of particular note is a section entitled "FEMA: Capability Assessment for Readiness Terrorism Preparedness." In addition, the American Red Cross provides seminars, staff training, and immediate emergency response to crises. Many other countries have their own version of the Red Cross and may be available to assist if college students and faculty are affected by a terrorist act abroad. The Red Cross Web site (www.redcross.org) contains a section titled "Terrorism Preparedness" that offers helpful information on specific steps individuals and organizations can take to help in case of a terrorist attack.

4. *Create Web sites that offer terror alert information and safety precautions and advertise them to the university community.* One excellent such site is www.ready.gov. The U.S. Department of Homeland Security has designed this site to assist the

American public in planning for a terrorist act and for dealing with the crisis if it should occur. Two other important resources have been designed by the American Psychological Association: "Managing Traumatic Stress: Tips for Recovering from Disasters and other Traumatic Events" and "Resilience in a Time of War" (see www.apahelpcenter.org/articles). These articles answer questions about what types of reactions and fears might be experienced after a terrorist attack or during times of war.

5. *Keep up with pending legislation that may deal with university issues related to terrorism.* State legislatures and the federal government have responded to terrorism and continue to introduce new laws that have an impact on college campuses. Identify someone on the CRT to track legislation and inform other members of the group if the university needs to modify its own policies and procedures as a result of the changes.

Making Important Plans

Members of the CRT can plan ahead for strategies designed to maximize human and technological resources. The very nature of terrorism is that it is generally unforeseen. The American Psychological Association (2001) describes the impact that terrorism has on people: a sense of fear and helplessness resulting in acute stress and trauma. The better a campus's advance planning the better the community will be able to deal with the resulting problems.

Here are some examples of planning strategies:

1. *Maintain up-to-date records on staff contact information.* Key individuals include staff in plant services, housing departments, counseling centers, health centers, university ministry offices, communications, university relations, campus security, the dean of students, and other members of the administration. These records should be kept both on campus and in

an off-campus location with the chair of the CRT, director of campus safety, and other appropriate staff.

2. *Have an off-site records management program plan in place to ensure that important records are preserved in the event that everything on the campus is destroyed.* The information technology department can be instrumental in planning for such a situation.

3. *Make sure CRT members communicate effectively with members of their own households about emergency plans and discuss each individual's responsibilities in advance of any crisis.* In the case of single-parent homes with young children, CRT members should plan ahead for child care. They should pack overnight bags in case responsibilities dictate that they spend several nights away from home.

4. *Have evacuation procedures in place.* Each building should have a posted plan for evacuation and clearly identified exits marked. Faculty, staff, and students, while possibly familiar with the buildings they frequent, may not know where to go if visiting a facility for the first time. Visitors to campus will most likely be unaware of what to do in the event of a terrorist attack, so visible directional signage is critical.

Attending to Displaced Students

Students who attend college represent a wide array of populations. Evacuation plans should take into consideration whether students are from out of state or foreign countries. Some students may also have families living on campus and their children may need special attention if the campus is attacked.

The housing department should keep a master roster of students living on campus, their permanent contact information, and an emergency contact list in its offices and also at an easily accessed off-campus location. The list should enumerate residents who have spouses or children living on campus.

It may be difficult to determine if students are lost or injured, particularly because many students leave campus on a regular basis without informing anyone. A practice that may help locate residential students quickly is to encourage them regularly to put an envelope with their off-campus plans on the inside of their residence door. The campus may be flooded with inquiries from friends and family members seeking information about their loved one. The contact information could prove vital in locating students and informing their family if inquiries are made.

Bus companies may be needed to help transport students to safe locations away from campus. Students most likely will leave with only the clothes on their back if they have to go in a hurry. It will be necessary to equip the students with basic necessities if they are to make it through the interim period without their belongings.

The Red Cross will be an important agency to work with to help coordinate donations of clothing, food, personal hygiene items, and even money. Some corporations might be able to provide assistance for the displaced students in the form of long distance calling cards, sleeping bags, and other needed tangible items.

The counseling center and other mental health agencies from the community can provide support to those in need. It is important to coordinate efforts to provide for emotional health in a timely fashion.

Making Personnel and Safe Spaces on Campus More Visible

The campus community needs to know the location of designated safe areas in the event a terrorist act occurs. University maps should identify safe location options and the campus Web site should provide instructions and directions about where to go. Particular attention needs to be paid to individuals who have physical disabilities and cannot move without assistance.

One can only imagine the potential chaos that would result after any kind of a terrorist attack. The university community will need to know that someone is in charge of making decisions and looking out for the common good of its members. Here are a few strategies:

1. *Create a command center equipped with technology that allows the CRT to communicate effectively and respond to the crisis.* The center should be stocked with battery-operated radios and televisions, extra batteries, flashlights, maps of the area, backup generators, bottled water, contact information, and crisis response plans. Other helpful items to include are first aid kits, kitchen items and food, and can openers. It would be wise to have a secondary location in place, in case the primary center is destroyed.

2. *In chaotic times it is best to have something by which people can recognize members of the CRT and other key volunteers or decision makers.* They might wear easily identifiable windbreakers, armbands, name tags, or hats.

Attending to the Safety of Specific On-Campus Groups

The September 11 attacks generated a backlash against Muslims studying and teaching in the United States. Ecoterrorists may impugn the work of nonviolent activist groups on campus. The existence of research laboratories housing dangerous chemicals that could be used in terrorist attacks may call into question safety procedures and the legitimacy of conducting such research on a college campus.

Strategies for dealing with the revenge mentality include educational outreach on personal safety and compliance with recent legislation.

1. *Conduct safety briefings for on-campus groups who may be targeted.* Providing information about areas to avoid, services available to assist those feeling vulnerable, strategies to address suspicious behavior, and what to do in case one is targeted empowers individuals and groups to take care of themselves. This is particularly important for international students who may not be familiar with American subgroups, cultural norms, and police procedures. Working with students

and staff to restore their personal sense of safety and keeping a situation in perspective while providing a realistic picture of what is happening are all important to containing escalating hostility.

2. *Educate key campus personnel in legislative actions resultant from terrorist attacks.* The so-called U.S. Patriot Act was written into law shortly after the attacks of September 11. The Family Education Right to Privacy Act (FERPA) has been affected by this new law. Under the guidelines, "(1) The Attorney General may obtain an ex parte order from the courts requiring an institution to permit the AG to: (a) collect educational records that are relevant to an authorized investigation or prosecution of an act of domestic or international terrorism, (b) retain, disseminate, and use (as evidence at trial or in other administrative or judicial proceedings) such records. (2) In order to get the order, the AG must certify that there are specific and articulable facts giving reason to believe that the education records are likely to contain information related to acts of domestic or international terrorism." (Lowery & Gehring, 2003, p. 2). It is also important for staff to be aware of the Student and Exchange Visitor Information System (SEVIS). This is a Web-based system for maintaining information on international students and exchange visitors in the United States (U.S. Immigration and Customs Enforcement, 2005). The Student and Exchange Visitor Program (SEVP), a division of U.S. Immigration and Customs Enforcement (ICE), the largest investigative arm of the Department of Homeland Security, administers SEVIS. SEVIS seeks to balance homeland security with facilitating foreign student and visitor participation in America's academic and cultural exchange programs. It is also imperative that university officials understand how to handle inquiries from the FBI. These most often include information that allows them to track patterns and movements—what a student or

faculty member is studying or researching, connections to others, addresses and phone numbers, citizenship, place and date of birth, and foreign contact information (Lowery & Gehring, 2003).

Suspending Bureaucracy and Academic Structures

A significant crisis challenges all aspects of campus life, including academic schedules, policies, and procedures. In the case of a terrorist attack, classes may be disrupted for an extended period.

To deal with this, it is important to negotiate means by which academic schedules and requirements can be modified to accommodate the disruption of a crisis event. In addition to classes being suspended, some students may even choose to drop out for a semester or longer. Plans for meeting the required student contact hours may need to be devised and may require negotiation with the state department of education. Departing students may want to be refunded tuition and fees. Predetermined institutional policies can help prevent conflict over these issues during a crisis.

Making Sense of Senseless Acts

After the initial shocking stages of a terrorist act and the imminent danger have passed, the long-term psychological recovery process begins. Our inability to make sense of a senseless act compounds our collective confusion and anger. According to Adams (2003), increasing levels of threat and expansion of acceptable targets are hallmarks of contemporary terrorists.

Throughout history, terrorists have used violence and destruction to spread fear and panic throughout society in pursuit of their multifaceted objectives. Traditionally, terrorist tactics such as bombings and assassinations have targeted military and government officials; civilians such as women, children, and the elderly have generally been immune from direct targeting, although not from so-called collateral damage. However, today terrorists' motivations, objectives, and modus operandi have radically changed.

Whether operating in foreign lands or the United States, terrorists now consider schoolchildren and university students as targets for opportunity (Adams, p. 1).

Given the current circumstances, assisting the campus community in making sense of these senseless acts is essential to the healing process.

1. *Do not underestimate the power of symbolic leadership*. Modeling and maintaining campus civility is an essential role of campus leaders. Students, staff, and faculty take their cues on how to behave in part from the actions of campus leaders. Demonstrating compassion, communicating actions taken to maintain or restore campus safety, and sponsoring dialogue to promote healing are all ways in which administrators can make their leadership visible. Rituals are another important element of symbolic leadership. Vigils, memorials, and community bonding experiences are critical.

2. *Channel the emotional tenor of the campus into positive productive activities*. Provide resources for faculty to lead classroom and campus discussion, identify roles for student leaders, and gauge the levels of stress on campus.

3. *Use information to combat fear*. It is not enough for administrators to manage the crisis created by an act of terrorism, they need work to understand it and help others understand it as well. This does not mean agreeing with the motives of those who perpetrated the act. It does mean uncovering the underlying objectives of terrorists. Adams (2003) provided the following explanation of the motives of many contemporary terrorists.

Terrorists seek to spread fear and anxiety throughout society—beyond the direct physical impact of an actual attack—in order to either influence government policy in a certain direction or to punish the government and its citizens for a myriad of reasons. By the randomness and unpredictability of their acts, or, in other instances, by directly targeting a society's most vulnerable citizens, such as children and university students, terrorists seek to undermine public confidence in the government's ability to protect its citizens. Terrorists hope the resulting insecurity and panic will increase public demand for government concessions to the terrorists in order to stop the terrorist acts. [p. 3]

Armed with insight into the objectives of those who perpetrate senseless acts, individuals can choose not to allow themselves to succumb to the psychological effects, and work toward regaining normalcy.

Summary

Several years after the September 11, 2001, terrorist attacks on the United States, colleges and universities continue to realize the implications. Stringent visa restrictions make it more difficult for foreign students to attend American schools, and they are opting to attend schools in other countries (Sidel, 2005). There is heightened awareness of race, religion, and nationality. We have yet to determine the effects on learning for students who live with constant reminders of the potential for terrorist attacks.

Although no plan can account for every possibility, institutions of higher education do have the power and ability to protect themselves to some degree. School and university administrators and teachers need to become aware of potential threats and take the necessary preventative measures to ensure that their campuses and students are properly protected. Preparing to defend against a terrorist attack can help prevent it. If terrorists know that their efforts to do harm to our schools and universities will likely fail, they will have little incentive to strike (Adams, 2003).

Conclusion

This chapter explored four contemporary issues in crisis management. Several themes became clear.

First, collaboration between universities and external agencies is critical. Teaching about local, state, and federal agencies and their resources is essential in the campus crisis response team's training. These relationships also have implications for the roles campus leaders will play during a crisis. The contemporary crises discussed in this chapter can affect the surrounding community and may tax their resources as well as those of the university. Relationship building is essential.

A second theme is the internal preparedness of the institution. Employee training, plans and procedures, internal communication, and crisis audits should be well developed. The university community should be aware that a crisis response team exists and who is on the team. Students should be informed of crisis response strategies and resources. Communications, technology, and safety personnel are key players during a crisis and their roles should be well defined before a crisis hits.

Finally, the more effective a campus is at staying connected to and addressing the needs of stakeholders (students, parents, the media, and others), the more quickly it can emerge from a crisis.

Our exploration of these four types of crises represents the ever-evolving nature of campus crisis management and confirms what those in crisis management have always known: although no plan can account for every unforeseen event that may transpire, prior planning can save precious time, and potentially, save lives.

References

Adams, J. A. (2003). *Protecting schools and universities from terrorism: A guide for administrators and teachers*. Alexandria, VA: ASIS International.

American Psychological Association. (2001). *Resilience in a time of war*. Retrieved July 31, 2005, from http://www.apahelpcenter.org/articles.

An adequate response to missing students? (2004, March). Magna Publications' *Perspective* Newsletter.

Andrews, D. W., & Buettner, C. K. (2003). *The Ohio State University task force on preventing celebratory riots: Final report.* Columbus: The Ohio State University.

Bouchard, M. (2005). *Securing internal networks: The final frontier.* Retrieved March 1, 2006, from http://www.checkpoint.com/products/downloads/ Check_Point_BouchardInternalNetworks.pdf.

Canter, D. (1989). *Football in its place.* London: Routledge.

Carr, J. L. (2005, February). *American College Health Association campus violence white paper.* Baltimore: American College Health Association

Coakley, J., & Donnelly, P. (2004). *Sport in society: Issues and controversies.* New York: McGraw-Hill.

Epstein, J. (2002). Breaking the code of silence: Bystander to campus violence and the law of college and university safety. *Stetson Law Review, 42*(1), 91–124.

Franz, L. (2003). *Disaster recovery planning.* Retrieved March 1, 2006, from http://www.educause.edu/ir/library/pdf/DEC0301.pdf.

Geraghty, J. (2005). The political/social dimensions of the NBA fight. Retrieved November 28, 2005, from http://www.nationalreview.com/kerry/ kerry200411221353.asp.

GQ names the top ten worst college sports fans. (2005, March 15). *Gentlemen's Quarterly (GQ) Magazine News.* Retrieved October 16, 2006, from http://www.digital50.com/news/items/668/gq-names-the-top-ten-worst-college-sports-fans.html.

Helping campus heal in the wake of a national tragedy. (2001, September 13). Special Fax Report. Garfield, NJ: PaperClip Communications.

Hong, L. (2002, May). *Understanding and preventing violence on our campuses: A comprehensive student affairs initiative.* Paper presented at the annual meeting of the American College Health Association, Washington, DC.

Improving our response to missing student reports. (2004, March). *National On-Campus Report, 32*(6), 1, 4.

Littleton, R. (1983). *Crisis management: A team approach.* New York: American Management Association.

Lowery, J. W., & Gehring, D. (2003). *Under construction: New legislative issues for judicial affairs.* Paper presented at the Association for Student Judicial Affairs (ASJA) annual conference, Clearwater, FL.

Lyall, D., & Lyall, M. (n.d.). *Campus safety. . . . Are you concerned?* Retrieved July 15, 2005, from http://criminaljustice.state.ny.us/missing/aware/ campus.htm.

McCarthy, J. D., Martin, A. W., McPhail, C., & Cress, D. (2002, August). *Mixed-issue campus disturbances, 1985–2001: Describing the thing to be*

explained. Paper presented at the annual meeting of the American Socio-
logical Association, Chicago.

Missing college student cases: An investigative guide. (2002). Retrieved July 18,
2005, from http://www.state.ny.us/governor/press/year02/nov20_1_02.htm.

NCAA. (2003). *Report on the Sportsmanship and Fan Behavior Summit*. Retrieved
June 1, 2006, from http://www.ncaa.org/sportsmanship/sportsmanship
FanBehavior/report.pdf.

Newman, M. (2004, April 6). *Barely over last night's party, UConn hopes for
another*. Retrieved April 8, 2004, from http://www.nytimes.com/2004/
04/06/sports/ncaabasketball/06CND-STOR.html.

Sidel, M. (2005). *Fallout from the war on terror: Antiterrorism policy has taken its
toll on foreign enrollment in U.S. universities*. Retrieved July 25, 2005, from
http://yaleglobal.yale.edu/display.article?id=5865.

Snider, R. (2004, June 24). Maryland sets policies for fan conduct. *Washington
Times*. Retrieved January 30, 2005, from http://www.washingtontimes.com.

U.S. Immigration and Customs Enforcement. (2005). *Student and exchange visitor
program (SEVP)*. Retrieved July 31, 2005, from http://www.ice.gov/sevis/
index.htm.

Zdziarski, E. L. (2003, March 17). Responding to the threat of campus terrorism.
NASPA NetResults. Washington, DC: NASPA. Retrieved March 30,
2006, from http://www.naspa.org/membership/mem/nr/article.cfm?id=995.

13

Where Do We Go from Here?

J. Michael Rollo, Eugene L. Zdziarski II, and Norbert W. Dunkel

There is no substitute for a well-developed plan that can be used to train and inform staff of their roles and obligations in the event of a crisis. When a crisis unfolds, or a tragedy overwhelms staff and resources, it is not the time to begin making lists of needed actions. It is not the time to begin searching for that three-ring binder that some of the staff put together a few years ago after attending a workshop or living through a different experience. Crisis management is a continuous process of experience, learning, training, evaluating, developing, and implementing the best practices that can be identified in order to be prepared for many different circumstances.

There is an often-stated criticism of planners when we begin to deconstruct our response to the latest crisis. Most of us tend to be well prepared for the previous crisis but not for the one in which we find ourselves. The challenge, it would seem, is to prepare for the crisis we have not yet anticipated by putting all of the pieces of the plan in place so that the necessary response for any circumstances can be crafted from the various components already assembled and for which we have trained. Both physical and human assets should be poised to respond in any direction and even in multiple directions if needed.

In this book, we have suggested an approach that we think will serve higher education institutions well if implemented in the context of each individual institution. An honest assessment of the resources at hand for response and a broad view of potential crisis situations will serve as the best starting point if a campus has not previously addressed crisis management in a coordinated fashion. What is a realistic expectation of the institution's staff to respond to the different types of events that occur? What assistance can be expected from the community, the state, or the federal government in the event of a large-scale disaster? Any plan that will ultimately succeed must start with a foundation of what one already knows about one's institution, personnel, and the overall challenges.

Once current circumstances are understood, it is time to begin to put together what needs to be done and fill in the holes in coverage that an assessment has revealed. The crisis matrix outlined in Chapter Two provides a model that allows readers to enter different sets of facts and begin to hypothesize about the types of resources and the scale of response mechanisms that would be needed to adequately address different incidents. The matrix provides a common language for all staff to use when planning and responding on-site. The flexibility it provides to address any set of circumstances allows staff to fit it to any size campus or any type of incident and to address changing or expanding circumstances. Whether consciously or intuitively, we can use the crisis matrix as a centerpiece for preparation, training, and response when a crisis affects us.

The crisis matrix can also serve as a template for developing protocol manuals for identified threats. None of us can see into the future, but we can extrapolate the possibilities that can occur by using the matrix to identify connecting issues and the interaction of resources and events, and brainstorming potential scenarios that can occur when natural forces, human behavior, and time interact in our communities and campuses. In this way, the crisis matrix may be the closest thing we will get to having the proverbial crystal ball.

Meeting regularly as a team provides the opportunity to share the collected wisdom and experience of interested parties, develop training materials, discuss experiences, develop relationships, review recent events, and look forward to potential crisis points. The more diverse the group is—representing a variety of departments, professions, and perspectives—the more effective it can be as a resource for training and planning for incidents just over the horizon. Each institution can develop its own model for how the team or committee should be structured and whether it has direct reporting lines to a specific department. No one particular structure will work on all campuses, and the campus culture seems to be a better guide to how best to organize a team around this issue. Some campuses have a loose confederation of committed professionals, others design committees based on clear reporting lines with specific authority and responsibilities. If there is no team or committee at present, an organizational workshop may be a good starting point to bring disparate staff together and develop a consensus over how to proceed. Whether the organization is developed from above, as a grassroots initiative, as a directive from some level of management, or as a hybrid comprising staff with differing reasons for contributing to the enterprise, it does not matter as much as the process of establishing a working group that can be a centerpiece for training through regular meetings and common interests viewed from multiple perspectives— facilities management, counseling services, campus security, communications, student concerns, and so on. This committee or work group becomes the action team during a crisis. Their knowledge, relationships, and trust for one another become key ingredients in the institution's ability to respond effectively or at all.

Professionals brought in from other campuses for training sessions and staff development workshops can be effective in jumpstarting a staff-training program. Recent incidents in departments or on the entire campus will raise interest and may be the impetus to provide a campuswide training opportunity. Regular training opportunities for first responders will most likely occur in departments as part of their own program, but cross-departmental training will be key to preparing for an incident with wider impact, where multiple resources may need to respond and interact. Learning our strengths and shortcomings in a training exercise (information as basic as the names of key staff in the various departments) is more productive and less stressful than trying to accomplish these tasks at the site of a tragedy or in the midst of a crisis. A full-blown real-time exercise can also be useful but expensive and time-consuming for both the planners and the staff involved. More limited exercises and tabletop exercises can be effective and provide valuable insights too. And campuses should not overlook the value of regular paper-and-pencil exercises as a way to keep the staff focused on preparation and training. In addition, they serve to regularly bring staff together in a less stressful environment with a clear task and result in improved interpersonal dynamics as staff learn together and about each other's skills and responsibilities. Working through problems in a classroom environment establishes relationships that will be needed when an actual crisis occurs.

A complete response plan must make use of resources and services dispersed among various entities on a campus. For instance, environmental health offices do not provide counseling services, residence hall staff cannot serve as police officers, and counseling staff cannot assist with storm preparation or cleanup. Allies on campus and throughout the community must be sought and relationships with them nurtured. Repeatedly, when tragedy strikes on our campuses and communities, we have seen a willingness among individuals to help in some fashion. Identifying key individuals in various constituencies—such as Greek life, students with disabilities, professional schools, international students, and so on—or with specific skills—such as language facility, interpretation for the hearing impaired, computer support, religious credentials, and so on—can be valuable, providing tools that can be brought to bear quickly if the alliance has been developed over time. Staff and citizens with these skills will be needed in any event, so it makes sense for planners to have them already tied to the plan and aware of the structure of response as they set about developing protocols. This network of allies also serves as a web of contacts for access to services on a daily basis and provides the community with a better support system even when there is no looming crisis or tragedy.

There are challenges when seeking allies and bringing them into the process, including keeping them connected at a meaningful level in periods when their services are not needed. The first flush of excitement that comes from helping in a crisis can diminish over time if one's services are not needed on a regular basis. Furthermore, constantly adding new personalities to the response teams requires paying attention to the interpersonal dynamics that can affect the ability of the team to respond effectively. The coordinating leaders of any crisis response program will have to pay attention to this or suffer the consequences when poor response, communication conflicts, and failure to provide a key service result. History shows that despite all the wonderful service and selfless acts of kindness and heroism that occur during a crisis or tragedy, there are also always organizational failures that surprise us and confound our efforts to respond.

Since the very beginning of the twenty-first century, the United States has been challenged by events that have shaped our culture and changed our society dramatically. These events, including the attack on the World Trade Center and the Pentagon in 2001, and more recently, the hurricanes that ravaged Florida and the Gulf Coast in 2004 (Charley, Frances, and Ivan) and 2005 (Katrina and Rita), resulted in the loss of billions of dollars and thousands of lives and the destruction of entire communities. The great human toll of these events, and all the more personal but just as tragic incidents, will ripple throughout our society into the foreseeable future. Families have been broken apart and uprooted, careers have been made or destroyed, and fortunes have been made or lost. The traumatic impact of these events has been felt by millions. Even the distant observer—thanks to the ever-present twenty-four-hour news channel—is affected profoundly by events that previously would have come and gone almost unnoticed. The San Francisco earthquake that occurred at the beginning of the twentieth century devastated that city and destroyed the lives of thousands of individuals. But the average citizen in the United States remained relatively detached from the experience, reading about it in the newspapers a day or more later. Contrast this with the recent experience in New Orleans, when Hurricane Katrina decimated the city. Millions of Americans watched on an hourly basis as the city was engulfed first by the storm and then by the floodwaters, and then as it sank into anarchy when governmental support structures failed one by one to maintain basic services to the community. Water, food, safety, self-respect, and a sense of community all disappeared before the nation's eyes. If ever we needed verification that Abraham Maslow's hierarchy of needs had validity, it was right there for us to observe and acknowledge (Maslow, 1970). Seeing how quickly we can lose the thin veneer of civilization provided an important lesson to keep in mind as we plan for the future.

This awareness by the entire country did foster some new and creative responses in the higher education community. Colleges and universities across the United States opened their doors to New Orleans students and faculty to bypass all the usual bureaucratic roadblocks so that individuals could continue their educational pursuits, their research, and some semblance of their previous lives. Interagency cooperation on this scale was unprecedented and offered new opportunities to learn how best to help individuals and institutions in crisis. More work and review will need to be done to see how effective this response was and what future responses might look like. As each institution reviews how it absorbed students and ultimately returned students to their home institutions, and how institutions can survive this level of disruption and destruction, there will be important learning opportunities for us to plan effectively for the next time a crisis of this proportion affects us.

This book is filled with ideas and guidance for professionals on how to prepare and respond to crisis and tragedy. The collective wisdom of our contributors can be used to develop an effective plan for an institution that is tailored to its unique characteristics. If there is one constant, however, throughout our discussions of crisis response, it is that what we learn by living through crises, and our ability to respond is heavily affected by the lessons we learn from the experience of others. Luckily for us, major crises do not happen to all of us with the same frequency, nor are we subject to the same forces of nature. Yet there are lessons that staff in the Midwest can learn from the experiences of those who prepare and respond to hurricanes on the Gulf Coast. Many of the campuses of the great Southwest have no need to plan for a blizzard or ice storm, but they can use the experiences of those in the Northeast and along the Canadian border to address concerns on their campus about resource deployment and disruption of services for extended periods of time. We can learn from each other regardless of the uniqueness of the experience or the campus on which the incident occurred. As we search for common themes across the experiences of university and college campuses, we find that each event provides new insights into how to respond more effectively. Changing conditions over time, new technology that either aggravates or mitigates our ability to respond, and changing staff and leadership at our own institutions dictate that we continue to search for new lessons so as to better prepare for the next incident.

Furthermore, we must not only seek to learn from others. It is imperative that those of us who experience firsthand such life-changing events share what we have learned with other professionals through presentations at conferences, consultation with peers, and publications in journals, newsletters, and reports. Smaller campuses with limited staff and resources may have no other way to access this valuable information in a systematic manner. Large campuses with thinly spread resources can enhance their training opportunities by relying on the expertise of others. Capturing the knowledge gained and sharing it with others will minimize human suffering, and in extreme cases, probably even save lives.

The end of one crisis is the beginning of the planning stage for the next one, which will inevitably arrive on our doorstep. In the world today, at the pace we live, and with the impending threat of international terrorism layered on top of the long-standing threats of accident or violence, we are bound as professionals to become ever more engaged in planning, preparing, and responding to the incidents that affect our campuses and communities. Our knowledge of incidents occurring around the world heightens our awareness of what is likely to occur at our own institutions. We cannot in good conscience ignore the possibility that something unthinkable can occur in our midst that will disrupt the lives of our students, faculty, and staff. As we prepare, we are best served by looking across our shared experiences to broaden our perspective, heighten our awareness, and in the end, better serve our constituents to minimize the disruption in their lives.

Reference

Maslow, A. H. (1970). *Motivation and personality* (2nd. ed.). New York: Harper-Collins.

Appendix

Crisis Debriefing

Daryl Johnston

A simple debriefing allows an institution to ask itself what it did correctly in responding to a crisis and what it discovered it can do better in the future when facing a similar situation. Depending on the intensity of the crisis, the institution may desire to go beyond the simple two prongs of what it did correctly and what it learned to do better by using a more complex review process. For institutions that want a more detailed process, we provide the following checklist.

Considering the Need for a Debriefing

Not every incident requires a comprehensive debriefing. In some institutions, incidents such as a student's natural death in a dormitory have happened recently enough that a clear series of actions are automatically taken to manage the crisis. In cases where the incident was handled satisfactorily, there may be little to be learned from the event. In such instances, debriefing may be limited to focus directly on the responders and the impact of the incident on them rather than to review the institutional process or departmental response capability. When individuals can "debrief" with a facilitator, it allows them to process their own emotional responses in the job context and in a safe environment.

It is most appropriate to consider a crisis debriefing when the situation is one that the institution has not experienced before or when there is a feeling that the institution could have responded better than it did. In situations where there is a concern that the institution's response did not meet a legal standard of care, the institution's legal counsel or risk management office should be approached for their input before beginning a debriefing.

When to Carry Out a Debriefing

Regardless of its scope, a crisis debriefing should be considered after the event is clearly over and the institution has had a chance to recover from it. Generally, several weeks should come between the event and the debriefing. This allows time for incident reports and safety reports to be written and reflected on. After a traumatic event it is also wise to consult with trauma response experts on the mental state of those involved and whether they should participate in a debriefing at all. Special consultation sessions with first responders may focus on the emotional impact; this will allow for better information to surface later, during the debriefing.

However, there is also a risk of waiting too long before beginning a crisis debriefing. If too much time separates the event from the review, the memory of those involved may not be so accurate. Some individuals have found it helpful to keep a log or journal during an incident to assist with this process and enhance information gathering when the debriefing occurs. A person's memory of specifics that occurred during crises that lasted over long periods of time also tend to be less reliable. Personal notes can therefore be very helpful.

Crisis Debriefing Checklist

The following checklist can guide the development of a crisis debriefing process. The coordinator or facilitator can judge the suitability of all items on this checklist for the task at hand and the granularity needed to meet the requirements of the delegating authority.

1. Determine who has authority to conduct a crisis debriefing.

   Consider the legal jurisdiction of the agency.

   Consider collaboration with other agencies.

2. Select the members for the review.

   Consider bringing multiple disciplines to bring diversity of thought.

   Consider personality type or style in the team selection.

   Determine if experts in a given discipline or body of study are needed.

   Consider bringing the diversity of the university-college community to the team makeup.

3. Determine a time line for the review to be completed.

   Balance the need to find answers with the time needed for a complete and accurate investigation.

   Consider resources needed to support the review: availability of clerical support; word processing and other graphic arts programs; visual image documentation requirements.

4. Consider how the report will be presented and to whom it will be presented.

   Security needs

   Need for legal counsel

   Budget for the review process

5. Conduct the investigation of the event.

   Conduct individual interviews.

   Conduct group interviews.

   Obtain reports.

Document the event.

Identify parties who have an interest in the event.

Determine if research is needed to assist in getting answers.

6. Organize the review.

What happened?

Who was involved?

What was the sequence of events?

When did it happen?

Why did it happen?

How did it happen?

7. Document findings.

Create a taxonomy to track issues.

Keep issues to one focus for each finding.

Include "lessons learned."

8. Make recommendations.

Track recommendations to findings.

What actions are recommended?

Keep each recommendation to one issue.

Identify a discipline or group to respond to the recommendation.

Identify a suggested time for response to each recommendation.

9. Create an appendix.

Maps

Photos

List of agencies involved

List of those affected by the event

10. Document references.
11. Follow up.

    Assign personnel to accomplish a recommended action.

    Determine a time line to accomplish a task or action.

    Manage media relations.

    Identify a spokesperson.

    Coordinate the message.

    Ensure the message is consistent and accurate.

Index

A

Abent, R., 50, 189

Adams, J. A., 314, 323, 324, 325

Administrators: crisis roles and responsibilities of, 6, 80, 111, 115–116, 191; early presence requirement of, 106; emergency agencies' relationships with, 128–129; and group outreach services, 165; and intervention services, 175–176; and lines of authority, 80–81; media training for, 188–189; and responder burnout, 175–176

African-American universities, Hurricane Katrina's impacts on, 20–21

Aguilera, D., 158, 172, 175

Allen, C., 231

Alpaslan, C. M., 200

Amateur Radio Emergency Services (ARES), 104

American Council on Education (ACE), CampusRelief.org of, 21–22

American Psychological Association, 318

Andreski, P., 150

Andrews, D. W., 293, 294, 297

Archer, J., 146, 174

Aronson, E., 175

Association of American Universities (AAU), Hurricane Katrina victim arrangements of, 225

Auerbach, S. M., 30

B

Bailey, K., 207

Balk, D. E., 164

Ball State University, crisis management team at, 58, 66, 67–68, 69

Ballew, A. C., 189

Barrios, L. C., 147

Bartlett, T., 147

Barton, L., 23, 25, 55

Beckley, S. L., 148, 171

Benton, S. A., 146

Benton, S. L., 146

Bickel, R. D., 4, 148, 153, 260

Billings, R. S., 25

Birch, J., 46

Bird, L. E., 255

Bisson, J. I., 161, 167

Blom, S. D., 148, 171

Blythe, B. T., 69

Bonanno, G. A., 150, 151, 161, 174

Borodzicz, E., 185

Bouchard, M., 303

Bowen, G., 159

Boyd, V., 148, 171

Brandel, I. W., 148, 171

Brener, N. D., 147

Breslau, N., 150

Brodsky, S., 175

Bromet, E., 150

Brooking, A., 59, 63, 64

Brown, P., 8

Brown, T., 231

Brunner, B., 20

Buckles N., 148, 171

Buettner, C. K., 293, 294, 297

Bundy, Ted, 12–13

Business continuity plan: description of, 299; hands–on testing of, 302; maintenance of, 301–302; and needs assessment, 300; rationale for, 299–300

Business Roundtable, 105

C

California State University—Northridge earthquake, emotional and financial impact of, 14–15

Campus phone books, and information dissemination, 104

Campus Security Inc., 10

Campus security operations, 122, 129; crisis management authority of, 88–89; and crisis plan development, 91; maintaining contact information on, 92; organizational structure and jurisdiction of, 131; outside agencies' relations with, 89; services provided by, 130

Campus tragedies: accidental death and injuries in, 231–245, 255–263, 263–268; and campus crime disclosure requirements, 9–10; caused by natural disasters, 14–15, 20–21, 140–141, 207–211, 216–222, 224–229, 236–245; and communication problems, 16, 17; lessons learned from, 6–22; terrorism and, 268–274; and trust between students and institutions, 9. See also Criminal acts; Student suicide

CampusRelief.org, 21–22

Canter, D., 286

Caregivers, healing process for, 49

Carr, J. L., 291

Case management team, for crisis interventions, 173–174

CEIO COM LINK (telecommunications bridge), 105

Celebratory violence, 291–297: common elements in, 294–295; injuries and property damage resulting from, 291; legislation and reports on, 293–295; Ohio State University's Task Force on, 293–294; and preventative strategies for, 292–293. See also Sport spectator behavior

Cell phone communication, 104–105, 258

Central crisis planning office, establishment of, 92

Ceremonial events, as healing process, 49

Chancellor, and crisis communications plan approval, 111

Chickering, A., 160

Chilcoat, H., 150

Clement, L. M., 40

Clery, C., 9–10

Clery, H., 9–10

Coakley, J., 289

College deans, and crisis management planning, 77, 92

Colorado State University, effective crisis management at, 62

Community colleges, crisis management teams in, 57

Community Emergency Response Team (CERT): FEMA's development of, 141; training for, 135. See also specific university

Compassion stress (CS), phenomenon of, 175–176

Concordia University, crisis definition of, 29

Conlon, A., 150

Conneely, J., 231

Coombs, W. T., 23, 25, 46, 195, 197

Coordinator of crisis planning, 80, 94

Corazini, J., 146

Coulter, L. P., 148, 171, 174

County emergency coordination, 135–136

Cress, D., 291

Crime Awareness and Campus Security Act of 1990, 10

Criminal acts: multiple responses to, 43; resources for addressing, 44; student and staff deaths from, 7–10, 12–13, 15–16, 274–281. *See also* Sport spectator behavior; Terrorist attacks

Crisis communication plan: approval of, 111; assessment of, 118–119; four-step development process for, 109–119; and long-term corrective action, 116–117; and media engagement, 106–107; practice/testing of, 114; research for, 109–110; response process in, 114–116

Crisis communication: budget and resource availability for, 110; channels for, 99, 100; "community" intranet site for, 99; consistent and factual information in, 100, 101; demographic issues in, 100; and disenfranchised constituents, 101; with external audiences, 99; goals of, 107; in initial response period, 114–115; to internal audiences, 99; and media relations, 87–88; methods, 101–106; partner and stakeholder support for, 113; in recovery period, 116–118; release of information responsibility in, 111; target audiences of, 97–101, 107; team, creation of, 110–111; and university image, 109. *See also* News media; Telephone-related communication tools

Crisis debriefing: for crisis teams, 176; and legal standard of care, 338; need for, 49–50, 337; protocols for, 166–168, 176, 261; in psychoeducational group interventions, 166–168; for stress reduction, 166–167, 261; timing of, 338. *See also* Psychological debriefing

Crisis intervention: assessment in, 158–159; clinical intervention/chronic illness support approaches in, 147–148; and collaboration across disciplines, 156–157; continuum of precipitating events and, 150–151; and developmental transitions, 147; disposition process in, 160; early, core concept behind, 151; goals of, 152–153; and institutional ethic of care, 148–149, 156; models of practice for, 158; multidisciplinary teams in, 156–157; multiphase process of, 157–161; and normalization of reactions, 156; preplanning for, 157; rationale for psychological first aid in, 146–149; referral and follow-up, 160–162; and restoration of physical and emotional security, 152, 153, 154–155, 158; rising need for, 146–149; safety plans in, 160; and situational crises, 147; six-step model for, 158–161; standards for, 148; triage around safety and security in, 158–159; and victim's natural support system, 155. *See also* Psychological first aid

Crisis management plan, 73–90; action steps in, 81–82; activation responsibility and coordination in, 79; administrators' personal style and, 73; and built-in redundancy, 87; and business resumption, 89–90; campus culture and, 73–74; campus security and outside agency roles in, 88–89; campuswide, 77–78; and command center creation, 86–87; and communication methods 86; and coordination among units, 77–78; defining crisis in, 78–79; distribution of, 93; electronic formats for distribution of, 83–84; establishing responsibility

for, 90–91; and existing plans/
protocols, 77; facilities issues in,
89–90; formal versus informal,
73–75; general outline for, 78–82,
94–95; and human resource needs,
76; identifying key response modes
in, 85–86; key stakeholders involvement in, 75; lines of authority
established in, 80–81; maintenance
of, 91–93; and media responsibility,
87–88; and recovery phase operations, 89–90; and resource assessment, 76; scope of, 85; starting
point for, 330; and threat assessment, 315–315; unit-specific,
77–78, 80

Crisis management team (CMT),
55–71; and action plan responsibility of, 68–69; activities and roles
of, 56–57, 65; adverse demands on,
63; assessment and, 60; barriers to
good teamwork in, 61–62; and
campus education efforts, 69–70;
and crisis plan implementation, 77;
communication flows in, 69; community resources for, 57; and current job responsibilities, 60; and
crisis plan development, 75; diversity-communication skills in,
59–60; divisional, 77; external
constituencies and, 191–192; first
response activities of, 66–68; formation of, 156–157; foundational
and qualitative skills needed by,
184–185; and incident debriefing,
176, 201–202; and individual motivation, 60; and institutional size
and setting, 57–58; interpersonal
dynamics in, 333; jurisdiction and
authority of, 65–66; knowledge
objectives for, 186; leadership,
62–64; and membership criteria,
57–61; and membership flexibility,
61; order of succession in, 65; orientation and training, 59, 70, 187;
personnel, 58; and personality type
suitability, 61; and positive out-

comes, 64; protocol for activating,
66; skills assessment for, 197; skills
and competences needed by, 57,
58–60; as support team, 65–66;
team player mindset in, 59; territorial issues in, 61; typical areas of
concern for, 58

Crisis management training,
183–203; active training design
in, 189–191; case studies in,
200–203; crisis management cycle
and, 196–197; for crisis prevention, 187, 201–202; feedback in,
190–191; for handling media,
187–189; for incidents with significant risk, 200; learning from and
relying on others' expertise in,
335; objectives of, 185–187; personal attitudes addressed in, 187;
planning for, 184–191; preparing
staff to become trainers in, 187;
and principles of effective training,
189; resource needs of, 185; sample
activities for, 196–198; simulations
and tabletop exercises in, 192–196;
skill development in, 186; task
assessment tool for, 197–198; and
team members' attitudes and characteristics, 187

Crisis management: and critical
thinking, 185; defined, 55; families'
expectations of, 5; FEMA's approach
to, 46; five-phase cycle of, 46–50;
human element as focus in, 37;
identifying constituencies and special skills needed in, 332–334;
injuries and illnesses as point of
contact in, 42; and institutional
mission, 56; and institutional size,
5–6; of intentional crises, 43, 44;
learning from successes and failures in, 49; and level of crisis,
37–40; and limited response time,
25–26; and organizational disruption, 26; and preventative actions,
48; safety and well-being objectives
of, 27, 38, 41; management versus

response in, 45; mitigation in, 46; of unintentional crises, 42–43. *See also specific institution*

Crisis matrix, 36 (*Fig2.1*); and audit process, 75–76; dimensions of, 36–43; and crisis management training, 198–200; and protocol development, 45; purpose and uses of, 36–37, 330; vectors of response in, 44–45

Crisis protocols: crisis matrix and, 45; for debriefing, 166–168, 176, 261; development and format of, 45, 82–84; for voluntary/involuntary transport, 163–164

Crisis recovery: closure events and memorials to aid in, 49; operations, 89–90; time frame for, 48–49. *See also* Healing process; Psychological first aid

Crisis responders: conflicts between, 48; death notification training for, 164–165; debriefing and support for, 49–50; job description for, 185–186; joint training of, 280; transport protocols for, 163–164

Crisis response, 37–40; to human crises, 41–42; and infrastructure needs, 38; initial activities in, 66–67; and institutional bureaucracy, 5; institution-wide, 38; lessons learned from, 118; and perception of event, 28; planning for, 48; at smaller/nonresidential institutions, 38; target audiences' opinions of, 115; timeliness of, 25–26; using smaller events as practice for, 36. *See also specific incident*

Crisis: audit, 315–316; definition and common characteristics of, 22–29, 149–150; inevitability and unpredictability of, 24–25; perceived as negative event or outcome, 24; as threat to safety and well-being, 26–27

Critical Incident Stress Debriefing (CISD), 166–167

Critical incident: and agency roles, 88–89; defined, 37; evolution of, 43–45; intentional, resources for addressing, 44; and stress debriefing process, 261; as test for large-scale events, 37–38

D

Dannells, M., 200

Davidshofer, C., 148, 171

Davis, G., 150

Daykin, A., 255

Deaking, S., 148, 171

Death notification, training for, 161–165

DeGirolamo, G., 150

Department heads, and crisis plan management, 77, 92

Department of Homeland Security, 126, 226–227; agencies housed in, 139–140; and bioterrorism, 14; campus contact with, 140; Crisis Action Team of, 105; establishment of, 139

Department of Justice, and terrorist threats, 315

Departmental crisis management plans, 77

Dewane, S., 159

Diamond, M. A., 200

Dillard University, Hurricane Katrina's impact on, 20–21

"Disaster Readiness University" classification, 214

Disasters: and command structure models, 89; lack of preventive controls for, 201–202; Red Cross response to, 137. *See also* Hurricane Katrina disaster; *specific crisis*

Disease-related crises, 13–14, 102

Divisional crisis management plan, roles and functions of, 77

Donnelly, P., 289

Duncan, M. A., 184, 189

Dunkel, N. W., 35, 121, 156, 186, 200, 205, 329

Dyregrov, A., 167

E

Eastern Kentucky University's power failure response, 245–253; challenges in, 246–247; communication and public relations issues in, 248–250; food issues in, 247, 251; lessons learned from, 250–251; media's crucial role in, 250; reimbursement policy in, 248, 251; student relocations in, 247–248

Edelwich, J., 175

Educational institution, as legal guardian versus caring educator, 3–4

802.11G communication system, 104

Eitington, J. E., 195

Ellen, E. F., 147

Ellet, T., 255

Elsinga, L., 308, 309, 311, 312

Emergency Alert System (EAS), 103

Emergency contact information: circulation of, 92–93; dual purposes of, 92; review and updating of, 92; sources of, 99, 104

Emergency Operations Center (EOC), establishment of, 81, 86–87

Emergency personnel and agencies, 121–143; and advanced preparedness measures, 125; and city police operations and jurisdiction, 131; and county sheriff's services, 132; first responder functions of, 122; and joint information systems, 125–126; and mitigation activities, 125; and mutual aid agreements, 129–135; and pre-event outreach and cooperation, 128–129; staff's work with, 130; and state police services, 132–133. See also Incident Command System/Unified Command (ICS/UC); specific agency

Emergency, defined, 38. See also Crisis; Critical incident

Employee Assistance Program (EAP), 86

Environmental audit, 25

Environmental crises: personal accounts of, 207–211, 216–222, 224–229; types and localized aspects of, 40–41

Epstein, B., 159, 167

Epstein, J., 297

Ercolano, M., 159

ERMS (Emergency Response Management System), 102

Ershine, C., 148, 171

Ethic of care, as basis of institutional actions, 4–5

Everett, S. W., 147

Everly, G. S., 151, 157, 158, 162, 171

Experiential learning: as adult learning approach, 196; cycle, training process and, 189–190

External consultant, for crisis management training, 185

F

Facility crises: and business continuity plan, 41, 299–302; and debriefing sessions, 250–251; defined, 41; and infrastructure protection and repairs, 41; need for contingency plans in, 41; personal accounts of, 231–253; student safety concerns in, 38, 41, 250; unpredictable nature of, 250; updated information as critical need in, 249, 250

Family Education Right to Privacy Act (FERPA), 310, 322

Federal Bureau of Investigation (FBI), 322; agency and staff overview, 137–138; campus involvement with, 138–139; priorities of, 138

Federal Emergency Management Agency (FEMA): and campus natural disaster plans, 140–141; crisis management approach of, 46; history of, 140; response capabilities of, 39

Felice, J., 207

Figley, C., 175

Fink, S., 23, 24

Fire and rescue services: access issues in, 134; emergency medical services of, 134–135. See also Emergency personnel and agencies

First responders: and individuals' personal needs, 5; and post-traumatic symptoms, 167; safety and security as primary focus of, 152; training opportunities for, 331–332
Flace, S. E., 14
Foa, E. B., 155, 159, 167
Franz, L., 299
Frazier, P., 150
Fukuyama, M. A., 156, 204

G
Gaines, N., 159
Gallagher, R., 146
Garden, A. M., 175
Gehring, D., 322, 323
Georgia State University, crisis management team at, 56
Geraghty, J., 286, 288
Gewertz, K., 192
Gill, A., 146
Gilliland, B. E., 149, 152, 158, 163, 171, 172
Glaser, T., 150
Good, C., 231
Gorton, K., 159
Gray, J. J., 151, 156, 159, 161, 166, 167
Greenstone, J. L., 158, 160, 172
Griffin, W., 145, 156, 186, 200
Guillery, J. M., 40, 46
Guth, D. W., 46

H
Harper, K. S., 28
Harrington, L. K., 75, 82, 195
Hattauer, E., 148, 171
Healing process, 39, 118, 261–262; bereavement and, 164–165; for caregivers, 49; for victims of terrorism, 323–324. See also Crisis intervention; Services of remembrance
Health crises: communication methods for, 102; institution's ability to respond to, 14; student deaths from 13

Health Information Portability and Accountability Act (HIPAA), need for staff knowledge of, 310
Hellwig-Olson, B., 285
Hensley, T. R., 9
Heppner, P., 146, 171
Hermann, C. F., 23, 25
Hoff, L. A., 150, 163
Holsti, O. R., 25
Homicide, assessing lethality for, 159, 163–164
Hong, L., 296
Hughes, M., 150
Human crises: defined, 41; healing process in, 151, 152, 154, 261–262; personal accounts of, 255–282, 305–313; responses to, 41–42; sources and support systems for, 41–42
Hurley, G., 148, 171
Hurricane Andrew, higher education institutions impacted by, 19. See also University of Miami's hurricane disaster
Hurricane Katrina disaster, 19–22; and constituent disenfranchisement, 101; fiscal and human resource losses from, 19–21; institutional recovery clearinghouse for, 22; and interinstitutional collaboration, 21–22; legacy of, 40; overwhelming impact of, 39; and residence hall protocols, 214; response and recovery tasks in, 39. See also Tulane University's hurricane disaster response
Hurst, J. C., 16

I
"In Harm's Way: Suicide in America," 147, 149, 164
In loco parentis, 3–4
Incident action plan, overview of, 126–128
Incident Command System/Unified Command (ICS/UC): elements and features of, 125–126; and emer-

gency response functions, 124; establishment of, 275, 276, 277–278; and NIMS integration center, 126; purpose of, 123; responsibilities and structure of, 124–125

Indiana University, crisis definition of, 28–29

Indiana University—Purdue University, crisis definition of, 29

International Association of Counseling Services standards, 148

International students: legislation related to, 322; security, 226–227; and terrorist acts on United States, 325

International terrorism, and 1988 Pan Am Flight 103 bombing, 10–11. *See also* New York University's 9/11 response; Terrorism response

Internet. *See also* Technological crisis; Web and e-mail services

Irvine, R. B., 25

J

Jackson, S. E., 175

Jacobsen, M., 285

James, R. K., 149, 152, 158, 163, 171, 172

Jeanne Clery Disclosure of Campus Security Policy and Campus Statistics Act, 10

Johnson, C., 20, 21

K

Kadison, K. D., 148

Kanel, K., 158, 172

Kent State University shootings, 8–9

Kessler, R. C., 150

Kilmann, P. R., 23

Kitzrow, M. A., 147, 148, 172

Konigsmark, A. R., 21

Koovor-Misra, S., 25, 40, 46

Kruckeberg, D., 42

L

LaGrand, L. E., 164

Lake, P. F., 4, 148, 153, 173, 175, 260

Lapan, R., 146, 171

Lawson, C. J., 97

Legislation: concerning international students, 322; for disclosure of campus crime statistics, 9–10; and mandatory sprinkler systems, 241; and student privacy rights, 307–308; resulting from terrorist acts, 302–303

Lehigh University rape and murder case, 9–10

Lerner, M. D., 149, 158

Leviton, S. C., 158, 160, 172

Lewis, J. M., 9

Lewis, L., 156

Lindell, B., 149, 158

Littleton, R. F., 75, 315

Litz, B. T., 151, 156, 159, 161, 166, 167

Locher, L. L., 148, 171

Loewendick, B. A., 192, 194

Lowery, J. W., 322, 323

Lyall, D., 305, 307

Lyall, M., 305, 307

M

Macleod, M., 7, 8

Martin, A. W., 291

Mascher, J., 148, 171, 174

Maslach, C., 175

Maslow, A. H., 152, 334, 336

May, T., 146

McCarthy, J. D., 291

McFarlane, A., 150, 161, 157

McKelfresh, D., 55

McNeil, F., 159

McPhail, C., 291

Meadows, E. A., 155, 159, 167

Medical plan, as component of incident action plan, 128

Memorial services. *See specific institution*

Meyers, G. C., 40, 46

Mian, A., 285

Milburn, T. W., 25

Millar, D. P., 25

Miser, K. M., 184, 189

Missing College Student Cases: An Investigative Guide, 307–308

Missing student crisis response: and anniversary events, 313; crisis ownership question in, 308–309; defining institutional role in, 309; external agencies' cooperation in, 312; federal actions in, 308; hindrances to, 306–307; historical waiting period for, 307; legislation on, 307–308; and public scrutiny of campus safety, 313; staff stress and burnout in, 312; and student privacy rights/laws, 309–311; volunteer operations oversight in, 311–312

Mitchell, J. T., 167

Mitchell, T. H., 46

Mitroff, I. I., 23, 26, 40, 46, 75, 82, 185, 195, 201

Moore, S., 25, 26, 192

Murks, S. M., 255

Murphey, J., 146

Murphy, S. K., 68

Mutual aid agreements: with external law enforcement agencies, 130–133; with fire and rescue services, 133–135; legalities of, 129; with nonconcurrent jurisdiction, 129

N

National Association of College and University Business Officers (NACUBO), 21–22

National Center for Health Statistics, 147

National Collegiate Athletic Association (NCAA): and good sportsmanship, 290, 296; and Katrina hurricane victims' arrangements, 225

National Institute of Mental Health (NIMH), 154; early intervention program recommendations of, 154–155

National Interagency Incident Management System (NIMS), 123

National Organization of Victim Assistance: crisis intervention focus of, 151; and death notification training, 164

Natural disasters, response and recovery assistance for, 140–141. *See also* Environmental crises

Nelson, C. B., 150

New Orleans educational system: in Hurricane Katrina's aftermath, 20–22. *See also* Tulane University's hurricane disaster response

New York State Campus Safety Act, 307

New York University's 9/11 response, 268–274; air quality concerns in, 271; convening of stakeholders in, 269; communication challenges in, 269–271, 272; lessons learned from, 272; public relations issues in, 271; safety and housing concerns in, 270; and staff stress and burnout, 272; Web technology function in, 269–270

Newman, M., 294

News media: and crisis aftermath, 118; cultivation of good relations with, 112; and disruptive fan behavior, 287; electronic intercepts used by, 17; institutional communication with, 106–109, 114–115; management of, 112–113, 187–189; methods for communicating with, 108; and onsite coverage impacts, 7–8, 9, 11, 12, 16, 17; providing access to, 107; and services of remembrance, 169; and speed and accuracy of coverage, 108–109, 114–115; and twenty-four-hour coverage, 12–13

Newsom, D., 42

Newton, F. B., 146

O

O'Connell, J., 146

Office of crisis planning, 91, 94

Office of Domestic Preparedness, 315

Offutt, C. A., 148, 171, 174

Ogrizek, M., 40, 46

Ohio State University, celebration riot response of, 293–294

Oklahoma State University's off–campus tragedy response, 263–268; agencies and individuals involved in, 263–265; communication success and failures in, 265; counseling provision in, 266–267; media and public relations issues in, 265–266; memorial service and healing process in, 264–265, 267; travel policy and emergency plan revisions in, 266

O'Malley, K., 146

P

Pan Am Flight 103 bombing, 10–11

Park, S., 174

Patterson, B. G., 28, 255

Pauchant, T. C., 23, 26, 40, 46

Paul, G., 159

Pearson, C. M., 75, 82, 185, 195, 201

Personal crises. See Human crises; Student suicide

Pfeiffer, J. W., 189

Phelps, N. L., 25

Pickrell, J., 20

PIER (Public Information and Emergency Response), 103

Pines, A. M., 175

Piorkowski, G., 148, 171

Pledge, D., 146, 171

Portable transmission towers, 104

Power, P., 59, 62–63

Preece, F., 7–8

President/CEO: and crisis communications plan approval, 111–112; crisis declaration responsibility of, 79; crisis team relationship with, 62, 69

Pritchard, R. S., 193

Protecting Schools and Universities from Terrorism: A Guide for Administrators and Teachers, 314

Psychoeducational group interventions: administrative concerns in, 165–166; and formalized psychological debriefing protocols/guidelines, 166–168, 176; identifying affected parties for, 165; leadership requirements for, 166

Psychological first aid, 149–156; basic types of interventions in, 162–170; best practice strategies for, 154–156; and cathartic self-disclosure, 163; competences and credentialing for, 171; defining basis of need for, 150–151; and early interventions, 166; and effective intervention characteristics, 153; focus of, 152; formal programs in, 171; and group interventions, 165–168; immediate phase of, 163; initial response to, 154; and interagency communication, 173–174; and interventionist attributes, 171; language issues in, 172; legal and ethical concerns in, 172–176; mandatory reporting and confidentiality in, 172; post–trauma, 154; professional standards and codes for, 174; for secondary victims, 162; and services of remembrance, 168–170; and staff burnout, 174–176; and student bereavement, 164–165; and transport protocols, 163. See also Crisis intervention

Public e-mail response service (PRS), 102

Public relations officers/staff: and crisis communication plan, 112, 113, 114, 115; crisis role of, 15; and missing student cases, 310–311; and new media handling, 188' risk management role of, 10

R

Radio communication plan, 128

Raphael, B., 152, 167

Red Cross: crisis intervention focus of, 151; death notification training by, 164; services provided by, 136–137; and terrorism preparedness, 317, 320

Residence hall staff, maintaining contact information on, 92

Rhatigan, J. J., 4

Rickard, S. T., 40

Rivier College, crisis definition of, 28

Robbins, S., 146

Roberts, A. R., 158

Robertson, J. M., 146

Rodolfa, E., 174

Rodrigue, C. M., 14

Roehlke, H., 146, 171

Rollo, J. M., 3, 35, 73, 329

Romano, L., 20

Rose, S. R., 161, 167

Rovsi, E., 14

Rudolph, J. M., 159

S

Safety concerns, as focus of crisis management, 38, 41. See also Student safety

Schaalman, M. L., 25

Schoenherr, S., 18

Schultz, L., 150

Scott, J. E., 74, 186, 200

Scott, J., 156

Secondary stress disorder, prevention of, 175–176

Secret Service, campus involvement of, 141

Self-inflicted injury, facilitative model of support for, 148

Senior administrators. See Administrators

September 11 terrorist attacks, impacts on students and campuses, 18. See also New York University's 9/11 response; Terrorism response

Services of remembrance: and anniversary rituals, 170; inclusiveness in, 169; general purpose of, 168; news media collaboration in, 169

Seton Hall University's fire disaster response, 236–245; communication methods in, 239–240, 243; crisis management plan implemented in, 237–238; and fire safety improvements, 241–242; legislation resulting from, 241; media relations in, 240–241, 243; responders to, 237; student affairs' roles in, 238–241; student deaths and injuries in, 236–237; and students' basic and emotional needs, 238; volunteers' roles in, 237, 238–239

Seymour, M., 25, 26, 192

Shalev, A. Y., 167

Shepard, Matthew, 15–16

Sherwood, G. P., 55

Shrivastava, P., 40

Sidel, M., 325

Silberman, M., 186, 189, 190, 196

Simon, T. R., 147

Simono, R. B., 148, 171

Simulations, 195–196; and crisis communication plan, 114; and group-level crisis response, 197

Siren systems, 103

Smaller institutions: crisis management teams in, 57; family expectations of, 5–6; Hurricane Katrina response of, 38; and terrorism preparedness, 317

Snider, R., 288, 297

Snow, R. L., 8

Sodders, L. M., 14

Sonnega, A., 150

Special Weapons and Tactical Teams (SWAT), creation of, 8

Speck, Richard, 8

Spillan, J. E., 55

Spivack, J., 148, 171

Spokespersons and experts, training requirements for, 112

Sport spectator behaviors, 285–298; alcohol as factor in, 287–288, 289;

and bans on games, 286; and bystander policy, 297; of disruptive fans, 285–291; documentation of, 296; European research on, 289; glorification of violence in, 286; history of violence in, 286; law enforcement approach to, 296, 297; legislation relating to, 293; local media coverage of, 287; offensive clothing and signs in, 290; and poor sportsmanship, 288–291; preventative and crowd management strategies in, 287–293, 296–296, 297; and school–sponsored commercials, 289–290; and student governing group input, 289; and suspension policies, 293; using crisis matrix to analyze, 295. *See also* Celebratory violence

Sportsmanship and Fan Behavior Summit, 296

Staff: and business continuity plan, 302; CERT training for, 135; crisis impacts on, 89–90; and FBI investigations, 138; and Homeland Security Department contacts, 139–140; with special needs expertise, 332–334; stress and burnout, 174–175, 212, 312; workshops and training programs for, 331

Stage, F. K., 200

Stamm, B. H., 159

Steel, C., 148, 171

Stone, G., 146, 174

Stressful Life Experiences Screening Short Form, 159

Stubbart, C. I., 75

Student affairs: and crisis plan development, 91; facility crisis roles of, 238–241; and incident debriefing, 201–202; risk management role of, 10

Student and Exchange Visitor Information System (SEVIS), 322

Student and Exchange Visitor Program (SEVP), 322

Student safety: families' expectations of, 5; in facility crisis, 38, 41, 250; and missing student cases, 313; and terrorism response, 270, 319–320

Student suicide: assessing lethality for, 159, 163–164; facilitative model of support for, 148; prevalence of, 147

Stump, L. J., 121

Suzanne's Law, 308

Syracuse University, and 1988 Pan Am Flight 103 bombing, 11

Sysko, H., 146

T

Tabletop exercises, 192–195; design and development of, 194–195; for crisis plan assessment, 192; sample of, 193 (*Ex8.1*); for technological crises, 301–302

Technological crises, 298–304; and backup recovery testing, 301–302; and business continuity, 299–302; costs and consequences of, 300; data restoration and storage strategy concerns in, 302; data security and disaster recovery in, 298–300, 301; and downtime evaluation, 300–301; internal security concerns in, 302–304; and IT continuity, 301; and updated system data availability, 301; virtual security threats and vulnerabilities in, 303

Tedeschi, R. G., 150

Telephone-related communication tools: campus phone books banks, 259; cell phones, 104–105, 258; 800 numbers, 102; hot lines, 99; reverse 911 call system, 102; securing and dedicated lines, 104, 249; telephone banks, 259

Terrorism response: bioterrorism concerns in, 14, 316; and campus vulnerability, 315; command center created for, 321; crisis response team (CRT) training for, 314–316; evacuation procedures in, 319;

Homeland Security's role in, 139, 317–318; housing options in, 317; international students and, 325; legislation resulting from, 318, 322; modified academic schedules/requirements in, 323; planning strategies in, 318–319; power of symbolic leadership in, 324; predetermined university policies in, 323; psychological recovery process in, 323–324; safety briefings and safe location options in, 319–320; and terrorism preparedness, 315–325; and understanding of terrorist motives, 324–325; utilization of outside resources in, 316–318. See also New York University's 9/11 response

Texas A&M's Bonfire tragedy response, 16–17, 255–263; agencies and individuals involved in, 256–257; coordination and communication in, 257–260; Critical Incident Response Team's role in, 256, 257, 260, 261, 262; debriefing in, 201–202, 261; healing process and services in, 261–262; independent commission's investigation of, 259; media coverage of, 258; protocols for, 256, 258, 260–261; risk management program instituted in, 260

Traffic plan, 128

Trauma: and early crisis intervention, 151; and individual coping and healing, 151, 152, 154; and mental health problems, 150; and post-trauma complications, 150–151; and psychological first aid steps, 156

Tribbensee, N., 173, 175

Tseng, W. C., 146

Tuchman, G., 9

Tulane University's hurricane disaster response, 20, 21, 224–229; agencies and individuals involved in, 225;

call center established for, 225; and communication systems failure, 225–226; and continuing education provisions, 226; coordinated evacuation in, 225; corporate partners' collaboration with, 225; and international students' needs, 226–227; lessons learned from, 227–228; media spokespersons for, 227; university's personal evacuation plan in, 224, 227–228; university's Web site utilization in, 226; and visiting arrangements at other universities, 226

Turk, J. V., 42

U

University of Arizona College of Nursing's crisis response: CERT's role in, 278–279; communication difficulties in, 276–277; critical incident stress debriefing in, 278; and first responders deployment, 274–276, 279–280; healing and counseling assistance in, 279; importance of collaboration in, 279; Incident Command System (ICS) in, 278–279, 280; media staging area established for, 277; outside agencies involved in, 276; protocol observation and revision in, 278–279; unified command center established in, 275, 276, 277–278; university president's efforts in, 277

University of Florida, Gainesville, student murders at, 12

University of Illinois at Urbana–Champaign, meningitis health crisis at, 13–14

University of Maryland—College Park's tornado disaster, 216–222; agencies involved in, 217; communication in, 217–218, 221–222; counseling and mental help support in, 219; incident response team's role in, 218–219; and lessons learned, 222; and protocol revisions, 221–222; public-private partnerships in, 219–220, 221; public relations staff's preparations in, 220; residence life officials' planning in, 221; university Web site utilization in, 220

University of Memphis, crisis management teams at, 58

University of Miami's hurricane disaster, 207–211; campus closing decision in, 209; communications issues and system improvement in, 209–211, 213; counseling provision in, 209; and crisis management team reorganization, 211; Emergency Operations Center activated for, 210–211, 213; FEMA's role in, 214; and payroll/business operations, 214–215; and protocol revisions, 212–215; public relations strategies in, 211–212; roles of resident assistants and resident coordinators in, 209, 212; rumor control hot line in, 213; senior leadership team meetings on, 208, 209–210; and staff contact information, 213; and university's community volunteer efforts, 212

University of Texas at Austin, Texas Tower shootings at, 7–8

University of Wyoming, and Matthew Shepard's murder, 15–16, 17

V

van Haperen, K., 185

Vesta, L. C., 164

Virginia Tech's balcony collapse response: academic relief requests in, 232–233; agencies and individuals involved in, 232; and crisis definition, 29; family notification in, 233; and liability issues, 234; media presence and rumor control efforts in, 233; and protocol effectiveness, 235; Student Affairs' Care Team involvement in, 234

Volpe, J. S., 149, 158

W

Washington, C. K., 255

Web and e-mail services, 102; as crisis information management and source, 16–17, 239, 249; overloading of, 83–84, 86; public, 102; and terrorism preparedness and relief, 317

Wheeler, I., 146

Whitely, P., 207

Whitman, Charles, 7

Wilson, M. E., 183

Wireless Internet communication system, 104

X

Xavier University, and Hurricane Katrina recovery efforts, 21, 22

Y

Young, M., 152, 153, 158, 167, 171

Z

Zdziarski, E. L., 3, 28, 35, 73, 74, 315, 329

Zhang, B., 146